OVER MY DEAD BODY

UNEARTHING THE HIDDEN HISTORY OF AMERICA'S CEMETERIES

Greg Melville

ABRAMS PRESS, NEW YORK

Library of Congress Control Number: 2022933716

Paperback ISBN: 978-1-4197-5486-9
eISBN: 978-1-64700-304-3

Printed and bound in the United States
10 9 8 7 6 5 4 3 2 1

Abrams books are available at special discounts when purchased in quantity
for premiums and promotions as well as fundraising or educational use.
Special editions can also be created to specification. For details, contact
specialsales@abramsbooks.com or the address below.

Abrams Press® is a registered trademark of Harry N. Abrams, Inc.

ABRAMS The Art of Books
195 Broadway, New York, NY 10007
abramsbooks.com

To Joan and Dave
with love and gratitude

GRAVEDIGGER: Come, my spade. There is no ancient gentleman but gardeners, ditchers, and grave-makers. They hold up Adam's profession.

—*HAMLET*, ACT 5, SCENE I

CONTENTS

PROLOGUE

Shawsheen Cemetery

Bedford, Massachusetts

Established: 1849

THE FIRST TIME I put a body in the ground was on a clear June morning before my senior year of college. I was in my hometown of Bedford, Massachusetts, sitting behind the wheel of a pickup truck dressed in blue jeans, steel-toed work boots, and my favorite Aerosmith T-shirt. I generally saved the Journey T-shirt for nicer occasions.

From the truck, I watched the claw of a yellow, exhaust-belching backhoe tear a hole into a patch of grass about fifty feet away, between granite gravestones. To my right sat my nineteen-year-old coworker, Billy, leafing through the pages of an adult magazine. Above the backhoe's rumble, Billy gave me—unsolicited—the synopsis of a short story that caught his attention. Ever the literature lover, he was. Billy and I both worked as summer employees for the Bedford Department of Public Works, our main job being to mow the grass at the local Shawsheen Cemetery and help dig graves for the occasional funeral.

Gravediggers, as I know firsthand, get a raw deal. In return for doing society's dirty work, society looks down its nose at them. The job title equates in people's minds to low-wage, menial labor. Never mind the fact that just about all of us will hire one someday. Abraham Lincoln once worked as a gravedigger. So did rocker Tom Petty, who said he took the job because "you didn't have to look too sharp." Amen.*

---

* See: T-shirt, Aerosmith, above.

After the backhoe finished scooping out the Shawsheen Cemetery soil and depositing it onto a piece of plywood, Billy and I exited the truck, reached for our shovels, and dropped into the newly dug hole. Machines do much of the heavy work these days, except in hard-to-reach nooks where only a shovel can reach. The smell of fresh earth enveloped us as we shaved the grave shaft's sides and leveled the floor to the proper size—about eight feet long, three feet wide, and five feet in depth.

I was surprised to discover that Shawsheen's graves weren't six feet deep, as horror movies led me to believe. The six-foot rule likely originated during a plague outbreak in mid-fifteenth-century England, when London's mayor required all bodies to be placed at that depth in the vain hope of preventing the spread of disease—and to stop animals and grave robbers from unearthing the corpses.

But six feet also made the job much harder. It takes five or six hours for a skilled person to shovel out a single grave of that depth in ideal conditions, when the soil is relatively soft and rock free. Six-foot graves were also more prone to cave-ins, which eventually meant abandoning the rule. Now, most graves dug in American cemeteries are four to five feet deep, which leaves a layer of between one and two feet of soil above the casket or burial vault.

As I stood in the fresh grave, I couldn't help but feel a little claustrophobic. Or maybe I was just freaking out—a little—about the prospect of someday being deposited in a hole like this one for eternity, or at least a long time.

We completed our task and climbed out of the grave before a crane lowered a concrete vault into the space, to house the casket. Shawsheen required that all caskets be placed within a concrete vault, to prevent the ground from collapsing over time. This is a standard rule for many modern American cemeteries, and one enthusiastically backed by the opportunistic funeral industry; it adds anywhere from $1,000 to as much as $10,000—for the over-the-top, needlessly ornate models—in expenses piled onto a grieving family. Billy and I then unfurled rolls of artificial turf around the rectangular hole's edges to hide the bare ground and placed a polished aluminum casket holder above it. As far as graves go, it looked almost inviting.

Thirty minutes later, the ceremony went without a hitch, and after the last lingerers faded, Billy and I joined a couple of public works colleagues in lowering the casket into the ground and depositing dirt on top of it. That's about when we realized we had dug the grave in the wrong place. But that's a story for another time.

The grave digging that summer didn't spark my interest in cemeteries as much as the mowing. I spent hour upon countless, sweaty hour pushing a lawn mower between graves, the machine's wide blade cutting the grass down to two inches and mulching the clippings. During my first couple of days on the job, I mowed with energy and ambition, as if I wanted to cut all forty-four of the cemetery's acres single-handedly. In one day.

One of the year-round employees quickly set me straight. "You get paid by the hour, not the square foot," he said. "There's no rush."

The words came out more as a threat than a suggestion. The permanent guys who made their living from the job didn't need some summer kid setting new productivity records.

From that point onward, on every weekday morning, except the Fourth of July, I came to Shawsheen to mow deliberately. And my reasonable pace gave me time to consider the surroundings. The cemetery, established in 1849, reveals itself in chronological order. The oldest, most garden-like sections come first, just past the front entrance, residing on a hillside where the light is dulled beneath a canopy of mature hardwoods and white pines. The headstones there sprout from the ground like rows of crooked teeth, their etchings worn by the endless cycle of harsh New England winters. The family names on these surprisingly artful monuments often match the ones attached to the town's parks, schools, and historic homes. This area's overgrown landscape was modeled after the garden-like design of Mount Auburn Cemetery in nearby Cambridge, which opened to much fanfare more than a decade before Shawsheen.

As my lawn mower dipped and rose over the shallow depressions in front of these ancient graves, the town's past came alive. I learned who died rich and who died poor, who was blessed (or cursed, depending on how you look at it) with many children, who lived full lives and whose were cut short. I became familiar with the long-forgotten names of war heroes, and I contemplated the tiny, ornate monuments dedicated to infants who left their families too early. I imagined colorful stories for the May-September romances, and for the widows who lived for decades past their husbands.

Every gravestone seemed like a mystery waiting to be solved. The gravestones provided me with the first and last pages of a story. From there I was left to find clues to piece together information on who the person was. I considered information provided in the inscriptions, and through the size, shape, and ornateness (or not) of the markers, and who else was buried in the vicinity. Every life holds an epic tale, even if no one alive remembers it.

My mower's path—and curiosity—inevitably pulled me eastward and progressed in time. I went from beneath the tightly clustered canopy of thick-trunked older trees, past the meadowy late nineteenth century, and through the gently maple-shaded eras of the Spanish flu pandemic, World War I, followed by the Depression, and World War II. Farther east, starting in the 1950s section, the trees largely disappeared as the cemetery took on a more modern—and easy-to-mow—lawn style, where the plots were tidier and more orderly. It wouldn't be until years later that I learned cemeteries acted as the first suburban subdivisions, employing this layout style.

Rambling across the decades among these gravestones, I occasionally passed the monuments of great-grandparents, grandparents, and even occasional parents of my friends, neighbors, and former school-mates. By regulation, the cemetery allowed only town residents to be buried within its confines. In Shawsheen's easternmost section lay about five acres of grass-carpeted land yet to be filled. As I cut a fresh path through the overgrown turf, I couldn't help but wonder who from Bedford would someday fill these grave sites, and when. I'd thought, *How many of them do I know right now?*

Today, a quarter century later, the answer has been revealed somewhat—and in short, it's too damned many. The potent lesson I learned during those months inhaling the scent of fresh-cut grass mixed with small-engine exhaust, and working on my sick farmer's tan, was that Shawsheen is the soul of my hometown. It reveals to anyone

willing to look the breadth of Bedford's art, philosophy, religion, ances-
try, politics, sense of the natural world, and culture. It's a repository of
so much more than just the no-longer-living. It holds our buried history.

Shawsheen isn't unique, either. Graveyards across the country
are the time capsules of our communities, recording—and sometimes
even shaping—America's winding forward path. Every cemetery has
a story. Yet these treasure troves of Americana are almost completely
overlooked in the historical record. For whatever reason, journalists
and historians generally whistle past the graveyards in their research.
Maybe it's because burial grounds are so creepy, and remind us of our
mortality. Or maybe it's because they're so omnipresent that they tend
to be overlooked. A NASA scientist recently used satellite images to map
144,000 cemeteries in America, which is nearly ten times the number
of Starbucks in the country, and eight times the number of McDonald's
restaurants. Put all of America's cemeteries together, and their square
acreage would be larger than the state of Delaware. That's a lot of stories.

Cemeteries have served as America's first public art museums and
parks. They acted as the first form of free, open religious expression in
America. They gave birth to landscape architecture and inspired the
layout of Disneyland. They moved our greatest poets and authors—and
not just in their written works. Ralph Waldo Emerson and Henry David
Thoreau undertook the country's first conservation project by establishing a cemetery in Concord, Massachusetts, to protect a natural area near
their homes.

New York's Central Park is a giant cemetery, of sorts, having been
built atop burial grounds without the remains being removed, and now
actively serving as a popular repository for cremated remains. Cemeteries have been used as political tools to rally the nation and were once
used to flip the proverbial bird at General Robert E. Lee during the Civil
War. They served as the Cold War's first cultural battlegrounds. They
have defined, and redefined, what it means for an American to die a
"good death."

They're also unsparing in their reflection of us. Cemeteries offer
painful evidence of the removal of Indigenous peoples from their ancestral lands. They stand as a surviving visual record of the contributions
Chinese Americans made in building the West, and the concerted

effort the country undertook to erase this page of our history. They reveal the sins of slavery and the conscious lengths to which enslavers, including Thomas Jefferson, went to hide them. Many cemeteries today remain racially segregated and unequally treated, as historic Black burial grounds struggle to survive due to a lack of public protections and support. Cemeteries have bred greed and corruption. They sparked the multibillion-dollar Death Industrial Complex, which too often takes advantage of the grief-stricken in the name of paying proper respects to the dead. Cemeteries capture the Great American Narrative like nowhere else—showcasing a combination of religion, race, ambition, democracy, identity, imagination, money, and the never-ending quest for justice.

Most recently, American graveyards have reached a critical phase in their existence. Cemeteries as we've known them for the last 150 years are reaching the end of their life cycle. They're filling to capacity, and we're running out of new real estate—especially in cities—for the dead. Many older cemeteries, which haven't seen a new burial in generations and receive scarce visitors, are struggling to find revenue. In New York State alone, an average of about eight cemeteries a year have gone bust and been abandoned this century, to be adopted by a local municipality. At the same time, more Americans are now cremated than buried. We're seeking out more environmentally friendly alternatives. Graves are like mini Superfund sites. Almost 4 million gallons of embalming fluid are placed underground with the dead each year, and these chemicals eventually seep into the groundwater. Then there are the preservatives used in making caskets, the mercury from dental fillings and pacemakers, and the bacteria and viruses we leave behind. And the need for cemeteries as permanent reminders of our existence is becoming obsolete in the face of the Digital Immortality metaverse, where we can be memorialized with infinitely more data than what can be carved into a piece of granite. If you consider a cemetery to be the resting place for the essences of people's lives, then Facebook is the largest cemetery in the world, housing the accounts of 30 million dead people and rising. Cemeteries in turn are seeking new strategies to stay relevant and solvent to keep their gates open.

Since my days of mowing Shawsheen's grassy expanses and digging the occasional burial plot, I've maintained my relationship with cemeteries, these places where life and death collide, where I'm reminded that time and nature always win. I jog through them frequently, drawn by their beauty, solitude, and lack of vehicle traffic. I've appeared at them in uniform as a U.S. Navy officer, bearing the flag at funerals with military honors, and I have stood in them to watch fellow service members receive a final goodbye. I visit them on work trips to new towns, and on family vacations, with limited luck in convincing my wife and two kids to join me among the graves. I've also visited them as a journalist.

Here, I try to tell the story of American graveyards—these vast outdoor archives of art, history, literature, religion, life, and death—before they disappear. I write as a reporter and a traveler, not as a scholar. Yes, this is a love story of sorts, but be aware: It's not a blind or always romantic one. Love outside of Hallmark movies is imperfect. It requires being unafraid to recognize the object of your affection's flaws.

I recently returned to Shawsheen. Many fresh graves have sprouted in the space that was so empty and open a quarter century ago. One now bears my father's name. It's etched with a cross and the words UNTIL WE MEET AGAIN, from the Irish blessing. I miss him every day. I just hope the gravediggers buried his ashes in the right spot.

Crosses mark the spot where the remains believed to belong to
Jamestown's first settlers lie, by a statue of colony leader John Smith.

1. CANNIBALS, A COFFIN, AND A CAPTAIN'S STAFF

Colonial Jamestown's original graves reveal
America's distinctly uncivilized beginnings

—

The 1607 Burial Ground
Historic Jamestowne, Virginia
Established: 1607

SOMETIMES YOU FIND a graveyard, and sometimes it seems like a graveyard finds you—as if it's yearning to tell you its story. The morning my family and I pulled into Virginia's Historic Jamestowne for a quick tour, an astonishing graveyard found us. My kids were still in elementary school, and we were in the midst of a two-week family summer road trip—from hell—in our station wagon, driving up the East Coast from Florida to New Hampshire. Along the way, we visited a mix of amusement parks, state parks, and historic sites. We'd spent the day before at Colonial Williamsburg, the Disney World of American historic districts, about ten miles up the road, which the kids loved.

Historic Jamestowne wasn't on our original itinerary, but my wife spotted it on a tourist map and decided it would be worth the side trip. After all, it's the site of England's first permanent North American settlement, but we didn't realize that its most significant artifacts aren't the crumbled stone foundations, or some centuries-old coins or pottery shards. Instead, they're what's inside the settlement's mass graves, which were lost and forgotten for centuries until recent times. They're marked now with a cluster of simple, skinny metal crosses that overlook the bank of the James River.

Jamestown is often called the stepping-stone to our present civilization. Yet the four-century-old burial sites here reveal the suffering, desperation, and even cannibalistic savagery at the heart of America's genesis story. They show with poignancy how uncivilized our country's beginnings were.*

WHAT'S MOST STRIKING about Historic Jamestowne is its gritty authenticity. The old James Fort site, established in 1607, hasn't been restored to theme-parky perfection like Williamsburg. There are no colonial cosplaying glassblowers, or town criers in puffy shirts, or bonnet-wearing butter churners, or bored teenagers selling ye olde fudge and taffy. Instead, the fort's ruins—and they are ruins—are slowly, carefully being uncovered and restored. This effort began in 1994 under the direction of a nonprofit organization called Preservation Virginia, which owns the property and keeps it open to the public in conjunction with the National Park Service.

Historic Jamestowne is the kind of place where you're not as much stepping into the past as stepping around, between, and on top of it. Visitors tend to speak in hushed, somber voices—even on bright July mornings like the one when we visited. Which makes sense considering how grim life, and death, were for the English who established the settlement—and given that a dozen years after the first settlers arrived, Jamestown became the gateway to human slavery on the continent.

The James Fort site is surprisingly compact. Its original triangle-shaped footprint occupies an area about the size of a high school baseball field. Period-looking wood-planked walls now trace much of the perimeter, where its old ones once stood, spilling into the James River. A path from the visitor's center, which crossed a broad marsh, led us through a gap in one of the fort walls, and into the grassy infield that houses what remains of the original settlement.

During our visit, a handful of tourists milled about between the dozen or so stations of archaeological significance that had either been

---

* Jamestown or Jamestowne? The original spelling included the *e* at the end, which is why Historic Jamestowne, for authenticity's sake, has kept it. The common modern spelling drops the *e*.

recently dug up, were in the process of being dug up, or were waiting to be dug up. Two large objects stood above all others at the site: a decaying redbrick church tower built in the late 1600s on the fort's edge, and a bronze statue of original colonist Captain John Smith erected in the early twentieth century. Smith stands dressed in a swashbuckling Shakespearean outfit, looking like the essence of civility. But when the real-life Smith and the other Jamestown settlers first anchored their three ships sixty miles up the James River in April 1607 to establish a European foothold, they must have seemed like savages to the Algonquian-speaking confederacy of Native peoples who filled the region. Smith and the other 103 English men and boys were dirty, violent, and unable to survive without the locals' help. They brought rats and illness, spoke a strange language, and fired loud, powerful weapons. The English were aliens, illegally staking their claim to a place.

And it was a tragically bad landing place. Although it provided a strategic vantage point to protect the new European arrivals from possible attack from Spanish ships, it was mosquito-infested and marshy, with no nearby source of fresh running water—leaving them without reliable irrigation methods or drinking water. In turn, death called frequently and without mercy during the colony's first winter, stealing the settlers through disease, starvation, and the elements.

The privately held Virginia Company, which funded the Jamestown venture and expected a handsome return on investment, told the settlers to bury any of their casualties in unmarked graves just inside the fort's walls in order to obscure the mortality numbers from all enemies—both Spanish and domestic. The settlers complied, not only for security reasons, but because they couldn't spare the precious time or energy for proper interments.

One exception was the burial of Captain Bartholomew Gosnold, one of the settlement's leaders who was granted Jamestown's charter by the king and raised much of its funding. An experienced mariner and explorer, he gave Cape Cod its name during a 1602 journey, and named Martha's Vineyard after his daughter. Gosnold died four months after landing in Virginia. In 2002, researchers discovered his likely remains, buried about twenty-five feet outside the fort's walls. He was laid to rest inside a wooden coffin—a privilege reserved for the elite—with a captain's ceremonial staff placed above it. It's believed that the settlers buried him openly and with fanfare because his absence wouldn't have escaped the notice of the local Native inhabitants.

Aside from Gosnold's burial, the settlement's mass unceremonious and hasty body dumps contrasted with the elaborate burial traditions of the surrounding Algonquian-speaking peoples, who interred their dead with useful tools, weapons, and food for their journeys to the afterlife. High-status Algonquian dead were sometimes first placed on a ceremonial platform, or scaffold, where their remains stayed for up to two years before the bones were interred in a burial mound.

The region's Algonquian-speaking population consisted of about 15,000 people belonging to 30 tribes, whose territory stretched from what's now northern Virginia to North Carolina. They were led by an emperor named Powhatan, head of the Pamunkey, who gave the leaders under him protection and relative autonomy for pledging their allegiance.

Despite a few violent skirmishes between Jamestown's settlers and local Native people, the two sides maintained relative peace at first—and Powhatan even came to the assistance of his new neighbors on occasion. For instance, when English food supplies ran out during that first September, he gave them the staples they relied upon through the following spring. Even so, he didn't trust the English, fearing they might eventually try to seize his people's land, and kill or forcibly remove them—a chillingly accurate assessment.

In the middle of the settlers' first winter, Powhatan and Smith cemented an uneasy peace between the local Native people and English. Nonetheless, the fort's field of unmarked graves kept growing. By the time Virginia Company ships arrived in the spring with supplies and more settlers, half of the original settlers were dead.

The English's troubles didn't end there. The region soon entered the worst drought in centuries, turning their meager garden plots to dust. They were plagued during that second summer by a lack of clean water and steady food, an abundance of bugs, and malaria and other diseases. In fall 1609, Smith left for England, and in his absence, relations with the local Native people soured, turning to outright hostility, and placing the fort residents under almost constant siege.

Desperate, the settlers dispatched small groups on missions to steal food stores from Powhatan's people, but often never returned, and conditions inside the fort's claustrophobic walls turned disastrous. That winter became known as the starving time. Jamestown's famine-stricken people first resorted to eating their horses to survive. Then the dogs and cats. Then the rats and mice. Then even their own dead: A few firsthand accounts from that winter referred to desperate residents digging fresh bodies from their burial spots and cannibalizing them. Researchers in 2012 confirmed these stories when they unearthed the skeleton of a fourteen-year-old girl whose bones showed the distinctive cuts and scrapes of butchering. Her flesh had been stripped, like livestock at a butcher shop, and her skull deliberately cracked for hungry fingers to claw at the brain. Her bones, once cleaned, were tossed into a trash pit. By the time three ships of reinforcements arrived from England in the spring of 1610, only 60 of 215 colonists had survived the winter.

The settlers in their desperation returned to almost prehistoric simplicity with their burial practices, discarding the rituals they previously believed were necessary for salvation and had evolved over the course of millennia.

I WISH I could start this brief history of burials by revealing that the act of humans depositing their dead in the ground was some major developmental turning point for our species many thousands of years ago. Or that the earliest cave people's burials somehow provided evidence of the unique regard that our socially, morally, and spiritually advanced kind began to pay to those they lost. But then I learned that some ants bury their dead. Some bees and termites do, too. Elephants have been known to throw dirt, leaves, and branches over the remains of the dead in what seems to be a ritual attached to the mourning process, and dogs have been observed doing the same.

What's unique to humanity is graveyards. Termites and elephants don't establish group burial sites. They don't use gravestones to memorialize those they've lost. Graveyards reveal how humans are singularly symbolic-minded creatures. (At least until we someday stumble upon dolphin graveyards deep beneath the sea.)

The world's oldest known graveyard lies just south of Nazareth in the fertile Jezreel Valley of Israel, in an ancient mountainside rock shelter called Qafzeh Cave. The remains of twenty-seven *Homo sapiens* dating as far back as 100,000 years were found ritualistically deposited—all decorated with shell jewelry and coated in red body paint made from the iron-rich powder ocher. They were accompanied by stone tools left, it's believed, for them to take to the Great Beyond, which is not too different from the traditions of Native peoples who met the first Jamestown settlers.

The oldest burial site on record in Europe lies in a limestone cave on the edge of the Bristol Channel in Wales. It dates back about 33,000 years. Deposited inside its diamond-shaped mouth were the remains of a man in his twenties, bathed in red ocher—like the bones at Qafzeh— and accompanied by shell necklaces and mammoth-tusk bracelets.

Strangely enough, ocher also covered the oldest buried human remains found in North America. They belonged to an infant boy who died about 12,700 years ago and was part of a tribe of woolly mammoth hunters whom anthropologists call the Clovis people. His bones were found in a high alpine meadow in Montana's Shields Valley, northeast of Bozeman between the sawtoothed ranges of the Absaroka, Bridger, and Crazy mountains. The landscape, carpeted by wildflowers in the spring and buried beneath a deep mantle of snow in the winter, still looks like a living diorama for the herds of woolly mammoth and American camels that roamed there during the boy's time.

Two construction workers found the remains in 1968, interred with spear tips, knife blades, and other tools made from bone and stone. The boy's skull was cracked. Researchers originally thought the ocher showed a connection between the boy and mammoth hunters who they theorized had migrated from Europe over pack ice that stretched across the Atlantic from France to Virginia. Yet his DNA, mapped in 2014, told a different, more amazing story.

It turns out that the Clovis boy's genetic markers align with 24,000-year-old human remains found in Siberia, meaning his ancestors likely came from Asia, crossing the Bering Strait land bridge. Even more remarkably, his DNA is shared by more than 80 percent of Indigenous people alive today in the Americas, all the way down to Chile. Around the same time the Clovis boy was being placed in the ground in Montana, a tribe in the coastal mountains of northern Israel was establishing even more elaborate burial rituals. Researchers in 2020 discovered the first known grave marker in a place called Raqefet Cave: a 13,000-year-old stone slab etched with the figure of a dancing person. The site served as a mass burial spot for the Natufian culture, one of the earliest groups of people to transition from hunter-gatherers to farmers.

Raqefet was a cemetery in its truest form, featuring multiple individual graves intentionally dug into the bedrock. The burials spanned generations. Many of the bodies in its five chambers were ceremonially placed inside beds of bright and aromatic flowers, like sage, mint, and figwort. Just as important, the cave offers the earliest evidence of beer—or any fermented drink—ever produced. Researchers believe it was brewed to be drunk for mourning rituals. This means it's quite possible, even likely, that the birth of the world's first alcoholic beverage was connected to an ancient graveyard. The sacred link between funerals and inebriation seems to have been carried down across the ages, from Raqefet Cave in the Middle East to members of my own Irish American family.

But why burials? Well, practicality for starters. Burials seal off the smell of decomposition and prevent animals from scavenging the remains, as long as the hole is dug deep enough. Burials, although labor-intensive, do require less equipment and effort than many other ritualistic methods, like cremation. Then there are spiritual considerations. About 7,000 years ago the people of Sumer reasoned that burials placed the dead closer to the spirit's ultimate destination in the underworld, making for a shorter journey. The Greeks thought the same. It's true that they used funeral pyres to cremate the dead—but probably not quite as often as lore or *The Iliad* tells us. Cremation in the ancient world was difficult and dependent on an ample supply of trees. The human body is two-thirds water, after all, and it takes about 1,000 pounds of wood to produce enough heat to turn one person to ashes.

Ancient Egyptians interwove astrology with the placement of the dead. The Great Pyramid of Giza, which is basically a 450-foot-high, 4,500-year-old limestone-and-granite tomb, is situated so that its four corners point precisely in the directions of true (not magnetic) north, south, east, and west. Egyptians believed human spirits were transported after death to the Field of Reeds, a paradise that closely mimicked a person's life and existence on earth, minus conflict and suffering. People were traditionally buried with food, jewelry, games, weapons, and other objects that could be useful to them in this mirrorlike Good Place. For royalty, this sometimes meant sacrificing court advisers, artisans, and servants to keep as company. Egyptians believed in a strong connection between body and soul in the afterlife, so even the poor tried to preserve the flesh and bones of dead loved ones by embalming and mummifying them. The rich went so far as to build their tombs before their death to ensure the structures would meet their tastes and standards in the hereafter.

Elaborate Egyptian burial requirements and customs gave rise to a vast and profitable funeral industry—the likes of which the world wouldn't see again until America in the nineteenth century. If the expensive balms that preserved the body couldn't be afforded, salt could be substituted. A stone sarcophagus could be skipped for a wooden casket or even a linen shroud. Whatever the mourning family could afford. As an Egyptologist told *National Geographic,* "Dead people are money. That's basically it." That's barely different from the United States today.

In America in the 1800s, an obsession with Egyptian culture, including burial art and architecture, known as Egyptomania swept through the country from Europe. It was sparked by the discoveries of scientists and artists who accompanied Napoleon's Egyptian expedition, and was further fueled by the translation of the Rosetta stone in 1822. Many American cemeteries established during this time boast Egyptian Revival–style entryways, their grounds are decorated by elaborate tombs shaped like mini pyramids, and they are filled with obelisks—which for Egyptians linked the dead's spirit with the sun god Ra—that serve as gravestones.

During the waning days of the Egyptian empire, farther east in China, royalty were traditionally buried in locations with powerful feng shui, like near rivers and mountains. China's most famous burial site is that of the First Emperor, Qin Shi Huang, who brought several kingdoms together under one throne and built the Great Wall of China before he died in 210 BCE. He was interred in the world's largest underground tomb complex, which lies at the base of 4,200-foot-tall Mount Lishan. Discovered by farmers in the 1960s, this sprawling subterranean metropolis of vaults and caverns took four decades and an estimated 720,000 workers to build—some of whom were sealed inside it alive. Standing guard outside the massive pyramid-shaped central tomb where the emperor is still believed to rest were 8,000 lifelike terra-cotta soldiers. Because the technology is still beyond our grasp to unearth and preserve the site without severely damaging its contents, only 2,000 of the terra-cotta soldiers have been removed, and the emperor's tomb—and all the potential wonders that lie inside it—remain untouched. For now.

The rise of Christianity shifted the paradigm for burials in the Middle East, North Africa, and Europe. The faithful tried to imitate the interment of Jesus, who was placed in a cave, and according to the Book of John, wrapped in linen and spices and buried "in accordance with Jewish customs." This particularly meant following the Jewish ban on cremations, so that a dead body could remain whole in preparation for the messiah's arrival. In Rome, burials were banned within the city walls, which led some Jewish mourners to excavate underground tunnels to use as cemeteries. Christians continued the custom until early in the fifth century, creating most of what is known as the Catacombs, which contain 375 miles of passageways, and the bones of possibly 1.5 million people.

In aboveground burial grounds, early Christians borrowed from sun-worshipping European pagans the custom of interring bodies with the head facing west and the feet facing east—reasoning that Jesus would return for Judgment Day from the east, and the dead will need to rise in the proper direction to meet him. To quote Matthew 24:27, "For as lightning that comes from the east is visible even in the west, will the coming of the Son of Man be."

The burial sites of martyrs became sacred places for Christians, giving rise to cemeteries established around them and filled with the faithful. Churches, basilicas, or chapels would then be built on site, sometimes with the martyr's tomb as an altar, to accommodate funeral services. In the sixth century, the Catholic Church ordered that burials must be performed only on consecrated churchyard or cathedral grounds. Of course, this meant fees had to be paid to the local parish for each interment, creating a burial monopoly. The dead were buried without coffins and only remained in their resting places for a few years while the worms did their work. The bones were then removed to make space for new residents, and placed in a charnel house, which is a glorified name for a bone storage shed. (Charnel houses are still in use in parts of Europe, including Greece.)

Islam's founder, the prophet Muhammad, was buried in the city of Medina, in what is now Saudi Arabia, just after his death in 632 C.E. His tomb is protected today by the green dome of the Prophet's Mosque, a sacred house of worship that he partly built himself but that has been expanded over the centuries. Following his lead, Islam's believers—like the Jews and Christians before them—required burial for the faithful and forbade cremation.

In the same century as Muhammad's death, the Wadi-Al-Salam, or Valley of Peace, burial ground opened in what's now known as the holy city of Najaf, in present-day Iraq. It was established next to the shrine of Muhammad's son-in-law, the first imam of the Shia branch of Islam. The graveyard is the world's largest, taking up a swath of desert land about twice the size of New York's Central Park. It's crammed with rectangular brick tombs and vaults that hug crooked, ancient streets and alleyways, with a population that stretches well into the millions—and it's still active, holding an estimated 75,000 burials annually.

The rise of Protestantism played a transformational role in European burials, especially with King Henry VIII's creation of the Church of England in the sixteenth century. As part of his religious divorce from the Vatican, the new church barred English elites from buying indulgences to atone for their sins. Looking for a substitute get-out-of-hell-free card, they turned to burial practices.

Since the graveyard was the earthly interface between life and the hereafter, they decided it was the best place to stake their claim for heaven. Ornate funeral processions leading to the church and graveyard came into fashion, in order to advertise the newly dead's good deeds and stature to the powers watching from above. Purchasing prime burial placement in the churchyard, or better yet, within the church or cathedral building itself, became essential. The use of gravestones arose, so the memory and status of the well-to-do could live on after death. And the elites paid more attention to the preservation and burial of their bodies, in hopes of an easier rise-and-shine upon the Rapture's arrival. This led to a more prevalent use of coffins—made from stone, wood, or lead—rather than simply interring the bodies in a shroud.

All these strategies for salvation slowly trickled down to the common folk. By the early seventeenth century, no English burial, for rich or poor, was considered proper unless it included a coffin. This is what made the hasty, haphazard, and desperate interments of Jamestown's original settlers during that period so jarring.

JAMES FORT'S FORTUNES finally turned in 1614, when settler John Rolfe married Powhatan's young daughter Pocahontas, whom the English had kidnapped and held prisoner. The union sparked a truce between the chief and Jamestown's people—enabling the settlement to spread, and Rolfe and his countrymen to establish tobacco farms. Their tobacco crop, cured using traditional Indigenous methods, quickly became popular and highly profitable in London, which saved the colony financially. The success of the tobacco fields motivated the English to continue to expand their lands along the coast and push the area's Indigenous population westward. To meet the labor demands, the farmers turned to captive African workers. Rolfe wrote in 1619 that "20 and odd" enslaved people from Angola were "bought for victuals" and brought to the settlement.

Powhatan died in 1618, and his mourners wrapped his body in skins and placed it on a scaffold in the traditional way. Sometime around 1620, his bones were placed inside an ancestral burial mound that lies within what's now the Pamunkey Indian Reservation, due east of Richmond. It's one of the few known Native burial sites that still exist in Virginia. Nearly all others have been plowed over, destroyed, or looted over the centuries following the removal of Indigenous peoples from their lands in the region—as Powhatan had feared.

Later in the seventeenth century, the Jamestown population dissipated as the colony's capital moved to Williamsburg, and the land that had held the settlement turned to plantation fields—with its artifacts, ruins, and bodies forgotten beneath the soil. The land was occupied briefly by Confederate forces during the Civil War, who built a fort there and reported seeing human bones poking out of the eroded riverbank, likely belonging to some of Jamestown's first fateful residents.

The property was donated to the charity now known as Preservation Virginia in the late 1800s, though another century would pass before formal, extensive archaeological efforts would take place on the twenty-two-acre site. Those efforts, begun in 1994, continue to uncover the truths behind the original settlement. Nothing among the relics reveals with such clarity the nature of Jamestown's beginnings or the way of life there like the graves and bones within them do.

When my family and I first crossed onto the fort site, my son clung to my side. His eyes darted from place to place as he searched in vain for reenactors, and maybe some ye olde taffy for sale like the day before at Colonial Williamsburg.

"Where's Thomas Jefferson?" he asked, frowning.

I paused, becoming aware for the millionth time of my complete failure as a parent. "Jamestown was founded a bit before Thomas Jefferson came along," I said. "You know what? Later today, we're gonna have a little talk on history."

Actually, a big talk. But not yet. At that moment, what captured my attention were the twenty-nine dark, waist-high crosses, huddled near the James River. I scurried to them to scan the information panel. It said this spot is believed to have been the site of the original settlement's burial ground during its fatal first winter in 1607. It's here where the first James Fort settlers hastily buried the dead just within its walls, the graves lying unmarked and forgotten. Only a handful of plots have been excavated, while the others remain undisturbed, carrying an unknown number of remains. Even with so few having been disinterred, the sites and bones within them paint a portrait of the first permanent English settlers in what would become the United States as a group of people who cast the norms of civilization aside in the name of conquest and survival.

The 1607 Burial Ground at Historic Jamestowne exposes remarkable truths, but its revealing nature isn't unique. All graveyards reflect—both above and below the surface—how the people who created and populated them approached death, and life. There's an honesty to these places, if you're willing to look, because the dead don't have a deceitful bone in their bodies. That's one of the reasons I seek out graveyards on my travels. And that's why I'm happy, like on that morning, when a graveyard happens to find me.

Burial Hill, the Pilgrims' first burial ground

2. PILGRIM'S PROGRESS?

To trace America's long, ongoing history of
desecrating the Native dead, start at Plymouth Rock

—

Burial Hill
Plymouth, Massachusetts
Established: 1622

I'M THE WORST tourist when it comes to visiting historic or important places close to wherever I'm living—and I've lived in a bunch of
places. I always tell myself, *I can see that anytime; there's no need to do
it now.* Then I never do, and suddenly, I'm packing moving boxes and
wishing I had gone to this place or done that thing before leaving.

When I lived in New York for a stretch, I never went to the trouble
of taking the ferry to the Statue of Liberty, which I now regret. Nor did I
ever ride the elevator to the top of the Empire State Building. The same
went for my first couple of years living on Cape Cod—that windswept
arm of land jutting off the New England coast. It wasn't until years later
that I visited the nearby historic Burial Hill burial ground in Plymouth,
Massachusetts.

Burial Hill, maybe the oldest maintained graveyard in America, is
home to some of the *Mayflower's* original passengers, and is rightfully
listed on the National Register of Historic Places. I drove near it all the
time to drop off my kids at various sports practices and games, but for
the longest while, I never quite made it there. My window of escape
always seemed too short, or the weather wasn't quite right, or something
else popped up. I also knew I'd have to go there alone because my wife
and kids don't share my fascination for graveyards. In fact, they feel the
exact opposite. The weirdos.

The spirit finally moved me to visit one dank November afternoon in 2017. After dropping my teenage daughter at an athletic facility, I made the fifteen-minute drive northwest, hugging the shore of Cape Cod Bay until I reached protected Plymouth Harbor, where the *May-flower* first anchored in 1620, settling the Pilgrims in the so-called New World. It's here where they celebrated the first Thanksgiving in 1621 with Ousamequin,* leader of the Wampanoag, and his people, who taught them to survive. Driving through the tiny but charming downtown— the essence of an old, colonial-style New England port—I turned onto a narrow one-way street and slid into a parking spot beside a set of concrete steps that vanished upward into the steeply sloping, five-acre Burial Hill.

Climbing the steps, I passed a weathered historical marker that explained Burial Hill was first used for burials in the 1620s. The region's first European settlers, the Pilgrims, originally built a stone fort alongside the site, overlooking the village. The sign informed me that the graveyard's earliest stone markers are considered valuable historic documents and works of folk art. At the bottom it asked visitors to leave the gravestones untouched, for preservation's sake.

But there's an important element to Burial Hill that the sign leaves out. It should have said, somewhere: If you want to examine America's long and continuing history of desecrating the Native dead, start here.

BURIAL HILL AT dusk in November, without another soul in sight, is as spooky as a graveyard gets. The newly fallen leaves dance restlessly in the cold breeze, as if pulled by strings. The smell of woodsmoke and damp soil fills the air. The graveyard's gnarled beech trees wave their arms back and forth, as if summoning the spirits. Beneath and between them stand the Gothic gravestones, crumbling mournfully back to the earth. This type of setting must have suited the Puritans, who believed that pretty much everyone was damned to hell. As for me on that November evening, not so much.

I kept a fast pace as I zigzagged up the steep, soggy grounds until reaching its highest point, where I turned to face the wind-chopped

---

*   Also commonly called Massasoit, which means "great leader."

bay. The earliest settlers built their first fort near this spot because it offered a prime vantage point for fending off possible attacks by the surrounding Wampanoag people. I turned on my phone's flashlight—which barely made a dent in the encroaching darkness—and began to seek out some of the older gravestones.

Burial Hill's markers span from the late 1600s all the way to the 1950s, when the graveyard finally stopped taking new boarders. The oldest gravestones stand out because they're made from rounded, two-foot-tall slabs of purple slate or granite, and are engraved with creepy images—like a winged skull, or skull and crossbones, or a skeletal grim reaper carrying a scythe. The inscriptions are still surprisingly readable. HERE LYES BURIED YE BODY OF MR. THOMAS LITTLE, says one, and HERE LYES YE BODY OF MRS. HANNAH COTTON, says another. There's a haunting number of infant graves from Burial Hill's early years, an indication of how difficult life was, and how often and early death called. It's no wonder why the graveyard is the Plymouth Colony's longest enduring remnant.

European explorers, traders, and fishermen had been visiting present-day New England and the fertile, cod-teeming waters off its shores for decades before the *Mayflower*'s arrival on December 18, 1620. What prevented them from staying ashore for too long was the hostility they received from the bustling population of Indigenous peoples who lined the Northeastern coast. For instance, Samuel de Champlain visited Plymouth Harbor fifteen years before the Pilgrims, where he was met by a thriving village of the Wampanoag who had occupied the southern Massachusetts coast for millennia. They made sure Champlain understood that he and his crew were unwelcome, so he didn't linger.

What drastically changed the conditions to allow the Pilgrims, and ultimately other Europeans, to settle throughout the area was a catastrophic pandemic, called by Native people the great dying. It arose in 1615, a mysterious, fatal illness that swept from what's now Maine to Rhode Island and struck with devastating lethality. In its wake, villages looked like they had been hit by an invisible gas attack, with bodies strewn everywhere, and no one left alive to bury them. Researchers long theorized the culprit was maybe the bubonic plague, or smallpox, or a flu strain brought by the crew of a French ship that ran ashore on Cape Cod, who were killed by the Wampanoags.

In 2010, disease researchers published a new theory, that a blood infection called leptospirosis (also known as rat fever) carried by infected European rats was the likely cause of the mass die-off. The signature gruesome symptoms—headaches, fever, jaundice, nosebleeds—described by survivors are more consistent, the researchers noted, with leptospirosis than any other possible disease. Regardless of the cause, the results were devastating. The pandemic ravaged for three years, killing 90 percent of the region's estimated 60,000 Indigenous inhabitants, and ending shortly before the Pilgrims arrived.

English explorer Captain Thomas Dermer described the carnage as he witnessed it in Maine in early 1619. "I passed along the coast where I found some ancient [Native] plantations not long since populous, now utterly void; in other places a remnant [of people] remains, but not free of sickness."

Captain John Smith—of Jamestown fame—made this observation during an expedition to the region around that time: "Where I had seen 100 or 200 people, there is scarce ten to be found."

The Pilgrims benefitted directly from the mass die-off, establishing Plymouth on the site of a once-thriving Wampanoag farming village that had been obliterated. The spot gave them ready-made fields for growing crops, and tree-cleared land for building homes along the protected harbor.

Still, their arrival onshore on the cusp of winter made survival difficult to the extreme. They had assumed that Plymouth's location—five degrees in latitude below England on the map—meant that it enjoyed mild weather. They were wrong. The elements, malnutrition, and diseases caused 50 out of the 102 original *Mayflower* passengers to die before spring arrived. What saved the rest from extinction during this time was grave robbery.

Before anchoring in Plymouth Harbor, the Pilgrims first stopped at Cape Cod in November 1619. Weak, hungry, and exhausted from a longer-than-expected journey on the cramped ship, they lingered at what is now Provincetown Harbor on the Cape's dune-filled eastern tip for the better part of five weeks. Time was largely spent scouting the area to decide whether its freshwater sources and land could sustain them—and what riches it might allow them to reap. Though the

Pilgrims largely consisted of Puritans who came to the New World seeking religious freedom, the Plymouth Company in England that funded their trip demanded a healthy return on investment within seven years. The settlers would soon discover what anyone who has spent time in Cape Cod knows: The only treasures to be found are the beaches and sunsets, neither of which could be sold in London or have much luster in November when winter Atlantic storms blot the sky and pound the sea.

During one of the first expeditions from the anchored ship, a group of sixteen Pilgrim scouts stumbled upon what looked like a grave freshly dug by the local Nauset tribe of the Wampanoag. The men, hoping for jewels or precious metals, unearthed it to find something more directly valuable: an underground granary containing winter stores of corn, wheat, and beans. They emptied it and began searching for other sites of freshly covered soil. The next one they found turned out to be a grave, holding two bodies—an adult and a child, accompanied by a sizable cache of corn. It was common practice among many Native peoples in North America to bury the dead with food. The Pilgrims left the bodies but took the corn. They promised in their journals they would come back someday and replenish what they had pilfered, out of respect for the dead. They never did.

The Pilgrim scouts raided some more graves and emptied the contents of a few homes—likely left vacant by the great dying—returning to the *Mayflower* with ten bushels of corn, wheat, and beans, which provided the bulk of their sustenance through the long, cold, miserable winter. In the words of one of the colonists, "And sure it was God's good providence that we found this corn, for else we know not how we should have done."

The Pilgrims made almost no contact with what was left of the Native population during their Cape Cod stopover except for a volley of arrows shot at them by the Nauset—these seemed to be more of a warning than aimed to hurt or kill. In December, they pulled the *Mayflower*'s anchor and sailed across Cape Cod Bay to the mainland and Plymouth Harbor, which offered a source of running water and better protection from storms.

But the Pilgrims' meager practical survival skills soon turned problematic. Cutting lumber from the forest and building homes atop the frozen New England ground was slow work, forcing nearly all the *Mayflower's* crew and passengers to spend the first winter aboard the ship—which had to be anchored a mile from shore, just beyond the harbor's muddy shallows. Scurvy and pneumonia soon began taking victims—and taking, and taking, and taking.

The first building the settlers erected was a thatch-roofed wooden shelter that doubled as an infirmary and living quarters for the small construction crew. Local members of the Wampanoag watched, and sometimes made their presence known in the distance, but never directly approached. By February, death became an almost daily event for the settlers. Burials took place under the cloak of night to avoid local Native people, with the bodies placed in unmarked graves on a rise now known as Coles Hill. The Pilgrims later planted crops over the graves to further mask the spot as burial grounds.* The dead were forgotten there for more than a century until floods peeled back the soil to reveal sets of remains, laid in an east–west orientation, to the surprise of locals.

In spring 1621, the surviving settlers made contact with Ousamequin. He came to the village accompanied by fifty warriors, communicating to the English that he wanted to coexist. He was under no illusions about Europeans—their hostile, imperial aspirations and their enslavement of Indigenous people. But the Wampanoag, devastated by the epidemic, found themselves under dire territorial threat from the rival Narragansett to the south. So Ousamequin needed a powerful ally.

The Pilgrims, on the other hand, needed assistance to keep fed and alive. The two sides reached an agreement, which led Ousamequin's people to help the settlers plant, grow, and hunt the food necessary to sustain them. That fall, the Native leader and about ninety of his men joined about fifty colonists during a harvest feast in what's known as the first Thanksgiving.

More firmly established, the early Pilgrims built a stone fort that doubled as a church on the steep hill that rose above the village and overlooked the harbor and Cape Cod Bay. They planted Burial Hill beside it with little decoration to mark the individual graves—none of them

---

*   More practically, bodies can help crops grow. In 2019, Washington became the first state to legalize human composting.

permanent. The Puritans considered the human body as little more than a temporary vessel for the soul, to be discarded after death. An overly elaborate burial or burial space wouldn't change the ultimate spiritual landing spot. Gravestones didn't begin to appear at Burial Hill until the late 1600s, leaving it a mystery as to who, exactly, was buried there in those early days, or precisely when the burial ground first opened to residents. For that reason, the Myles Standish Burial Ground, a cemetery in nearby Duxbury, Massachusetts, which conclusively traces its roots to 1638, dubiously claims being America's oldest maintained cemetery ahead of Burial Hill—not to mention scores of Native sacred burial grounds.

Peace between the settlers and the Native population held but slowly deteriorated over the years—in direct proportion to Indigenous lands lost—before collapsing upon Ousamequin's death in 1661. By then, Harvard University had been teaching students for nearly three decades and the expanse of the region's English settlements stretched from Maine to Connecticut. A year later, Ousamequin's second son, Metacomet, became leader of the Wampanoag. Called King Philip by the English, Metacomet led an alliance of tribes in an immensely bloody, two-year revolt that left no person—settler or Indigenous—safe, and towns in smoldering ruins. The death toll, as a percentage of the population, was higher than the American Civil War. The hostilities of King Philip's War, as it's now known, ended in 1676, when Metacomet was fatally shot in a Wampanoag village in Rhode Island.

By then, more than half of the Wampanoag people had been killed, and nearly all their land, encompassing much of eastern New England, was lost to the settlers. The English, in an act of vengeance, sold Metacomet's wife and surviving son into slavery in the West Indies. They hanged Metacomet's lifeless body and had it drawn and quartered—then they cut off his head, placed it on a pike, and displayed it publicly in Plymouth as a warning to any other Native person who might harbor ideas of resistance. His desecrated skull would stand there for a quarter century. In front of the old fort building. At the top of Burial Hill.

Ousamequin didn't avoid desecration to his remains, either. His people laid him to rest with his ancestors in a 2,500-year-old sacred burial ground in Warren, Rhode Island, but his bones and those of

Burial Hill, circa 1922

forty-two others were unearthed in 1851 to make way—in an act thick with irony—for the construction of a new railroad. The rest of the site was looted by so-called pothunters, who dug up sacred spaces looking for treasure. Native people's remains and the tools and weapons buried with them had become highly sought-after curiosities by museums and private collectors in the nineteenth century, and continue to be today. Not until the 2000s were the descendants of the people whose remains and valuables were stolen from the site allowed to reclaim many of the items. Finally, in 2017, Ousamequin's bones were returned to their original resting place and marked by a teardrop-shaped sandstone boulder etched with his name and accomplishments. It stands in what is now a city park.

The Wampanoag leader's reburial is a rare story of semi-redemption when it comes to the desecration of Indigenous burial grounds. The American tradition of looting and destroying Native graves that began with the Pilgrims robbing the Nauset dead in 1620, then the display of Metacomet's head on a pike at Burial Hill, has never ended. The expansion of European powers on the continent, followed by rapid west-ward settlement, became an extended exercise in Indigenous people's grave destruction. One of the most tragic examples took place in the mid-1800s in St. Louis, when ambitious developers leveled a cluster of earthen pyramids on the bank of the Mississippi River, destroying what some considered the greatest ancient human-made wonder in the country. These twenty-five towering structures existed for more than 1,000 years and were built within what was once an ancient bustling city of 30,000 inhabited by the Mississippian people. Its centerpiece was the three-story-tall Big Mound—which St. Louis construction crews tore down to use its contents as fill for building a nearby railroad bed.

As the carnage to Native burial grounds continued into the late twentieth century, a sliver of guilt began to percolate within the American public. It displayed itself in popular culture—particularly horror movies, with the story line of developing land on top of an "old Indian burial ground." The bestselling 1977 book *The Amityville Horror* told the supposedly true—but not really—story of a young couple driven from their Long Island home by the ghosts of Shinnecock Indian Nation members buried on the site. The movie version released in 1979 was nominated for an Academy Award and became the second-highest-grossing film of the year, behind *Super Man*, and ahead of *Rocky II* and *Star Trek*. In 1983, Stephen King published the classic book *Pet Sematary*, about a Maine town that suffered under a curse after local residents placed a graveyard for pets above a Native burial ground.

The federal government responded to growing public concerns in 1990 when Congress passed the Native American Graves Protection and Repatriation Act. It called for the safeguarding of all Native graves on federally owned land, and it empowered recognized tribes to reclaim hundreds of thousands of items—including human remains—from the collections of museums and federal agencies. It was through this law that Ousamequin's bones finally made their way back to their rightful home. Not that this halted the frenzy for Indigenous artifacts; in 2014, the FBI raided the home of a ninety-one-year-old man who kept 42,000 items from Native burial sites, including the bones of as many as 500 people, in his home, southeast of Indianapolis. Prosecutors didn't charge him with a crime, and in

January the following year, the Indiana Archaeological Society gave him its Lifetime Achievement Award for his decades of pothunting. He passed away two months later.

This century, big-box retail chains have become the newest predator of Native burial grounds, winning lawsuits allowing them to build atop ancient Indigenous sacred sites in Nashville, Tennessee; Canton, Georgia; and Anderson, California, to name a few. In other instances, these companies have simply acted without seeking permission. In 2009, construction crews for a retail giant in Oxford, Alabama, tore a giant gash through the center of the state's largest burial mound, which was at least 1,500 years old and stretched nearly twenty stories high. Protestors stepped in before the entire ancient structure was leveled.

In 2016, the Obama administration took the most sweeping action in American history to protect endangered Native sacred lands and burial grounds by creating Bears Ears National Monument in southeast Utah. The new preserve encompassed a crescent-shaped, 2,000-square-mile swath of land that was once the site of a collection of ancient villages, connected by a vast network of roads that can still be traced today. A rolling quilt of red rock mesas, juniper forests, open desert, and mountains stretching as high as 10,000 feet, it's decorated by ancient rock arches, narrow sandstone canyons, and two identical buttes that gave the preserve its name.

The monument's creation was seen as a rare moment when the U.S. government listened to, and worked together with, the country's Indigenous people to prioritize their culture, heritage, and land over other interests, resulting in a victory for the Navajo, Hopi, Ute Mountain Ute, Pueblo of Zuni, and Ute Indian Tribe of the Uintah and Ouray Reservation peoples. The monument's subsequent protection was the result of nearly a century of efforts by these five sovereign Native nations, who consider it part of their ancestral homelands.

Within its new borders also rested a trove of more than 100,000 archaeological sites—including petroglyphs dating back thousands of years, and scores of ancient Puebloan cliff dwellings still strewn with objects like ancient feather blankets and baskets filled with corn—sheltered from the elements and preserved for centuries by the dry air. Once the home to maybe as many as 30,000 people, much of the area was abandoned suddenly about eight centuries ago, maybe due to drought, and the artifacts were left behind intact.

Bears Ears is pockmarked by clusters of Native American grave sites, which had become the frequent victims of robbery and looting by pothunters on all-terrain vehicles. By falling within the boundaries of the new national monument, the sites were given an added layer of federal protection. The government designation also protected Bears Ears from new road construction and the extraction of natural gas, oil, and uranium from rich deposits in the area.

Then Obama left office, and the next presidential administration arrived. Hostile to Bears Ears from the start, but barred by law from eliminating the monument altogether, they shrank the preserve's size by 85 percent, from 1.1 million acres to 200,000 acres. The administration was also actively destructive in 2019 to Arizona's Organ Pipe Cactus National Monument, a place considered sacred to more than a dozen Native nations. Contractors hired by the federal government to build a Mexican border wall plowed a broad path straight across it, using national security as justification to ignore environmental laws and the Native American Graves Protection and Repatriation Act.

The construction crews blasted and flattened an area known as Monument Hill, which once served as a burial site for the Cherokee and Tohono O'odham people, where bones and artifacts dated back 10,000 years. They toppled forty-foot-tall saguaro cacti older than the Declaration of Independence and drained an ancient and rare desert aquifer in order to mix cement. Objections from local activists were ignored. In 2021, the Biden administration reversed the reduction in size to Bears Ears, returning it to the borders created in 2016. The damage to Organ Pipe Cactus National Monument, however, couldn't be undone.

The United States isn't alone in its continual desecration of Native people's graves. In Canada, a cedar-tree-filled 2,000-year-old burial site was clear-cut by a logging company in 2021. The country's Indigenous peoples have long fought for greater protection to sacred sites, with limited success. In Australia this century, Aboriginal Australian activists

Big Mound in St. Louis, Missouri, circa 1854, in the midst of being leveled
by developers who used its contents to build railroad beds. The imposing
structure, oval-shaped and several stories tall, was constructed by Mississippian
people between 1,000 and 1,400 C.E. Crews dismantling it discovered two
long, plaster-walled burial chambers inside, containing centuries-old remains
of about thirty people, feet pointed west and adorned by copper jewelry
and seashells taken from the Gulf of Mexico, 1,500 miles away. Big Mound's
contents—bones and all—were looted by the time its destruction was complete
in 1869, and none of its artifacts are known to exist today.

have successfully repatriated the remains of thousands of ancestral bones from private collections, universities, and museums around the world, and the effort is ongoing. In New Zealand, the desecration and robbery of Maori burial grounds remain a continuing problem.

On that November evening when I wandered Burial Hill in the semidarkness, the events surrounding Bears Ears and Organ Pipe Cactus hadn't yet taken place. I didn't yet know that the puritanical heroes of my history books had beheaded and enslaved members of the Native family who gave America its first Thanksgiving. I didn't realize or fully comprehend the extent of neglect and destruction heaped upon important Indigenous people's burial grounds, compared to the regard we pay to many gravesites occupied by early European colonists—but later while researching I would. Mostly I was thinking that I needed to keep the trip short, or my daughter would be waiting. Just after the sun extinguished behind the hill, I walked to my car, passing the historic marker once again, contemplating its words of reverence for the Pilgrims, and unaware of its omissions.

The Colonial Jewish Burial Ground, also known as the Touro
Synagogue Cemetery, is perhaps America's most
enduring symbol of religious liberty.

3. ... OR GIVE ME DEATH

Jewish cemeteries are America's first and most enduring public expressions of religious liberty—which makes them targets for intolerance

—

Colonial Jewish Burial Ground
Newport, Rhode Island
Established: 1677

WHEN YOU WALK past the Colonial Jewish Burial Ground, you might think it's just another cozy, oak-shaded old cemetery. Or you might even miss it altogether among Newport, Rhode Island's maze of centuries-old, winding streets. Yet it's not to be missed.

The burial ground, established in 1677, holds an outsized place in history. It was the second Jewish cemetery established in North America and remains the oldest Jewish sacred space still standing in the United States. I first came upon it during a frigid March weekend years ago while serving in the navy on a training visit to Newport. I would have overlooked it completely if not for its Egyptian-style granite entryway catching my attention. Flanked by a tall iron fence, it's nearly identical, down to the inverted flaming torches on the sides, to the equally old and nearly as historic Granary Burying Ground beside the Park Street Church in Boston.

The Colonial Jewish Burial Ground's gate was locked when I found it, but through the gaps in the iron bars, I could take in nearly all its modestly sized grounds. The space the cemetery occupies is compact enough that its few tall trees—a maple, oak, and ginkgo—cast shade over most of it, even with bare branches. A row of four obelisks jutted from the center, rising above the cracked, faded slate gravestones and tabletop tombs mingling with the dormant grass. Ivy draped itself over the stone-block wall facing the gate from the property's far side. The Burial Ground's surviving monuments date from the early 1700s to the mid-1800s and carry inscriptions in English, Spanish, Portuguese, and the almost-extinct Judeo-Spanish language known as Ladino.

I would later learn that unlike Boston's Granary Burying Ground, which opens its gates to the public every day, the Colonial Jewish Burial Ground, alternately called the Touro Cemetery, in Newport opens only once each year, on the third Sunday in August, and only for three hours. Nearby Touro Synagogue, the oldest standing synagogue in the country and built after the cemetery, maintains it. Traditional Jewish graveyards, in contrast to predominantly Christian ones, draw a closer connection to the human body. These spaces are intended as houses of eternity where a soul is believed to linger above the grave until the person's remains turn to dust. Out of respect for the deceased, who may be present in the burial ground and can't enjoy earthly comforts, visitors are encouraged to wear modest clothing and refrain from life's pleasures, like laughing, eating, and open prayer. The humility and simplicity of the burial ground's markers are in keeping with the notion that riches do not define a person's life. As Proverbs 22:1–2 says, from a modern translation of the Hebrew Bible: "A name is chosen above great wealth; good favor over silver and gold. A rich man and a poor man were visited upon; the Lord is the Maker of them all."

The mere creation of this cemetery, a permanent spiritual fixture planted in the colonial Rhode Island ground, was an astonishing accomplishment by the Touro congregation. It came in the face of sweeping, repressive prohibitions against the practice of Judaism in both Europe and the North American colonies. Its creation was a milestone in free expression of religion, and directly influenced the First Amendment to the U.S. Constitution, protecting the right to worship without government restraint.

America's oldest Jewish cemeteries, particularly the Colonial Jewish Burial Ground in Newport, have stood for centuries as America's first and most enduring symbols of religious liberty—a status that gives them invaluable historical and spiritual importance, but also makes them distinct targets for intolerance.

ON THE SAME week in 1492 when Christopher Columbus sailed for the New World, his benefactors, Queen Isabella and King Ferdinand—the architects of the Spanish Inquisition—expelled all Jews from Spain. Somewhere between 40,000 and as many as 160,000 people likely fled the country as a result. The refugees spread along the Mediterranean to Portugal (which then expelled Jews five years later, in 1497), North Africa, the Italian Peninsula, and the Ottoman Empire. Where Jews didn't go—openly, at least—was the New World. Spain and Portugal dominated the early age of Atlantic exploration through the sixteenth century, enforcing the same anti-Semitic policies on the lands they conquered as on their home soil.

The other rising European colonizing forces were no better. England banned Judaism in 1290 and implemented this policy on its foreign territories. France expelled Jews in 1394 and didn't fully reverse its policy until the French Revolution of the late 1700s. The Netherlands was one of the few exceptions. The Union of Utrecht, written in 1579 as the legal foundation of the Dutch Republic, stated that "everyone shall remain free in religion and that no one may be persecuted or investigated because of religion." The Dutch didn't hold completely true to these words of tolerance, but they came closer than any other European power.

In the 1630s, the Dutch West India Company gained a foothold in the New World by seizing a sliver of northeast Brazil from the Portuguese. To gain immediate strength in numbers, they allied themselves with the Indigenous population and encouraged Dutch settlement—including Jews from the Netherlands and beyond—promising prosperity and freedom of religion. At its peak, the territory's Jewish community swelled to perhaps more than 1,000 people escaping European persecution.

The Dutch era in Brazil was short-lived as Portugal retook the territory in early 1654 and expelled the Jewish population. Most of them returned to the Netherlands, while a group of twenty-three set sail for the new Dutch colony of New Amsterdam on the island of Manhattan. The journey to North America was fraught with peril since the group couldn't land at any Portuguese- or Spanish-controlled ports for fear of being imprisoned, tortured, or executed.

In late summer, the group reached their destination, but the colony's governor, Peter Stuyvesant, refused them settlement, demanding in a letter to his bosses that "this deceitful race,—such hateful enemies and blasphemers of the name of Christ,—be not allowed further to infest and trouble this new colony." The Dutch West India Company took seven months to decide but, under pressure from the country's Jewish community, overruled him.

Stuyvesant in response placed heavy burdens on the new arrivals, denying Jews full citizenship rights, taxing them heavily, and forbidding them from building a place of worship. Undeterred, the group asked the Dutch West India Company for a plot of land to bury their dead, which they were granted in 1655, on a tiny parcel outside the village's wooden ramparts. The burial ground the new congregation, Shearith Israel, built was the first Jewish sacred site established on North American soil, long before the first synagogue was constructed.

As the city's boundaries expanded in the coming decades, the property was soon reclaimed, and the burial ground vanished—no one knows of its exact location anymore. Which brings us to Newport's Colonial Jewish Burial Ground. Rhode Island was established in the 1630s by outspoken abolitionist and Baptist preacher Roger Williams after the Puritans—who didn't tolerate dissent from their political and religious orthodoxy—kicked him out of Massachusetts for his heretical preaching on liberty and equality.*

Rhode Island became a kind of breakaway, religiously free territory for people of diverse faiths. As it grew in population, the town of Newport—founded by feminist Anne Hutchinson, also excommunicated by the Puritans—turned into one of the Northeast's most bustling ports. England's King Charles II incorporated Rhode Island and its economy into the British colonies in 1663, with the concession to its residents that they could continue to "freely and fully have and enjoy his and their own judgments and consciences, in matters of religious concernments." This type of liberty was known nowhere else on British soil, or in Europe, for that matter.

---

* The Puritans hanged Quakers for their beliefs. Who hangs Quakers?

The Jewish families of Newport, mostly of Spanish and Portuguese descent, created a congregation during these years, holding services in homes, and in 1677 left their lasting imprint on the town by buying a small piece of land, establishing the Colonial Jewish Burial Ground. Touro constructed its house of worship decades later in 1758 in Newport. Nearby in New York City, the Shearith Israel congregation built a tiny new burial ground in 1677 to replace the original one. It's now called the Chatham Square Cemetery, and it still stands in what is now Chinatown. It's closed to the public but can be seen through an iron fence and is New York City's second-oldest existing cemetery after Trinity Churchyard. Shearith Israel built its first synagogue—which was North America's first synagogue, for that matter—in 1730.

After New York and Newport, Jewish communities arose in Philadelphia, Pennsylvania; Savannah, Georgia; and Charleston, South Carolina, in the 1700s. In each case, burial grounds were consecrated before a synagogue was built. Savannah's first Jewish graveyard opened in 1733, and another was built thirty years later, on land deeded by King George III with the understanding that it "shall be, and forever remain, to and for the use and purpose of a Place of Burial for all persons whatever professing the Jewish Religion." Philadelphia's Congregation Mikveh Israel established its first cemetery in 1741, which still stands. Charleston's Kahal Kadosh Beth Elohim congregation built a cemetery in 1762, which is the South's oldest surviving Jewish burial ground.

But just as Jewish cemeteries have stood as America's most enduring symbols of religious freedom, their status as such has made them continual targets for desecration. There's a pragmatic reason why the historic Jewish burial grounds in New York, Philadelphia, Charleston, and other cities are closed to the public, and protected by high walls and fences. In recent times, headlines of hate-fueled vandalism at Jewish cemeteries have proliferated. News of swastikas defacing headstones in Fall River, Massachusetts; Hartford, Connecticut; and New York City. Dozens of tombstones being toppled in Philadelphia. Political slogans being spray-painted on headstones in Michigan, just hours before a presidential campaign rally nearby. The toppling of nearly two hundred headstones in Missouri.

While the Egyptian-style front entryway at the Newport cemetery remains closed for all but three hours a year, its nearly identical twin in Boston—fronting the graveyard where historical figures like Paul Revere and John Hancock lie—remains open in perpetuity.

THE TOURO CONGREGATION in Newport drew national attention after the Revolutionary War, when its leader, Moses Seixas, sent a congratulatory letter to George Washington, asking for assurances on the freedom of religion. He argued that the United States should empower "a Government which to bigotry gives no sanction, to persecution no assistance—but generously affording to All liberty of conscience, and immunities of Citizenship: deeming every one, of whatever Nation, tongue, or language, equal parts of the great governmental Machine."

The next day, Washington replied in a letter that religious liberty for everyone, and not religious tolerance granted by a ruling class of people, would be a fundamental principle in the new country, and government would not impose religious beliefs. It closed with, "May the children of the Stock of Abraham, who dwell in this land, continue to merit and enjoy the good will of the other inhabitants, while every one shall sit in safety under his own vine and figtree, and there shall be none to make him afraid."

Washington's response would serve as the basis of the First Amendment to the Constitution. Seixas was buried in the Colonial Jewish Burial Ground upon his death in 1809.

AFTER THE WAR of 1812, the members of Newport's Jewish community began to shrink as the town's vitality as a shipping port withered beneath the shadow of larger Northeastern cities. Soon the Touro Synagogue lay vacant, though it and the cemetery were maintained by New Yorkers who spent summers in the area.

Henry Wadsworth Longfellow, one of the most popular American poets of the nineteenth century, stumbled across the burial ground in 1852 and wrote an elegy to it called "The Jewish Cemetery at Newport." In it, he mourns the disappearance of the community's Jewish population as a metaphor for the Jewish diaspora losing its homeland of Israel. He concludes with the lines:

> But ah! what once was has been shall be no more!
> The groaning earth in travail and in pain
> Brings forth its races, but does not restore,
> And the dead nations never rise again.

The following decade, the young New York poet Emma Lazarus—and, in fact, the great-niece of Moses Seixas—wrote a response to Longfellow, using the same form and meter, titled "In the Jewish Synagogue at Newport." Her perspective is one of optimism, not loss. She describes a place where "green grass lieth gently over all," and while the synagogue may seem vacant, she adds, "Nathless the sacred shrine is holy yet."

In 1883, Lazarus wrote the sonnet "The New Colossus," which would be placed on the pedestal of the Statue of Liberty. It's partly influenced by the experiences of her immigrant descendants, who brought religious freedom to America's shores. In the poem, the "mighty woman with a torch" whom she calls the "Mother of Exiles" stands as a welcoming beacon to all.

> "Keep, ancient lands, your storied pomp!" cries she
> With silent lips. "Give me your tired, your poor,
> Your huddled masses yearning to breathe free,
> The wretched refuse of your teeming shore.
> Send these, the homeless, tempest-tost to me,
> I lift my lamp beside the golden door!"

Walk through Newport's Colonial Jewish Burial Ground, as I once did, and you'll witness it as the most enduring embodiment of this ideal of liberty.

Monticello's enslaved people's burial ground, discovered in 2001, lies largely undisturbed as a monument to the hundreds of captive workers who toiled under Thomas Jefferson for his profit.

4. WHERE THE BODIES ARE BURIED

Southern plantation owners concealed the evidence of their
moral crimes by hiding the bones of the enslaved

—

Monticello African American Graveyard
Charlottesville, Virginia
Established: Late 1700s

WHERE THE BODIES are buried. The *Oxford English Dictionary* says the earliest known use of this phrase comes from the 1941 Orson Welles movie *Citizen Kane.* In it, the widow of media mogul Charles Foster Kane tells a reporter digging into her late husband's past, "Look, if you're smart, you'll get in touch with Raymond. He's the butler. You'll learn a lot from him. He knows where all the bodies are buried."

The meaning of the phrase is clear: To know "where the bodies are buried" means to hold knowledge of someone's, or a group of people's, most shameful, incriminating, and secret acts. I mulled these words one stifling August day as I lingered on the neatly paved parking lot of a Hampton Inn in the heart of Charlottesville, Virginia, at the foot of the Blue Ridge Mountains. *Where the bodies are buried.*

There, about where I stood, was reportedly the spot where Eston Hemings, the six-foot-tall son of Thomas Jefferson and enslaved servant Sally Hemings, owned a small home after becoming free in 1827. I wondered what the soil under my feet could tell the world about America's third president.

My plan from there was to make the fifteen-minute drive to Jefferson's renowned mountaintop estate, Monticello. First stop on the property would be to see the Jefferson family graveyard, which houses Jefferson himself and some of his descendants. My second stop would be to get a look at the famed mansion house and explore the grounds directly around it. Finally, I would go to Monticello's African American Graveyard, the resting place for maybe as many as forty enslaved people who lived and died on the property largely during Jefferson's time.

The African American Graveyard's location—and even its existence—vanished from consciousness for more than a century until researchers uncovered it in a wooded area at Monticello in 2001. No written records had been kept of its whereabouts, and no permanent grave markers were placed at the site. The lack of a paper trail for an enslaved people's graveyard on a Southern plantation is striking but not surprising, even for Jefferson—a meticulous record keeper who left troves of documents detailing the tiniest day-to-day goings-on at Monticello. In fact, it's typical.

More than 6 million people died while enslaved on American soil between the early 1600s and the Civil War. Yet the whereabouts of a vast majority of their remains are unknown. This is partly the result of conscious acts by Southern plantation owners to hide the evidence of their misdeeds. Although the institution of human bondage was legal, the people involved in perpetuating it, including Jefferson, reveal through their concealment of enslaved people's graves that they understood its hideous immorality. Only now, through research and activism in places from New Orleans and Tallahassee to Monticello, are we finally uncovering a tiny fraction of these hidden burial sites. Only now are we learning where the bodies are buried.

MONTICELLO ISN'T THE flat, sprawling Southern plantation I had imagined. It's not Tara from *Gone with the Wind*, or George Washington's Mount Vernon, where a stately mansion lies in repose at the end of a long, flat, oak-shaded drive, surrounded in every direction by farm fields. Instead, it looks more like a posh, colonial-era mountain getaway with a stately, 11,000-square-foot mansion designed by Jefferson—from the foundation to the tall rooftop dome—occupying the summit of a rounded peak within the Blue Ridge of the Appalachians. It offers almost unimaginably vast, unimpeded views to the west of wooded hills and mountaintops—still seemingly untouched by the human hand—stretching without end into the horizon.

Realize it or not, you've actually seen Monticello's private mansion, built by enslaved people and kept afloat during Jefferson's time through the labor of enslaved people, many thousands of times. You've felt the edges of its image between your thumb and forefinger, as it has been engraved on the flip side of the U.S. nickel since 1938.

When I arrived at the Monticello estate, I parked in one of the lots beneath the visitor's center, which is separated from the mansion by a new-growth forest and nearly two hundred feet in elevation. The property has been owned and operated for the last century by the non-profit Thomas Jefferson Foundation and receives roughly a half million tourists a year. I bought my ticket at the ticket booth, housed within an impressive and relatively new, sustainably built structure. Then I ascended a steep path through the woods, with sweat immediately beginning to soak through the back of my T-shirt. After about a half mile the trees opened to reveal a grassy clearing and the Monticello Graveyard. There, Jefferson lies with about two hundred of his relatives, descendants, and a few friends, all surrounded by a tall wrought iron fence that keeps them insulated from the public.

America's third president chose this location for his family plot because he and a childhood friend used to spend their idle time there, sitting beneath a giant oak, studying and dreaming. The graveyard is littered with elegant markers of different dates, shapes, sizes, and designs—from long granite tabletop tombs with brick-and-mortar bases to tiny slate gravestones, from lichen covered and centuries old to shiny and relatively new. It's still an active burial ground, with its entire south-eastern half filled only with grass, waiting for future arrivals.

As you might expect, Jefferson's resting place is by far the most prominent within the graveyard. It's marked by a twenty-foot-tall granite obelisk, designed by Jefferson to be his memorial, and inscribed with words he penned himself to ensure future generations of Americans would know how he wanted to be remembered:

HERE WAS BURIED

THOMAS JEFFERSON

AUTHOR OF THE

DECLARATION OF

AMERICAN INDEPENDENCE

OF THE

STATUTE OF VIRGINIA

FOR RELIGIOUS FREEDOM

AND FATHER OF THE

UNIVERSITY OF VIRGINIA

Egyptian-style art and architecture were particularly popular throughout the nineteenth century, including in graveyards. Obelisks represent light, vitality, and rebirth; they're eye-catching without taking up much space. They were often built in town squares or prominent city locations—like the Washington Monument in Washington, D.C., and the Bunker Hill Monument outside of Boston—and used by the wealthy as grave markers.

There's also the obelisk's symbolic representation of the male anatomy, which shouldn't be overlooked. As my physician wife, who's never shy with talking about body parts, puts it when we walk through old cemeteries packed with firmly erect obelisks, "A lot of men were overcompensating for something around here."

Jefferson's towering obelisk rises from the edge of the graveyard. I spied it from the closest spot possible through the fence's ornate front gate. Above my head hung a gilded plaque that read: THIS GRAVEYARD PLOT IS THE PRIVATE PROPERTY OF THOMAS JEFFERSON'S DESCENDANTS.

A steady trickle of tourists flowed past as I stood there, headed either to or from the mansion. Not wanting to monopolize the best viewing spot, I moved to the side after a minute, uphill. A middle-aged father wearing a fanny pack—yes, an old-school 1980s-style fanny pack, but let's not judge—and his teenage son in a Kansas Jayhawks T-shirt walked up to the gate. The son shook it lightly with two hands.

"You can't go in there; it's chained," the father said.

The son looked at the padlocked chain that held the gate closed. He nodded. "Oh, it's chained."

Thomas Jefferson's grave in the locked and chained
family burial ground at Monticello

It was striking, and ironic, to see Jefferson and his relatives penned
inside an iron cage kept shut by thick chains. It felt isolating—physically,
and from the present time—rather than exclusive. The group of descendants who own and maintain the graveyard call themselves the Monticello Association. They're completely separate from the nonprofit that
runs the estate, and they're very particular about who can be interred

beyond the metal bars. The Monticello Association states that burials in the graveyard are open only to the direct descendants of children born to Jefferson and wife Martha.

Yet Jefferson had other children. He fathered at least six with Sally Hemings—who was Martha's half sister, by the way—beginning in 1790. Four of those children survived past youth to be enslaved by Jefferson, forced into labor as carpenters and textile workers at Monticello. When Jefferson was in his late seventies, he allowed two of his kids to go free, his son Beverly and daughter Harriet, followed by sons Madison and Eston upon his death in 1826 at age eighty-three, as directed in his will. Sally Hemings was never officially freed, but Jefferson's daughter Martha eventually allowed her to leave the plantation to live with Eston in downtown Charlottesville—at the spot where I began the day of my tour, where a hotel now stands.

The family graveyard grabbed national headlines in 1998. A DNA test of one of Eston Heming's descendants confirmed their genetic link to Jefferson, but the Monticello Association refused to recognize the mountain of evidence of the third president's paternity. When the Hemings side of the family asked for burial rights there, the other side voted in 2002 by an overwhelming margin—according to one of the people who participated—95-6, against. They suggested that the Hemings descendants ask the nonprofit that runs and owns Monticello for a separate but equal parcel somewhere on the estate for burials. The Hemings side naturally declined.

Anyone who knows this backstory can't help but be consumed by it when visiting the family graveyard. I caught my breath at the top edge of the graveyard for a few final seconds, looking down at Jefferson and his family, and the profound value they have all placed upon a proper, dignified burial.

Monticello's lone identified African American burial ground, by contrast, somehow vanished from consciousness in the years after Jefferson's death until it was discovered in 2001. It's unknown how many more enslaved people's burial grounds might lie on the estate, or where they may be. Southern plantation owners like Jefferson took active measures to keep African American graveyards and funeral practices on their properties out of general sight, and mind. They also did what they could to remove any semblance of ceremony from these burials. Funerals of more than a few gatherers were forbidden. Burials could only take place in the dark. No written grave markers were allowed. Burial grounds themselves were usually set far apart from the plantation house, on a patch that couldn't be farmed, grazed, otherwise used for profit—out of sight of any visitors. The locations of these spots were almost never put into any written record. This is why we only know the locations of a tiny fraction.

The route from Jefferson's grave took me uphill for maybe a quarter of a mile before depositing me into a clearing near the top of the peak. And there it was: the backside of Monticello mansion. I approached the house from a long avenue called Mulberry Row, which ran in a straight line along the side of the mountaintop, skirting the edge of the grand back lawn. This dirt street was the plantation's central vein but was hidden from visitors who arrived on the front drive.

I passed the remains of outbuildings dating from the plantation days: A charcoal burning shed. An iron storehouse. A joiner's cabin. At one time, seventeen structures stood alongside Mulberry Row, including a blacksmith shop, a smokehouse, a dairy, and a textile-weaving shop, all where enslaved people toiled from sunup to sundown to earn Jefferson his comfortable living. Among the educational displays posted on Mulberry Row, I found one with a paragraph labeled TREATMENT OF SLAVES. It noted that Jefferson "struggled to balance humane treatment of slaves with the need for profit at Monticello."

Struggled. If the Jefferson struggle was real, it was certainly hard to spot. *Humane treatment of slaves.* That's quite a contradiction in terms. Slavery by its very nature dehumanizes. Think of the mental gymnastics needed by the people writing, approving, printing, and finally displaying the words *humane treatment of slaves* on an educational board that 500,000 people pass each year.

The signboard went on to explain that Jefferson instructed his white foremen to minimize severe punishment. "On occasion," it read, "he ordered a whipping for repeated misbehavior as an example to other slaves."

Ah, well, misbehavior. More mental gymnastics. What, I wonder, was the definition of *misbehavior* for an American enslaved person?

Refusing to submit to forced labor? Trying to escape from being held captive and treated like property?

I was trained in the military to follow the Code of Conduct, which states, "If I am captured, I will continue to resist by all means available. I will make every effort to escape and aid others to escape. I will accept neither parole nor special favors." This type of misbehavior earns soldiers medals for bravery.

The educational sign addressing enslavement stood outside what was left of the nail factory—maybe the most infamous of Monticello's worksites. Jefferson opened it in 1794, the year he began construction on the mansion. He used enslaved boys starting at age ten to work inside the stifling-hot outbuilding. Those who needed extra motivation were whipped. In justifying the beatings, Jefferson wrote that some enslaved children "require a vigour of discipline to make them do reasonable work."

The factory soon churned out as many as 10,000 nails a day, the child labor putting so much money in Jefferson's pockets, it "now provides completely for the maintenance of [his] family." The institution of slavery kept him solvent and raised the very frame of his plantation house. During his life, Jefferson enslaved 600 people, 400 of them at Monticello, with a peak working population at any one time of 130. In all likelihood, scores of enslaved people died and were buried on the estate—from newborns to those who managed to exceed the Virginia enslaved person's average life expectancy of twenty-two years.

Early in his political career, Jefferson passionately opposed enslavement. He wrote a fiery 168-word passage protesting the "crimes" of the British colonial slave trade in the Declaration of Independence before it was deleted from the final draft. In it he accused King George of waging "cruel war against human nature itself, violating its most sacred rights of life & liberty in the persons of a distant people who never offended him, captivating & carrying them into slavery in another hemisphere or to incur miserable death in their transportation thither."

This language showed his keen understanding of "the hideous blot" of enslavement's "moral depravity." But after the revolution, Jefferson struggled to maintain his personal wealth, and so slavery and the brutality of enforcing its system—a system that left 6 million people of African descent dead and buried on American soil before the end of the Civil War—became all too acceptable.

Yes, 6 million. The figure was recently compiled by J. David Hacker, a demographic historian at the University of Minnesota. He relied heavily upon old census records, which were surprisingly well-kept, especially after the Three-Fifths Compromise of 1787, which established that each enslaved American counted as three-fifths of a person. In total, he calculated that the enslaved population in the country performed a staggering 410 billion hours of forced labor.

It's likely that the plantation owners in the South recorded the living enslaved people on their estates, but not the dead, because a well-marked graveyard would have offered lasting physical and symbolic evidence of slavery's human toll. They were intimately aware of the importance and enduring power of graveyards—and how they bear witness to history, good and bad. Jefferson was among them, as shown by the care he took to set aside an inviting patch of land at Monticello to create a family burial ground that would endure through the ages. And through the obelisk he designed for his grave site, and the epitaph he penned that he knew would likely be read by generations of Americans for centuries to come.

The story told by the bones beneath enslaved people's graveyards was equally damning to those involved in the institution, by revealing with concrete evidence its brutality. In 1991 in New York City, archaeologists unearthed the remains of 427 enslaved people upon the discovery of a mass African American burial ground also erased from the map and forgotten. They discovered that 43 percent of the remains belonged to people who died before reaching sixteen years old. The bones of those who survived into adulthood revealed severe malnutrition and exposure to repeated trauma. Researchers identified "huge, deadly fractures" on the remains of individuals forced to carry loads too heavy for their bodies to withstand—like instances of the spine pushed up into the cranial cavity. The project director told a newspaper the bones provided evidence that many enslaved people labored "at the margins of human physical capacity."

To assume plantation owners were ignorant to the greed and moral degeneracy embedded at the foundation of slavery is to give them more credit than they earned or deserved. There was no illusion of humane slavery. Their conscious efforts to obscure enslaved people's graveyards show they wanted to hide where the bodies were buried.

I TOOK MY time circling the Monticello house while a tour guide led a group of twenty people by a re-created enslaved person's cabin on Mulberry Row. Another guide welcomed two people into the mansion through the front door. The property was well-kept and so lush with green, all accentuated by the stunning wooded backdrop. It's easy to understand why Jefferson was drawn to this place. After a while, I retraced my footsteps down the mountain, slowly passing the Jefferson family graveyard again, and down to the visitor's center. I headed toward my parking spot, but along the way was the other important stop in my Monticello journey.

Descending to a spot between lots C and D, I found it: the estate's African American Graveyard. The graveyard was about one hundred feet by forty-five feet, enclosed by a split-rail wooden fence. A couple of rails had broken and fallen, and the posts were termite-eaten. A sign stood beside a narrow entryway that said at the bottom: PLEASE ENTER WITH RESPECT. No gates or chains or locks were there to keep people out.

Inside, a scattering of fieldstones peeked above the red, weed-garnished clay. A beech tree, a couple of oaks, and a few scraggly pines all stood within the enclosure. A few rectangular impressions were visible on the ground—each facing east–west—where the earth had been disturbed long ago for burial and had settled differently.

The African American Graveyard is the final resting place for an estimated forty enslaved adults and children who died at Monticello. A recent analysis of coffin nails unearthed in the acidic soil reveals that the burials took place during Jefferson's time. It's likely that members of the Hemings family were among them, as were those from the other main families who spanned generations on the estate—Gillette, Fossett, Hern, and Granger.

After the site was discovered by archaeologists in 2001, it was enclosed and rededicated. There are plans to enhance the area around it, to bring more attention to it and offer a better chance for people to lin- ger and contemplate as they make their way from the cars nearby to the visitor's center. If enslaved people's burial grounds were intentionally hidden from the view of Southern plantation visitors during Jefferson's time, they should be the first landmark we see now. Monticello's sits serenely between patches of pavement. The burial ground is the only part of the tour of Jefferson's estate accessible without buying a ticket.

Jefferson, who in his famous Farm Book diary took notes on nearly every granular detail at Monticello, from the daily temperature, to nailery productivity, to the precise number of yards of cloth used for enslaved people's clothes. Jefferson, who possessed enough moral clarity to write about the evils of slavery throughout his life. Jefferson, who gave the world the phrase *All men are created equal.* Jefferson, who yet somehow didn't manage to keep a single record on where enslaved people were buried on his property.

A MOVEMENT AMONG researchers and activists is now under- way to locate and unearth the lost resting places of enslaved Americans at former plantations throughout the South. Archaeological efforts like the one at Monticello have taken place at the Virginia estates of George Washington and James Madison, for example, where records also don't exist. (Washington himself, meanwhile, lies within a grand tomb designed at his request that allows people to view his sleek marble sarcophagus through a redbrick archway, and Madison lies in his family graveyard beneath a giant obelisk similar to Jefferson's.)

Researchers in Delaware have found 400 enslaved people's graves clustered together on state land once occupied by the 13,000-acre plan- tation of John Dickinson, considered one of the country's Founding Fathers and the namesake of Dickinson College. Archaeologists near Annapolis, Maryland, have uncovered what's left of an enslaved people's burial ground on a tobacco plantation owned by the relatives of Francis Scott Key, the man who wrote "The Star-Spangled Banner." Activists in Florida recently used ground-penetrating radar to locate a cluster of forty enslaved people's graves beneath the seventh fairway of a Tallahassee golf course, where a plantation once stood, after rectangular-shaped impressions in the ground appeared.

In Loudoun County, Virginia, a local pastor led a community effort to locate, restore, and preserve a nearby enslaved people's burial ground found hidden in the woods and marked with fieldstones. She did the same shortly after with similar sites on former plantation lands in other Virginia communities. In Louisiana, activists recently convinced an oil company to preserve an old burial ground on a sugar plantation west of New Orleans, containing maybe as many as 1,000 enslaved people's graves. Researchers in the area believe hundreds more like it are strewn throughout the industrial wastelands between the city and Baton Rouge—though countless more have already been plowed, paved over, dug up, or removed. Each one leaves a record of our past that has long been obscured.

After my Monticello visit, I drove back to Charlottesville, my route skirting the University of Virginia—another of Jefferson's local contributions. There, in 2012, the unmarked grave shafts of sixty-seven enslaved people were found when a landscaping crew was peeling back some topsoil for a construction project. I navigated the afternoon traffic and made my way back to that chain hotel, where Eston Hemings's house likely once stood. Getting out of my vehicle, I walked inside the lobby looking for . . . I'm not sure what. A plaque? A memorial?

Painted on one wall, above the front desk, was a mural of Montpelier, the plantation owned by James Madison where his family enslaved more than three hundred people. Painted on another was a mural of the Rotunda, the most recognizable building at the University of Virginia, designed by Jefferson himself and built by enslaved people from nearly 1 million bricks made by enslaved people. Outside, across the street, a small group of college students—a mix of genders and skin tones and clothing choices and tattoos—walked into Benny Deluca's pizza joint, "Home of the Virginia Slice," whatever a Virginia Slice is.

My mind turned to Sally Hemings. In the nineteenth century in Virginia, free African Americans in the South were usually buried in the yard where they lived, since they were not allowed to establish community properties like graveyards, or even churches. Sally Hemings died in 1835, in her early sixties, while still living with Eston. That much is known. Her final resting place is not recorded—no shocker—but there's a strong theory put forward by Lucian Truscott IV, a direct descendant of Thomas and Martha Jefferson. He supports welcoming the Hemings branch into the Jefferson family graveyard. Truscott wrote in an *American Heritage* article, "If indeed Sally was interred behind her sons' house, her body today lies beneath the parking lot of a Hampton Inn."

Maybe that place should go on the back of the nickel.

Mount Auburn Cemetery, considered America's first city park

5. OUT OF THE CHURCHYARD, INTO THE WOODS

Rural-style cemeteries transformed America's landscape, turning burial grounds into tree-filled tourist destinations

—

Mount Auburn Cemetery

Cambridge, Massachusetts

Established: 1831

NOT ALL BIRDS sing like angels. Take the black-throated green warbler. Its "zee-zee-zoo-zoo-zee" violates the air like a traffic cop's whistle from hell. At least the song from one particular black-throated green warbler did. The plum-size bird—actually more yellow than green—announced itself to me and the six others in my bird-watching group one late-spring morning at Mount Auburn Cemetery in Cambridge, Massachusetts. We spied it perched on the arm of a grandfatherly oak tree.

According to the person serving as our birding guide, a tall, raven-haired man named Brooks, that warbler had likely traveled thousands of miles from South America, mostly at night, flying over mountains and desert, tropical swamps and cities, and across the length of the Gulf of Mexico. It came to New England to spend the summer, and the cemetery offered a brief stopover before it made the final leg of its journey. Such a big trip for such a tiny creature seemed against the laws of physics and nature—yet there it sat, among the viridescent leaves. Singing. Poorly.

Though I believe that all guides—tour guides, river guides, museum guides, birding guides, whatever—fabricate most of what they tell their clients, I took Brooks at his word. After all, he was a

Harvard-trained naturalist. Or so he said. My group and I hung on his words, and as we did, none of us even bothered to consider the dead people resting below our feet. At Mount Auburn Cemetery, the formerly breathing can be an afterthought like that.

More than a quarter million living people pass through Mount Auburn's elegant Egyptian-style gates each year to look at the natural, parklike sights as if they're strolling through nearby Harvard Yard. They linger to enjoy the cemetery's fern-carpeted groves of ancient oaks and maples that adorn its glacier-carved hills. They sit beside its lily-filled ponds to smell the roses—and azaleas, and zinnias. They climb stony Washington Tower, which rises 125 feet above a bend in the nearby Charles River, to glimpse the to-die-for views of downtown Boston.

With so much to see on the grounds, it's not unusual for people to wander cluelessly past, or even above, the resting place of poet Henry Wadsworth Longfellow, or cookbook maven Fannie Farmer, or John Wilkes Booth's less murderous brother Edwin. If the season is right, the guiltiest grave trampers are the bird-watchers, always angling for a better view. Birding is one of Mount Auburn's biggest attractions because the cemetery is an important migration stop on the Atlantic Flyway—an inviting patch of green among a wasteland of overdeveloped asphalt.

Despite its present-day popularity, its essential role in American history remains largely buried. Opened in 1831 as a leafy escape from the bustle of the city for both the living and dead, Mount Auburn was the country's first "garden," or "rural," cemetery—sparking a rapid spread of imitators across the young country. Mount Auburn was the birthplace of landscape architecture in the United States, and the country's first public park, laying the first building block for the modern environmental movement. But just as notably, it untethered graveyards from houses of worship and turned them into freestanding entities, which transformed America's burial process and customs. Nearly every modern cemetery in the country shares the DNA of Mount Auburn.

I HAD ARRIVED at Mount Auburn shortly after dawn, and quickly met the other members of the tour. Brooks led us along a grassy fin of earth called Indian Ridge, pushed skyward by ancient glaciers, now garnished with oaks and maples. Throughout the spring, tens of thousands of travel-weary birds like the black-throated green warbler arrive for a brief rest at Mount Auburn. Brooks pointed out the calls of as many varieties as he could—like the "see-me, here-I-am!" of the blue-headed vireo, and the "you-hoo-you-hoo-you-hoo" of the Baltimore oriole. At this time of year, a sharp-eared person could single out all kinds of thrushes, vireos, sparrows, warblers, flycatchers, and sandpipers, and even the elusive scarlet tanager, which is my favorite bird.

The cemetery's 170 acres are so verdant because they're home to more than 10,000 trees and shrubs, which also shelter vibrant populations of frogs, turtles, lizards, and even coyotes—as well as a not-as-vibrant population of roughly 100,000 permanent human residents. Spread among the grounds lie 60,000 grave markers, from ornate nineteenth-century mini masterpieces to modern polished-granite, machine-cut plaques. Every pathway opens into a different landscape—a hidden pond, a towering hill, an open lawn, a dark, wooded thicket. And none of it would have existed, I must add, if it weren't for the French.

In the late 1700s, France's King Louis XVI faced a grave problem: Paris's aging burial grounds had finally reached such a point of overcrowding that people's remains began spilling out of them. The most populous graveyard lay beside Holy Innocents' Church, near the city's center. More than two million bodies had been deposited there over the course of six centuries.

During that era, the French in particular and Europeans in general were fairly unsentimental about a loved one's remains as long as they were placed on sacred ground. The rich, to gain a few extra steps ahead of the masses on the stairway to heaven, often paid to be deposited inside the church itself, in the basement crypts—or, if there was no subterranean level, beneath the floorboards. In this way, churches served more accurately as glorified tombs where people came to worship. And foul-smelling tombs, at that—it's hard to hide the scent of decomposition of so many bodies in so small of an area. To ease the problem, clergy often threw fragrant strewing herbs on the floor to act as air fresheners, but that's like putting a daisy on a manure pile and hoping it'll smell like flowers.

The poorer dead were relegated to interments in the churchyards—turning burial grounds like the one at Holy Innocents' into jam-packed landfills of flesh rather than pleasant, dignified graveyards. Gravediggers there did little more than dump bodies into mass pits, which may or may not have been covered with a sprinkling of dirt. As soon as the bodies decomposed enough, the bones were removed and stacked like kindling in a charnel house, to allow the process to begin again with new occupants. Sometimes for the sake of speed and space, holes were never even dug, and bodies were dumped one atop another aboveground.

On hot days, these mountains of the dead at Holy Innocents' created an oozing, gelatinous runoff of fat, and on breezy days, the *eau de* dead overpowered surrounding neighborhoods, keeping even the most God-fearing churchgoers home. Neighbors insisted that the gases of the dead were snuffing out candles and changing the color of clothes that came into contact with it. Making matters worse, in 1780, a spring season of biblical downpours pummeled Paris, softening the ground, causing an avalanche of bones to burst into the cellar of a house next to Holy Innocents' like a scene from a horror movie. It created a scandal, and King Louis XVI responded by banning all further burials within the city limits. Six years later, in 1786, an edict was issued ordering the removal of all human remains from the Holy Innocents' Cemetery, and for the church building itself to be destroyed.

The removal operation was remarkable in its efficiency. Night after night, skeleton crews placed human remains on carriages covered in black sheets and drove them through the streets of Paris. Chanting priests trailed the caravans, carrying incense and torches. The remains' ultimate destination was the vast network of limestone quarry tunnels dug beneath the city, which became known as the Paris Catacombs. Any usable fat from still-decaying bodies was turned into soap and candle wax, while fires burned constantly through the city's center in vain hopes of purifying the air until the removal work finished just two years later in 1788.

Soon afterward, the French fought their revolution, toppling the monarchy, and in 1799 elevated Napoleon to power. He ordered four new cemeteries to be constructed on the outskirts of the city, each one marking a point on the compass for easy access by all Parisians. The cemeteries to the north and south were built from existing graveyards, the one to the west was never created, and the one to the east became the famous Père-Lachaise.

Built on the sloped grounds of a lavish former home for Jesuit priests, the forty-three-acre Père-Lachaise was designed by well-known French architect Alexandre-Théodore Brongniart as a kind of country village for the dead. He decorated it with a network of winding cobblestone alleys and tree-lined main avenues that meandered through the property, all marked by street signs. There was nothing like it in the world. Père-Lachaise had the relaxing, pastoral feel of a European garden, splashed with rosebushes and vibrant beds of tulips and violets, and topped by newly planted maples, walnuts, willows, and blossoming cherry trees. It invited Parisians to stroll in wonder, and linger.

From the start, Père-Lachaise was nondenominational, accepting people of all faiths, which broke from long-standing European interment traditions. It was believed to be spacious enough that the proprietors could sell plots as permanent resting spots without overcrowding, and it broke the churches from their monopolies on the lucrative burial business. Père-Lachaise opened in early May 1804, and in June accepted its first resident, a four-year-old girl.

As revolutionary as Père-Lachaise was, it didn't attract many customers at first. It was set too far from the center of town, making for a long, expensive journey. Plus, the whole concept of a beautiful burying ground where people could visit just seemed too strange. Only fourteen people were interred on the property in its first year, and the numbers barely rose in its second year. So, in 1817, Père-Lachaise's desperate proprietors decided to inject some marketing flair to the project by buying, then burying, three long-passed famous residents: Molière, the beloved French playwright who died in 1673, and Héloïse and Abelard, the twelfth-century letter-writing lovers. The trick worked, as real estate around the celebrities became hot property among well-to-do dead Parisians. Soon Père-Lachaise's popularity soared. Today, its 110 acres are the final home to 1 million people, including composer Frédéric Chopin, novelist Marcel Proust, playwright Oscar Wilde, poet Gertrude Stein, actress Sarah Bernhardt, and overrated rock star Jim Morrison.

In fact, Père-Lachaise is now filled to capacity. To make space for occasional new burials, its administrators have begun declaring older, obscure graves as abandoned. If no surviving family members can be tracked down and reached, the plot is emptied of any remaining bones, which are placed in a bone house, and the site is resold. So much for the permanent residence. The cost of a grave for a new occupant who wants to stay in so-called perpetuity is $16,000, but if people want to occupy their plots for only a decade before bone removal, the cost is a more affordable $1,000.

The scant annual burial revenues only cover a fraction of the upkeep, so Père-Lachaise relies heavily on meager scraps of city funding, leaving the property in a state of near disrepair—a place that has long lost its vitality of youth. Still, the cemetery is breathtaking, with 700,000 mostly aboveground graves and tombs, and more statues than a half dozen Louvres. Some visitors will leave a bottle of whiskey for Morrison, or fresh-cut flowers for Chopin. People used to leave graffiti and lipstick-laden kisses in tribute to Wilde, the Irish poet and playwright who fled England in 1897 for Paris after serving two years in prison for loving another man, until a glass barrier was placed in front of his tomb in 2011 to protect it. Others stop to take pictures of Héloïse and Abelard. The couple lie together within what looks like an outdoor stone chapel, their altar-like tomb topped by granite likenesses of them, lying flat, eyes pointed at the sky. Héloïse is pressing her hands together as if in prayer. The cemetery is called the City of Immortals, because its crowded streets and cobblestoned paths feel like an urban area decorated by flowers and trees. And art.

The artistry adorning the plots across Père-Lachaise is as eclectic as it is weatherworn. Especially spellbinding are the many bronze, lifelike statues, greened with age. A wistfulness fills the cemetery that even the tree and flower blossoms of spring can't filter, which I guess is appropriate for a place that's crammed with so many tragic stories—of artists and heroes, the infamous and anonymous, the victims of wars, plagues, and the Holocaust. The mood is different from the one at Mount Auburn Cemetery, which is wilder, more untamed, and so bursting with life.

IN THE EARLY 1800s, cities in the United States faced the same problem with overcrowded burial grounds as in Paris and across Europe. Boston's three central burial grounds had become so stuffed with bodies that storm runoff seeped into the city's wells, polluting the water supply. Grave robbing among the shallow, overfilled graves became rampant. According to local legend, shortly after American Founding Father John Hancock was interred in 1804 at the Granary Burying Ground downtown, robbers dug up his body and cut off his hands to take the ornate rings off his fingers.

Sometimes entire corpses were stolen. Body snatchers, known as resurrection men, made a comfortable living working in small but speedy teams, emptying fresh graves and selling bodies to the area's rapidly expanding medical schools. There was no legal method to meet the demand for cadavers, and digging up graves beat the work alternatives for people struggling to make a living. A group of Harvard medical students went so far as to create their own secret corpse-grabbing society, called the Spunker Club, which snuck into Boston's various burial grounds using three-person squads to unearth fresh stiffs.* City graveyard caretakers, forced to respond to the problem, hired guards to patrol the grounds at night. In 1815, the state legislature stepped in, turning grave robbing into a felony.

The demand for "burial reform" became a popular political cause in Boston at the time. Until, in 1825, a Harvard professor named Jacob Bigelow proposed a solution: a sprawling graveyard on the edge of town that would double as a landscaped public nature preserve. The concept was inspired by Père-Lachaise but would be different in one major aspect—instead of mimicking a garden, it would be leafier, wilder, and more untamed, like a reflection of America itself. The plots would be spacious enough for families to share and decorate as they'd like. Instead of calling this new concept a burial ground, as nearly all American graveyards were referred to at the time, he gave it a more dignified and obscure European title: a cemetery.

---

* A custodian assigned to get rid of the stolen cadaver bones stashed them in the basement walls of Harvard's Holden Chapel, where they remained until being discovered by construction workers in 1999.

The concept seemed crazy to some at first. Americans in the early nineteenth century gave almost zero consideration to protecting nature. They considered it something to be defeated, not nurtured. Parks didn't exist in any form, either. Yes, there were some limited urban green spaces—like Boston Common—but they were generally used for livestock grazing, and as military encampments, and to hold public executions. Still, Bigelow was undeterred. A practicing physician who also taught at Harvard Medical School, he was a compulsive innovator—writing the definitive textbook on the medicinal use of plants, creating a new color-printing method for books, and even coining the term *technology*.

Bigelow began selling the idea of a stand-alone nondenominational "garden of graves" among Boston's elites, whose religious beliefs had taken a dramatic turn from the doom-and-gloom Calvinism of their grandparents and great-grandparents toward Unitarianism. This new brand of religion rejected predestination, original sin, the Holy Trinity, and a literal interpretation of the Bible. It instead embraced human free will, a benevolent Christian God unified with all living things, and salvation through good works.

Unitarianism didn't offer the same certainties of a heaven (or hell) that the Calvinists claimed, which meant Bostonians sought novel ways to immortalize themselves in an earthlier sense. Bigelow's cemetery offered them one. Here, their bodies could be laid to rest permanently, without threat of being lost, moved, desecrated, or completely forgotten. Here, they could etch their names onto the faces of monuments that would stand for centuries, maintaining an essence of their souls even if there was no guaranteed afterlife.

Bigelow spent the next several years searching for the right property. He constantly ran into local resistance because sellers generally weren't interested in their land being turned into a mega-graveyard, and due to the not-in-my-backyard attitude of the neighbors. Bigelow spotted the perfect property in 1830: an idyllic seventy-one acres in a largely undeveloped plot in Cambridge, near a bend in the Charles River. Named Stone's Woods, it was punctuated by a hill jutting above the leafy vegetation like a goose bump, which peered across the Charles River to downtown Boston only four miles away. The only people who ventured onto the property were nearby Harvard University students, who had nicknamed it Sweet Auburn after the deserted village in the aptly named poem "The Deserted Village" by Oliver Goldsmith, celebrating the joys of rural living. "How often have I loitered o'er thy green," Goldsmith writes in the opening lines, "where humble happiness endeared each scene!"

Among the great admirers of the Stone's Woods site was young Harvard student—and future poet and naturalist—Ralph Waldo Emerson. He enrolled at the college as a fourteen-year-old in 1817. "In Cambridge," he wrote in his journals, "there is some wild land called Sweet Auburn upwards of a mile from the Colleges & yet the students will go in bands over a flat sandy road & in summer evenings the woods are full of them. They are so happy they do not know what to do."

Bigelow and the property's owner settled on a sale price of $6,000, but he didn't yet have a concrete funding method, or a plan for selling the general Cambridge public on his concept. The solution to both problems came in the form of the hugely popular Massachusetts Horticultural Society, established in 1829, with a mission to create a repository of plants, seeds, books, and ideas for the Northeast's farmers and gardeners to improve their harvests. Bigelow approached the horticultural society's board with a proposal: If they lent the group's name, influence, and contact list to the cemetery sales project, he would set aside thirty of Sweet Auburn's seventy acres for the group's headquarters and experimental garden. They agreed.

Bigelow began marketing the project as the horticultural society's garden and cemetery (with the word *garden* intentionally placed before *cemetery*). Investors were recruited to pay $60, and in return, they received eternal rights to a family-size burial plot (twenty feet long by fifteen feet wide) at the cemetery, and a voting membership in the horticultural society. Within a year, by August 1831, Bigelow had raised the $6,000 needed to buy the property, which he decided to call Mount Auburn. The following month, on a sunny, unseasonably warm Saturday afternoon, the cemetery held its opening ceremony. Horse-drawn carriages brought 2,000 of the city's most influential people down the shaded central path for the event, which took place at the four-acre natural amphitheater, now known as Consecration Dell, that sits near the property's center. A sixteen-piece orchestra played on a small stage as people found their seats.

The crowd hushed when the master of ceremonies, Supreme Court Justice Joseph Story, rose to speak, "enabling him to be heard with distinctness at the most distant part of the beautiful amphitheater in which the services were performed," wrote a reporter for the *Boston Courier*. Story, like so many of his contemporaries, was no stranger to death. Only two of his seven children lived to adulthood. His voice broke with emotion as he described America's uncivilized ritual of placing "graveyards in the midst of our cities, and heap the dead upon each other with a cold, calculating parsimony, disturbing their ashes, and wounding the sensibilities of the living."

Only days after the event, the horticultural society's founder and president, Henry Dearborn, presented extensive blueprints for the cemetery. They called for a vast network of paths and roads that would cling to the contours of the landscape. Ponds and creeks would be dredged, meadows would be cleared, and hundreds of varieties of trees and shrubs would be planted to look like they had existed there since the dawn of time. It would be a Garden of Eden of graves. The proposal included construction of a Greek-inspired viewing tower atop Mount Auburn's tallest hill, and the still-present Egyptian-style entryway.

Upon approval of the plans, Dearborn and a civil engineer did much of the early marking, surveying, and earthmoving—undertaking the first true landscape architecture project in America. Meanwhile, plot holders began to take possession of their parcels, installing decorative iron fences to mark the boundaries and commissioning statues and monuments of different sizes and styles to be placed within them. Curious Bostonians swarmed to Mount Auburn before the plots were even ready. The sprouting artistry alone made Mount Auburn worth visiting as a first-of-its-kind outdoor sculpture gallery. More customers clambered to purchase burial space, and in July 1832, Mount Auburn received its first resident, an infant. Because the plot holders were given automatic voting membership in the horticultural society, they quickly formed a powerful bloc—led by Bigelow and Story—that decided an experimental garden wouldn't be necessary after all, and the entire property would be dedicated to the cemetery. Dearborn quit the group in a huff. The leaders of the horticultural society felt double-crossed and ultimately severed the group's affiliation with Mount Auburn. They suspected Bigelow had never planned on building the garden, and for the next three decades they excluded all mention of his name in the organization's publications, records, and histories. They ghosted him.

Regardless, Mount Auburn became America's biggest tourist attraction—this place where humans created their own paradise on the edge of urban civilization, to house the dead. An array of poets, writers, artists, celebrities, and even royalty joined the crowds who flocked there to see the novelty and gain inspiration. A sixteen-year-old Emily Dickinson described her visit in her letters to a friend and mentioned it in later poems. Henry David Thoreau praised the way Mount Auburn drew people to enjoy the outdoors in his essay "Autumnal Tints." Nathaniel Hawthorne used the cemetery's natural setting for a short story called "The Lily's Quest," which was included in an early Mount Auburn visitor's guide. Sir Arthur Conan Doyle described in his journals how he carried a bouquet of flowers on his pilgrimage to Mount Auburn to place at the grave of essayist Oliver Wendell Holmes Sr., whom he called one of his "spiritual and literary fathers." (Note the importance of Holmes's last name to Doyle.)

Not to be outdone, cities and towns across America began copying the Mount Auburn rural cemetery model, as people sought a nature fix they didn't know they needed. Philadelphia built magnificent Laurel Hill Cemetery north of town above the Schuylkill River in 1836. In 1838, construction was completed for New York City's first planned green space, Green-Wood Cemetery in Brooklyn. In 1839, Baltimore opened sculpture-filled Green Mount Cemetery.

By the close of the 1840s, rural cemeteries spread throughout the country, in towns big and small—from Richmond, Virginia; to Cincinnati, Ohio; to Bangor, Maine. The capital of Kentucky consecrated rural Frankfort Cemetery in 1844 on a scenic, wooded bluff above the Kentucky River. To make a splash—as the masterminds behind Père-Lachaise in Paris had done before them—the founders wrangled a huge celebrity resident by acquiring the bones of legendary conqueror of the frontier Daniel Boone, who had died a quarter century earlier and been laid to rest near his son's Missouri home. Frankfort declared a holiday

and closed downtown businesses for Boone's reburial ceremony in September 1845, luring thousands of spectators.

Two decades later, Frankfort Cemetery's proprietors placed a towering sandstone monument at the grave site, decorated by four carved
marble panels that capture the noble, all-American exploits of Boone
and his wife, Rebecca. The most eye-catching one shows Daniel beneath
a majestic oak tree, wearing his trademark coonskin cap. He's stepping
on the corpse of one Indigenous American while about to deliver the
mighty, fatal blow of justice to another with the butt of his rifle. It's not
clear what, if anything, his victims did wrong besides get in the way
of Manifest Destiny. The grave site is still one of the city's top tourist
attractions.

AS MOUNT AUBURN'S influence took root, the cemetery itself continued to grow and evolve—a living process that still hasn't ended. Its
Harvard physician founder, Bigelow, designed the boxy, Egyptian-style
front gates called for in the plans. And the sixty-foot-high, medieval,
turret-shaped tower atop the cemetery's tallest hill, which he named
after George Washington. And a granite Gothic Revival chapel that
modestly bears his name, and today regularly holds wedding ceremonies, as well as funeral services. In the late 1800s, the cemetery built a
second chapel of red sandstone decorated with elaborate stained glass
windows, in the style of an English country church. In the twentieth
century the cemetery continually acquired more land and developed
later sections in the grassy, memorial park style of today's cemeteries—
where the gravestones are embedded flat in spacious lawns to offer a
more open look.

Ironically, as Mount Auburn's novelty dimmed over time and
Americans turned their attention to the growing number of outdoor
spaces that didn't include buried bodies, the cemetery's beauty matured.
More monuments appeared with its growing permanent population,
tracing the country's history, its changing artistic tastes, and its shifting financial fortunes and population booms. The cemetery reached a
critical stage in 1993 when engineers discovered that it would reach full
capacity by the year 2000 if drastic steps weren't taken. Mount Auburn's

administrators responded by opening hillsides and other previously unused terrain for burials, encouraging cremation as an option, and building memorial walls for the aboveground placement of caskets.

Mount Auburn took an even bolder step in 2014 by becoming the first Massachusetts cemetery to be certified for natural burials. In a natural burial, a body is wrapped in a shroud, free of embalming fluid and other preservatives, and placed in a biodegradable wooden casket. It's then lowered into a four-foot-deep hole in order to return to nature, with no monument or gravestone marking the site. Mount Auburn was created two centuries ago because Bostonians specifically wanted to avoid ending up in shallow, unmarked graves—and now people are requesting it.

The natural burial sites hide themselves throughout the nooks of the older, historic sections of Mount Auburn, where my bird-watching group lingered the longest on that warm spring morning, beneath the canopies of the larger, more mature trees. Our guide, Brooks, ended our tour with a stop beside an hourglass-shaped pond at the base of Indian Ridge. A chestnut-sided warbler called to us from a maple, whistling, "Very pleased to meetcha. Very, very pleased to meetcha," while a brown thrasher flitted, socially, from branch to branch nearby. Suddenly, Brooks turned to me, pointed, and whispered, "Scarlet tanager!"

I looked atop a towering oak and spotted a blur of red. There it was, the baseball-size bird, its flamboyant plumage contrasting the green leaves. A woman scribbling in a sketchbook leaned next to me. "Makes you happy to be alive, doesn't it?"

I nodded. *Yes. It does.*

Stereoscopic image of Green-Wood Cemetery's brownstone Gothic Revival
main gate, in the late 1800s

6. UNDERGROUND ART

The Brooklyn cemetery that turned New York
into America's cultural capital

—

Green-Wood Cemetery
Brooklyn, New York
Established: 1838

THOSE STUFFY CURATORS at the Metropolitan Museum of Art.*
In late 2000, they unveiled a landmark exhibition called *Art and the
Empire City: New York, 1825–1861*. The intent was to chronicle the city's
"ascendancy to the position of the nation's primary art center, and its
capital of culture, a role it has claimed ever since." It featured works
borrowed from public and private lenders across the United States
and Europe.

But they made a grave omission. *Art and the Empire City* didn't
include cemeteries. Not in its displays, and not in its accompanying 636-
page, full-color catalog. Which is astounding because it's impossible to
paint the full portrait of New York's art history without including, at the
very least, Green-Wood Cemetery in Brooklyn.

Almost from its start in 1838, Green-Wood attracted New York's
finest sculptors and architects, who found steady commissions on its
grounds when the Met wasn't yet a twinkle in a philanthropist's eye. It
inspired writers and poets, including Walt Whitman. It lured painters
looking for a muse. It was the city's first major public art museum,
bringing a constant influx of sublime new art to the masses like never
before in America—and the people liked what they saw. The cemetery

---

* Or in local parlance, the Met.

later became the resting place of some of the country's finest artistic talents, and it continues to uphold the creative tradition today.

If New York is the country's capital of culture and primary art center, Green-Wood Cemetery lit a vital spark in the flame of its ascendance, while setting an artistic standard for all other American burial grounds to follow. Even if the people at the Met didn't realize it.

FOR ME, ROMANCE involves seeing dead people. For my wife, Ann Marie, a physician who generally likes to keep people alive, not so much. Yet she humored me with a quick detour to historic Green-Wood. It was a Saturday morning, and we were driving to Manhattan for a weekend getaway for two. She had two conditions for the side trip: Keep the pace fairly fast, and absolutely no other graveyard tours that day.

Upon our arrival, we were greeted by the cathedral-like brownstone entryway built in 1861. Its three tall spires serve as home to a small population of green South American monk parakeets, who, if the legend is true, are the great-great-grandbirds of a flock from Argentina that broke free from a cargo box at JFK airport in the 1960s.

We drove through one of the entryway's two arched passages, both built just wide enough for horse-drawn carriages in days past, and parked on the hillside to the left. After we stepped out of the car, I unfolded one of those big, touristy maps and placed it on top of the hood. It detailed the cemetery's entire 478 acres, highlighting many of its artsy attractions. "There." I pointed. "The Minerva statue."

Ann Marie shrugged. "Okay. It's your tour." She was already thinking about the extended sidewalk foodie excursion of Manhattan she had planned for us that afternoon.

The bronzed object of my desire, Minerva, the Roman goddess of war, stands on the tallest point in Brooklyn at 216 feet in elevation, her frozen stare aimed directly into the gaze of the Statue of Liberty across New York Harbor. Commissioned by a mogul in the fountain pen ink business, Minerva was unveiled in 1920 to a crowd that included Franklin Delano Roosevelt. The creator was one of the city's most prominent artists, Frederick Ruckstull, whose work also stands on display at the Met.

We began our spirited ascent to where the statue stands, the air around us perfumed by the pink blossoms of scores of Japanese cherry trees that lined our route. Near the top of the hill, we passed two young women striding quickly in the opposite direction as three preschool-age kids spun around them in constant orbit.

"I used to walk here every day during the pandemic," one of the women said. "So I decided I should get buried here someday, too."

The other woman nodded.

Ann Marie and I exchanged understanding glances. We were there shortly after COVID-19 vaccinations were introduced, and New York was recovering from the early pandemic wave of devastation. During the height of cases and death, Green-Wood experienced a sudden surge among the living population in Brooklyn looking to escape their apartments and find quiet outdoor space. In all, the cemetery received more than a half million visitors in 2020, a record. It's somehow fitting that during a massive wave of death, the city's living sought—and found—comfort in a pastoral cemetery.

We soon reached our destination: the larger-than-life Minerva, dressed in robes and a gladiator helmet. Her left hand was lifted in a frozen wave, pointing in the same direction as her eyes, directly at the tiny figure of the Statue of Liberty standing sentry over New York City's watery gateway on an island in the far distance.

I looked at my wife. "Could you imagine being anywhere else right now?"

"Yes. Actually, I could," she said.

If I were smart and good at comebacks, I would have said something like, "This cemetery is what gives me my sustenance, not some Michelin-starred Manhattan restaurant." But I'm not, so I didn't. Instead, I huffed, "Well . . . that's you."

Green-Wood originally sprouted from the Brooklyn soil as an answer to New York's dire need for a new, nondenominational graveyard. The city's population had exploded in the first half of the nineteenth century, and with this astounding growth came the same burial problems in Manhattan that plagued the other urban areas of the Northeast—namely overcrowding, grave robbing, foul smells, and the public's fear of disease caught through the acrid air. In 1822, the city completely outlawed all burials in Lower Manhattan.

The ban, though welcome, forced New Yorkers to look outward for burial options. And when Boston and Philadelphia established grand, magnificent new rural-style cemeteries on their outskirts in the 1830s, New York would not be outdone. One of Brooklyn's city fathers, who had laid out its grid of streets, led the effort to build a cemetery that would rival Mount Auburn in beauty and reputation.

Green-Wood was established on 178 fertile acres of corn and potato fields, on what was then the edge of Brooklyn, atop a high, glacially formed ridge where the bloody first battle of the American Revolution was fought and lost by George Washington's forces after the signing of the Declaration of Independence. The cemetery's designer was a famous civil engineer and Yale graduate, David Bates Douglass, who, it absolutely must be noted, would later become president of my alma mater, Kenyon College. He transformed the site over the next few years into a meandering spread of trees, ponds, and meadows that mimicked a virgin natural landscape, all interconnected by a serpentine network of paths and avenues that contoured the geography rather than plowed through it.

George Templeton Strong, whose diary of nineteenth-century life in New York City would become famous after his death, observed Green-Wood's construction in 1839, before any burials had occurred. He called Green-Wood

> a most exceedingly beautiful place . . . and I sincerely hope it won't turn out a bubble, for in this city of all cities some place is needed where a man may lay down to his last nap without the anticipation of being turned out of his bed in the course of a year or so to make way for a street or a big store or something of that kind, and this place, when it is a little improved and cleared up, will exceed Mt. Auburn.

Though Green-Wood opened to great fanfare and many tourists in 1838, it initially struggled to attract customers. It wasn't until 1840 that its first burial took place. Manhattanites were deterred by the cost and hassle of getting their deceased loved ones and an entire funeral procession to the edge of Brooklyn—a trip that involved taking a ferry across

Stereoscopic image of a grave-digging at Green-Wood Cemetery in the late 1800s

the East River followed by a three-mile carriage ride. Besides, with the cemetery being so new, there was no social cachet to being buried there.

So, following the lead of Père-Lachaise before them, Green-Wood's proprietors decided to acquire the remains of a dead celebrity, DeWitt Clinton, to bury on the grounds with the hope his presence would pump up the demand for its real estate. Clinton, who died in 1828, was a former New York City mayor, New York State governor, and U.S. senator. He granted New York City Catholics the right to vote, led the commission that laid out Manhattan's street grid, and, most famously, was the driving force behind the Erie Canal.

Clinton had been buried in Albany, but Green-Wood got permission from his son to dig him up and bring him to Brooklyn in 1844. Green-Wood's fortunes soared from there, as people clambered to become his next-door neighbor. Business boomed further in 1852 when a new law banned all burials beneath Eighty-Sixth Street in Manhattan. Suddenly Brooklyn's Green-Wood became the hottest place for New Yorkers to spend the afterlife. And the monuments for its new residents were unrivaled.

The spacious rural cemeteries of the early and mid-nineteenth century brought a new era of expression to America. Prior to their existence, crowded traditional burial grounds didn't offer enough space for gravestones to be placed atop every new resident. Trinity Churchyard on Wall Street in Manhattan, where Alexander Hamilton was laid to rest in 1804, for instance, is home to more than 100,000 permanent residents beneath only 100 markers.

Most early colonial gravestones were utilitarian in nature: hand carved, made from slate, rounded at the top, and containing a simple, brief epitaph. They looked like what you might expect Moses—or Charlton Heston—carried down from Mount Sinai containing the Ten Commandments. Sometimes the markers would be adorned with a scythe, winged skull, cherub, or hourglass to symbolize the soul's continuing journey.

After the American Revolution, as artistic and architectural trends bent toward Greek, Roman, or Egyptian Revival designs, so did grave markers. Their materials shifted to granite and marble, with urns frequently carved onto the top, or inscribed on the face. Markers carved in the shape of an obelisk also became popular—the bigger the better. With the emergence of rural cemeteries, everyone got a gravestone, and the elite often went to great lengths for their memorials to be memorable. Green-Wood took funerary art to a whole new level.

FUNERARY ART IS, in essence, art specifically created to decorate a burial space. This includes gravestones, cremation urns, and tombs.* The earliest known examples of funerary art are the previously mentioned 13,000-year-old figures etched into Raqefet Cave in Israel. The pyramids of Egypt are funerary art, as are the mummy cases inside them. The Taj Mahal in India is. So are the 8,000 terra-cotta soldiers that have stood guard for 2,200 years in front of Emperor Qin Shi Huang's tomb by Mount Lishan in China. Stonehenge, which was used as a burial site for cremated remains for five centuries, can very well be classified as funeral art.

Ancient Egyptians were magnificent funerary artists. Because they believed the dead could take objects from life to the Great Beyond, their tombs were stuffed not only with practical items (and sacrificed servants) but also art like jewelry, furniture, and figurines. Their elaborate coffins—made from wood, metal, or clay, depending on the buyer's budget—were often painted with the image of the deceased's face. Jars,

---

* Tombs are loosely defined as any kind of structure or chamber built to house a grave.

containing the body's organs, which were removed before embalmment, were buried with them.

The ancient Greeks were also prolific makers of death art. Starting as far back as 3,000 years ago, they erected tombs for the rich and powerful decorated with carved or painted reliefs depicting the dead, filled with statues, and marked by stone slabs etched with poetic epitaphs. In 2019, archaeologists uncovered two beehive-shaped tombs, each about the size of a New York studio apartment, embedded into a hillside in the ancient city of Pylos in southwestern Greece, constructed by the Mycenaeans around 3,500 years ago around the time when Homer's *Iliad* and *Odyssey* were supposed to take place. They were looted ages ago, so it's unclear what cultural riches they once contained, but their walls were lined with gold foil.

A tomb built by Greek architects around 350 B.C.E. to house the body of Mausolus, a ruler of a territory in what is today Turkey, became known as one of the Seven Wonders of the Ancient World. The rectangular marble structure commissioned after his death by his widow—who was also his sister—towered over the city of Halicarnassus, stretching nearly fifteen stories tall. Above its forty-yard-long base stood thirty-six columns, each one twelve yards tall, which supported a pyramid-shaped roof topped by the sculpture of a horse-driven chariot. The exterior was adorned with carvings of Greek myths and at least one hundred statues. An earthquake destroyed the structure in the Middle Ages, but it lives on in the word *mausoleum*, which means "a large, elegant tomb."

The ancient Romans initially opted for cremation as their primary body disposal method—and the focus of their art. They stored remains in vase-shaped urns made of stone, glass, or pottery, and placed in a public building for housing ashes called a columbarium. At home people kept busts, statues, and masks of the dead for remembrance. Most art privately commissioned—and seen in people's everyday lives—in the Roman Empire was funerary art.

Starting in the final two centuries B.C.E., Romans increasingly turned to burials. Because interments weren't allowed within city walls, rich citizens lined the sides of roads leading into towns with elegant tombs, the bodies inside them contained in lavish stone coffins called sarcophagi. The poor were buried without coffins in mass, anonymous graves, while the middle class formed burial societies to pool resources for funeral expenses among their dues-paying members.

Early Christians in Rome created their own distinctive funerary art by painting walls within the Catacombs that depicted religious figures and stories. The oldest surviving example is a portrait of the Virgin Mary nursing the baby Jesus. It's believed to have been created in the middle of the second century. The earliest churches, built after Constantine legalized Christianity in the Roman Empire in 313 C.E., were a form of architectural funeral art—built as shrines atop the tombs of martyrs. The most famous is the Church of the Holy Sepulchre in Jerusalem, built in 336 on the site where Jesus was said to have been crucified and entombed.

The transition of Catholic burials to churchyards and consecrated grounds in the sixth century brought about dark times for Christian—and European—funerary art that lasted almost 1,000 years. Limited space for burials meant that most people were buried without a coffin, a memorial marker, or any kind of ornamentation. Not until the rise of the Church of England in 1534 did conditions change. It revived the popularity of grave markers among elite worshippers, who could no longer buy Catholic indulgences and needed new ways to differentiate themselves as deserving salvation.

Then came Père-Lachaise in Paris in 1804, which detached burials from the churchyard, gave corpses room to breathe, and allowed more space for creative expressions of remembrance. In the United States, burial grounds—starting with Mount Auburn—did the same. But it was Green-Wood in Brooklyn, in the midst of New York's emerging cultural scene, that attracted and inspired creative minds and elevated American funerary art to its modern grandeur.

At the time of Green-Wood's establishment, a growing community of ambitious architects and artists had converged on the city to design the homes of the new upper class and create works to fill their parlors. The cemetery became the place where these creative types could secure side gigs. Statues and sculptures took root on Green-Wood's grounds, commissioned by New Yorkers eager to display their everlasting wealth and taste for generations to view with wonder. Mausoleums using classical design features were built. Handcrafted marble bas-reliefs sprouted like daisies. And obelisks, obelisks everywhere, of all sizes, reaching toward the sun. These masterful works lured larger and larger throngs of curious, awestruck visitors to browse, free of charge, at their own leisure.

The magnificently designed grounds also attracted writers, painters, and poets seeking inspiration through its natural beauties. One

The seven-foot-long bronze statue of a bride leaning despairingly on the steps of the Merello Volta Monument at Green-Wood Cemetery

of Green-Wood's most avid early admirers was a young Brooklyn poet who made a living as a newspaper reporter named Walt Whitman. He visited often to ponder what he called Green-Wood's "poetic beauties," and wrote several articles about the cemetery. In 1855, Whitman hired a nearby printing shop to publish his collection of poems *Leaves of Grass*, which the Academy of American Poets would one day call "possibly the greatest book of poetry ever written." Some scholars now believe its most acclaimed poem, "Song of Myself," in which Whitman sounds his "barbaric yawp over the roofs of the world," and where grass grows as the "uncut hair of graves," is actually a tribute to Green-Wood. The traditional interpretation has been that the poem is set in the untamed wilderness, and that it celebrates nature—and life and death—in its purest form, following in the tradition of Emerson and Thoreau. But if "Song of Myself" is instead set beneath the leafy canopy of a human-engineered rural cemetery, the poem takes on a different tone. In this light, he's poking playful fun at the transcendentalists, under the surface.

Around when *Leaves of Grass* was published, Green-Wood, with its ever-growing splendor, overtook Mount Auburn as the country's most-visited urban tourist attraction. Its popularity spurred the New York legislature to pass the Rural Cemetery Act in the mid-1800s, which permitted the creation of other stand-alone nonprofit, tax-exempt cemeteries—with the stipulation that they couldn't occupy more than 250 acres within a single jurisdiction.

In turn, groups of budding cemetery purveyors quickly bought real estate occupying both sides of the Brooklyn-Queens border and began to build burial grounds that stretched up to five hundred acres in size. This cluster of graveyards straddling the two jurisdictions is today known as the Cemetery Belt, housing fourteen Jewish, eight nondenominational, four Catholic, and three Protestant cemeteries. More than 5 million people are buried within the Cemetery Belt, eclipsing the living population of Brooklyn and Queens by about 200,000.

AFTER VISITING THE Minerva statue, Ann Marie and I continued our walking tour by stopping at the modest nearby resting place of composer Leonard Bernstein, who died in 1990. His grave is marked by a rectangular granite marker embedded flat into the grass. About twenty small stones lay atop it, placed by visitors paying their respects. Over the centuries, Green-Wood has become a sanctuary for no-longer-living artists. In addition to Bernstein, it's home to the painter Jean-Michel Basquiat and stained glass designer Louis Comfort Tiffany, to name a couple.

Our route took us east, down Mulberry Avenue, where my touristy map led us to Margaret Pine, the last person to die while enslaved in New York State, at the age of eighty in 1857. The original headstone is faded to the point that its inscription is no longer legible, but a newer, polished-granite one has been placed beneath it with her name and death date.

Our next stop took us up, down, and around to the grave of Boss Tweed, the corrupt New York City political power broker who embezzled millions of taxpayer dollars and was convicted in the late nineteenth century for larceny and forgery. After dying in jail in 1878, he was buried at Green-Wood in a small, rectangular family plot, which is surrounded by a polished-granite border. At the time of his interment, Green-Wood had banned all convicted felons, but he was rich and powerful, so, well, there he lies.

Ann Marie and I meandered a bit after that. We stumbled upon the cemetery's collection of catacombs. Dug into a hillside in the 1850s, its long, arched central hallway looks like an underground bunker, lit by round skylights. The chambers on either side hold thirty burial vaults. Entry is barred by a locked iron gate, but Green-Wood sometimes opens it to hold string quartet concerts and occasional art exhibits—in keeping with the cemetery's status as the birthplace of public art and culture in New York City.

Not that Green-Wood always kept itself accessible to the masses. In the late decades of the twentieth century, the cemetery suffered from neglect and dwindling funds; it closed itself and allowed only families of its permanent residents (who were given a special pass) and a smattering of visitors who signed up for its occasional guided tours to enter. Taking pictures was prohibited, and a sign hung outside its gate warning of "Armed Guards and K-9 patrols" to ward off trespassers. A *New York Times* reporter in 1996 described Green-Wood as "all but forgotten by most New Yorkers," its roads and paths "quieter than any country lane."

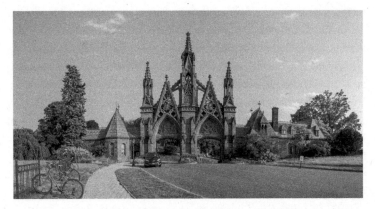

A modern view of Green-Wood Cemetery's brownstone
Gothic Revival main gate, built in 1876

By 2000, Green-Wood went into survival mode. Its leaders realized the cemetery would run out of space for burials—and with it, a bulk of its revenues—within six years. So it opened its gates to the public again, holding concerts featuring music composed by Bernstein and others buried there. It kicked off an adopt-a-statue program called Saved in Time, encouraging philanthropists to donate as much as $15,000 to restore a sculpture. It hired an architecture firm to design an expansion of its Hillside Mausoleum to add 2,400 burial crypts, and the construction of a columbarium that could hold the ashes of 8,000 people. It marketed itself as the gorgeous repository of art that it is. New Yorkers responded enthusiastically, and the cemetery has continued to expand its creative offerings.

Green-Wood now houses its own, ever-growing collection of more than 400 paintings, drawings, prints, and sculptures; 9,000 artifacts; and 1,000 published volumes related to the countless artists, authors, and musicians buried there. Almost a big enough set of holdings to make the Met blush. Most of it is stored beyond the public's regular view—except during its scheduled exhibitions in its chapel, catacombs, or other buildings. But the entire collection has been photographed and can be viewed online from the cemetery's website.

In 2021, a panel of five judges appointed by the cemetery's public programs and special projects office named Green-Wood's first (living) artist in residence, Heidi Lau, who specializes in ceramic art. Green-Wood provided her with a studio inside the gatehouse, a cash stipend, and access to its trove of documents, photographs, and archives.

As we made our way back to the car, I led Ann Marie on one last side hike, not too far from where we had parked, to Green-Wood's most interesting obelisk, and one of its newest. Made of a seven-foot-tall slab of white marble, it was placed in the cemetery in 2017, and doesn't belong to a grave. It's inscribed with the words, HERE LIE THE SECRETS OF THE VISITORS OF GREEN-WOOD CEMETERY. There's a slot at the base where people can place slips of paper containing their secrets that then slide into a buried vault. Once the vault is filled, all the secrets are burned. This, in its own way, is a sort of act of performance art, carrying on Green-Wood's legacy as a purveyor and conservator of the arts.

I can understand how old rural cemeteries eventually, inevitably, became overshadowed by art museums. The Corcoran Gallery of Art opened in Washington, D.C., in 1869 and became an instant sensation. It was created by wealthy banker William Wilson Corcoran, who had also founded a rural-style cemetery, Oak Hill, in Georgetown. The Met opened in 1870. The first object it acquired for its permanent collection was—of course—a piece of funerary art: an ancient Roman sarcophagus. At least the curators back then weren't quite as snotty about grave-related creative works. Or maybe only really old burial objects count as being worthy of display?

The art museums that emerged in the late nineteenth and early twentieth centuries gave artists a public venue where their works didn't have to be placed above dead bodies, draining the creative vitality somewhat from Green-Wood and other cemeteries. As time passed, a growing detachment from facing death among the American public began to avert audiences almost altogether from going to graveyards to appreciate art. Yet in recent years the crowds have returned to Green-Wood. They come for the sculptures, and tombs, and mausoleums, and the concerts and exhibits. And they also come to bask in the always-maturing landscape, designed by human hands, that embraces an eclectic array of nature—from monk parakeets to Japanese cherry trees to, as Whitman put it, the uncut hair of graves.

The sculpture *Silence*, erected in 1875, stands in the whites-only
section of Laurel Grove Cemetery in Savannah above
the graves of Confederate soldiers.

7. DEATH COMES EQUALLY TO US ALL

Racial segregation in American cemeteries is still very much alive

—

Laurel Grove Cemetery

Savannah, Georgia

Established: 1853

MOST PEOPLE AREN'T in a rush to get to the graveyard—for good reason. But on this particular late-March morning, I was. During a family spring break trip to Savannah by Georgia's semitropical coast, I escaped to Laurel Grove Cemetery. We were spending a few days camping at a nearby state park—my wife's idea of fun—and I cut away to explore the burial ground's ninety acres, promising everyone I'd be back before they finished breakfast.

Established in 1852, city-owned and -operated Laurel Grove was designed and landscaped as a rural cemetery in the model of Green-Wood, except that it's split into two adjacent sections: North and South, where more than a simple dotted line drawn by a surveyor on a piece of paper separates them.

The half called Laurel Grove North is the historically white section. It filled to capacity in the early twentieth century, with about 30,000 people, long before the city's facilities integrated. Laurel Grove South is known as the Black section. Its first residents consisted of free and enslaved African Americans who lived and labored in and around Savannah before the Civil War. The permanent population is more than double that of the North section, at about 60,000, and it still accepts some burials today.

Laurel Grove North is pure, genteel, Southern-postcard material, with each twist and turn along its wide, oak-shaded paths and avenues

Savannah's enslaved population was required by law to be buried in the
historically Black section of Laurel Grove Cemetery in the nineteenth century.

revealing new and interesting Gothic statues and flamboyant grave
markers. Taking a virtual tour is easy for anyone who can't physically
travel to Savannah because Google features panoramic Street View
images that trace every inch of the white section's roads on its Maps app.

Laurel Grove South feels much different. Divided from the northern half by a stretch of interstate highway, its resting places stand more
modest in decoration and design. The paths and avenues run narrower
in width, fewer trees and shrubs dot its expanses, and its patches of
grass are browned by the sun. Its beauty instead radiates from its simplicity and closer connection to the earth. To see what it's like, you'll
have to go for yourself, however. Google doesn't offer Street View panoramic images of the Black section's roads on its Maps app.

The disparity between Laurel Grove's two distinct sections is
an all-too-familiar sight in the southern United States—where racial
segregation of the dead is still very much alive and traditionally Black
cemeteries continually struggle to inhabit their rightful place on the
cultural, historical, and literal map.

LAUREL GROVE WAS built atop former plantation land in 1850 on what was then the city's edge. Savannah's need was dire at the time. Its white cemeteries were nearing capacity, and real estate developers wanted to build atop the centrally located African American burial ground downtown—where all Black free and enslaved citizens were required by local law to be interred. So city leaders decided to construct a municipal burial ground in the popular rural style.

The African American section of the new cemetery, which would become Laurel Grove South, occupied the lowest-lying, swampiest few acres. Crews removed the occupants from the old Black burial ground downtown and reinterred them there, planting the small, oddly shaped slate gravestones in orderly rows, but not necessarily atop the correct people. A small wooden sign that reads SLAVES BURIALS now marks the original burying spot. Within a decade, Laurel Grove South grew to fifteen acres and expanded outward to more than double that size in the twentieth century.

Its gravestones mark the passage of time within Savannah's Black community, revealing stories recorded and stored nowhere else but in their inscriptions. Like that of Jane Deveaux, a seamstress and "free person of color" who—at the risk of beating, imprisonment, and maybe death—ran a secret school for thirty years, illegally teaching enslaved people to read. She died in 1885, and her faded, lichen-covered stone reads, CELEBRATED AS AN EARLY EDUCATOR OF HER PEOPLE, SHE HAS BUILT FOR HERSELF A NAME MORE ENDURING THAN MONUMENTS OF STONE OR BRASS.

Or the story of formerly enslaved person Andrew Cox Marshall, who became a wealthy real estate owner and the pastor of the First African Baptist Church. Before he died in 1856, he had "baptized 3,776, married 2,000 and funeralized 2,400." Or the story of an enslaved twenty-year-old woman named Sarah, who "was drowned by the destruction at sea of the steamer Pulaski" in 1858.

Many memorials are darkened by the moist Georgia coast air, and they lean crookedly in one direction or another, victims to the sandy soil's movement. Walk among Laurel Grove South's twentieth- and twenty-first-century grave sites, and you'll see improving fortunes of newer occupants, through a small handful of aboveground burial vaults and gravestones made of granite. Nonetheless, this is not a place of grandeur. It was not initially planted with ornamental shrubs, its roads are almost entirely dirt, and routine maintenance doesn't appear to stretch beyond the occasional mowing.

It's a stark contrast to Laurel Grove North. Savannah paved the boundary between the two sides with an extension of Interstate 16 in the mid-1960s, an era when American city developers intentionally used highway construction to place asphalt moats around urban communities of color. Laurel Grove North looks like a different cemetery altogether—starting with its entryway. While the southern half's front entrance consists of two simple swinging metal gates attached to brick posts, the northern one is decorated by a tall iron archway bearing the words LAUREL GROVE CEMETERY painted in white and held aloft by two thick Victorian-style posts. It looks like the entrance to a London park.

Laurel Grove North's wide, concrete main drive leads through a stunning tunnel of moss-covered oaks, garnished at their feet by azaleas that bloom pink in the spring. A white gazebo, where visitors can rest in the shade, lazes on the right side of the drive, and just past it, at the first main junction of sandy roads, stands a gorgeous, impressively detailed Map of Laurel Grove Cemetery, etched into polished granite. But it's not a full map of Laurel Grove Cemetery.

Installed in 1998 by an organization called the Society for the Preservation of Laurel Grove, it shows the exact location of each individual plot in only the white section. There's no mention of Laurel Grove South. Instead, there's a line marking the interstate, and to the left is a smooth, blank space where the historically Black section lies, running off the edge. As if it doesn't exist.

Laurel Grove North, like so many other nineteenth-century rural-style cemeteries, became an instant tourist attraction upon its completion in the 1850s. Savannah's richest families bought large plots along its roads, built iron fences around them, and erected aboveground flat-topped vaults, statues of angels and weeping virgins, and mausoleums that looked like mini cathedrals.

One of the most famous statues on its grounds depicts a robed woman pressing an index finger to her lips while her other hand grasps the torch of liberty, upside down, by her side. The pedestal reads: TO THE CONFEDERATE DEAD. Laurel Grove North is the resting place to about 1,500 Confederate soldiers, including 700 who died in the Battle of Gettysburg. The cemetery's whites-only section is also the final home of Juliette Gordon Low, the founder of Girl Scouts of the USA, who died in 1927. Her grave, marked by a tall Celtic cross, is the pilgrimage site for thousands of Girl Scouts from around the country each year, who lovingly decorate the spot with flowers.

When Laurel Grove North ran out of plots for sale, the city bought a popular private burial ground, Bonaventure Cemetery, four miles due east, on the bank of the Wilmington River, in 1907 as a new option. In the 1990s, it became one of the country's most famous and visited burial grounds after it was depicted in the book, and movie, *Midnight in the Garden of Good and Evil*. At Bonaventure, the Gothic sculptures look like they're about to come to life, and the wild tangle of bushes and trees that sprout from the sandy soil are on the verge of swallowing all evidence of humanity whole. It should top every person's "10 Cemeteries to See Before You Die" list, simply for its looks. It still accepts burials, now for all people.

Because Laurel Grove South was owned by the city from the start, it's actually among the South's more well-kept historically Black burial grounds. Too many others have been cleared away, and among those that survive, few receive any meaningful federal or state funding, leaving them struggling to cover expenses through charitable donations. Drive through any town beneath the Mason-Dixon Line, and it's difficult to ignore the racial divide of the dead, and the disparity in resources doled out for white and Black. Take, for instance, Brewer Hill Cemetery in Annapolis, Maryland, and Mount Zion/Female Union Band Society Cemetery in Washington, D.C.

BREWER HILL CEMETERY roosts on a 4.5-acre bump of land on the outer fringe of downtown Annapolis, the capital city of Maryland. It was established in the late 1700s—its oldest known burial dates back to 1789—by a local judge named Brewer as a burial ground for local enslaved people and free Black citizens. After the Civil War, his descendants sold the parcel to members of the Mount Moriah African Methodist Episcopal Church. Brewer Hill is now home to 7,000 permanent residents and still conducts some burials. Like Laurel Grove South, the property is adjacent to a resplendent cemetery established for whites only: Annapolis National Cemetery. But instead of being divided by an interstate, a narrow, brush-filled ravine runs between them.

I lived in Annapolis while teaching at the United States Naval Academy. Early one Memorial Day morning, I visited the two cemeteries, stopping at the National Cemetery first. Initially created to house the dead from a nearby military field hospital early in the Civil War, it occupies nearly the same amount of land as Brewer Hill and holds the remains of about 3,000 military members, spanning from the 1860s to the present day.

I walked among the graves, browsing the names of people who died in Vietnam and World War II and Korea. Boy Scouts had painstakingly planted tiny American flags in the tidy rows between each chalky-white marble gravestone. In December, a charitable organization called Wreaths Across America enlists volunteers to adorn 90,000 veterans' graves at 2,500 cemeteries across America all with holiday wreaths, including every grave at Annapolis National Cemetery. I spent about fifteen minutes there, the thick green sod soaking my shoes. Frankly, there's not much to see. The cemetery's strict uniformity breeds monotony.

I then strode two minutes down the street and through the iron gates fronting the entrance to Brewer Hill, where nothing is monotonous or uniform. Unlike at the National Cemetery, where the primly trimmed grass looked like it belonged on the fairway of Augusta National Golf Club, it had been a while since a lawn mower had taken a pass on this ground, as the grass had grown long enough to brush dew against my calves. The families of a few residents had taken it upon themselves to cut neat rectangles of grass around their loved ones' resting spots—a tender, moving act.

Many of Brewer Hill's graves are unmarked, but where the simple crosses or gravestones or cracked stone tabletop vaults lie, the cemetery's soft ground is in the process of reclaiming them. Hardly a single human-made object stands perfectly level besides the flagpole rising from the center, a tattered American flag flapping from it. They're all teetering, or tipping, or toppling, or tilting. Yet they still stand.

A military marker caught my eye. It belonged to Hillary Johnson, born in 1886, who served in the army in World War I. It looked identical to the ones found in the National Cemetery next door, except it leaned forward and was stained green from algae, obscured somewhat inside a circle of tall grass. Hundreds of Black American war veterans are buried in Brewer Hill, some with federally supplied markers, some without. A vast majority were barred from being interred next door because the National Cemetery accepted only white residents until 1962.

The federal government still provides no funding for the care of Brewer Hill's military graves to keep them mowed, or to ensure the markers are board-straight and gleaming like the ones housed by its neighbor. The Boy Scouts don't plant American flags beside them for Memorial Day. And no wreaths are delivered here by Wreaths Across America to adorn them in December.

Brewer Hill receives its funding from two local churches, various state grants, and occasional fundraising efforts. Its upkeep is mostly from community-led cleanup efforts, as it operates on a shoestring budget. Unlike the millions of dollars the federal government sets aside annually for Confederate burial sites, the government allocates no money specifically to restore or preserve historically Black cemeteries. And there's no federal law protecting them from destruction, leaving ones like Brewer Hill under constant threat from real estate developers and road construction.

In rural areas, Black cemeteries are often the only remaining visible record of African American communities that vanished during the Great Migration, when more than 6 million people fled the South during the Jim Crow era. They're considered by the nonprofit National Trust for Historic Preservation as some of the country's most endangered historic sites. And yet few government, private, or charitable resources are allocated to preserve or maintain them, like is seen at Laurel Grove South.

I zigzagged my way around Brewer Hill, reading inscriptions, absorbing its past. Somewhere on its grounds lie the remains of John

Snowden, laid to rest in 1918. Wrongly accused of killing a pregnant white woman, he was the last person to be hanged at the Annapolis gallows. Maryland's governor pardoned him in 2001. Also occupying an unknown space in the cemetery is Henry Davis, accused and arrested in 1906 for "ravishing" a white woman. A mob broke into the Annapolis jail, dragged him into the street, hung him from a chestnut tree, then shot him one hundred times. His name and those of nine other victims murdered by lynching in Annapolis between 1891 and 1906 are inscribed on a bronze plaque attached to a granite pedestal. By starving these cemeteries of funding, maintenance, and attention, we obscure the important and ugly chapters from our past that they reveal and that should not be forgotten. Or maybe that's partly why we neglect them.

In Maryland, there has been some discussion within the state legislature about providing funding for historically Black cemeteries, although no votes on the matter have taken place. In 2020, Virginia passed a law dedicating as much money annually to restore Black cemeteries—about $5 per grave dug between 1800 and 1900—as it does to protect Confederate graves. On the opposite end of the spectrum, in late 2019, the Alabama Supreme Court upheld a provision in the state's constitution, added in 2017, that preserves Confederate memorials from destruction or removal. No such provision exists there for African American graves or monuments. On the federal level, the U.S. Senate unanimously passed bipartisan legislation to aid historic Black cemeteries, but the bill died in the House of Representatives without even coming to a vote.

THE MOUNT ZION/FEMALE Union Band Society Cemetery in Georgetown is the oldest existing Black burial ground in Washington, D.C. Established as two separate churchyard burial grounds in the early 1800s, it evolved into a graveyard for free and enslaved African Americans, and came to hold perhaps as many as 10,000 residents beneath its 310 existing markers before it stopped taking residents in 1953. A decayed redbrick hillside vault where bodies were stored in the winter for burial is believed to have doubled as a stop for runaway enslaved people escaping to freedom on the Underground Railroad. The property's three tree-shaded, corrugated acres of dirt and grass patches fell into a tangle of neglect for a while, but it's now regularly maintained by school groups and other volunteers under the direction of a charity organization founded by local activists for its protection in 2005.

Identical to Laurel Grove South and Brewer Hill, the cemetery shares a border with a more opulent neighbor. In this case, it's Oak Hill Cemetery, founded in 1849 for whites only, by wealthy banker and enslaver William Wilson Corcoran, who was also the namesake of the Corcoran Gallery of Art. It's landscaped in Green-Wood's classic rural style and listed on the National Register of Historic Places. Oak Hill's most striking feature is its stone Gothic Revival chapel, which looks like it belongs in the French countryside and was designed by the architect who drew up the Smithsonian Institution Building on the National Mall, and St. Patrick's Cathedral in New York City.

Mount Zion/Female Union Band Society Cemetery also shares a border with Rock Creek Park, a rolling nine-mile-long ribbon of woodsy green space that winds its way northwest into Maryland. Created in 1890, it's protected by the National Park Service, and its thirty-plus miles of paved, gravel, and dirt trails are popular with joggers and hikers in need of a quick escape from the city's congested trappings. In late 2021, construction crews employed by the Park Service and city department of transportation used tractors to slice two massive gashes in the ground alongside the cemetery, in a spot where human remains are believed to still lie. The director of the foundation preserving Mount Zion/Female Union Band Society Cemetery discovered the digging the next day and posted a video of the craters on Instagram. In it she narrates that no one at the cemetery was told about the digging, and no archaeologists were on-site overseeing it.

"It's a cemetery, for god's sake. We don't ever touch Oak Hill, though, do we?" she said.

The construction was immediately halted, and the cemetery foundation's director met with Park Service officials, who, during the

Brewer Hill Cemetery in Annapolis, Maryland, the city's oldest Black graveyard, was established in 1789 as a burial ground for enslaved people and is now home to seven thousand permanent residents, including hundreds of veterans. Its maintenance and preservation rely upon the support of donations and volunteer efforts.

discussion, spread out a map highlighting federal park lands in the city.* Oak Hill was marked on it. But all too familiarly, Mount Zion/ Female Union Band Society Cemetery was not.

THERE'S ALSO THE segregational element of burials, like at Laurel Grove, Brewer Hill, and Mount Zion/Female Union Band Society, that lie in plain sight but are so seldom mentioned. In the same way that unequal treatment for Black burial grounds continues in America, so does the actual division of the dead along racial lines. Although such practices are, of course, illegal, the law isn't necessarily enforced, so cemeteries have become the islands that civil rights forgot, to an extent. For instance, it took until 2016 for a 140-year-old city-owned cemetery in Waco, Texas, to tear down a chain-link fence separating its two racially divided sections, where the historically Black side suffered from significant neglect and unequal resources. A few months later, a woman two hundred miles south, in Normanna, Texas, sued the local cemetery for enforcing its whites-only policy and refusing to allow her Latino husband's burial. As recently as 2021, the family of a Black sheriff's deputy in southwest Louisiana who died of cancer was barred from burying him in the local cemetery that enforced an illegal whites-only policy.

The poet John Donne wrote, "Death comes equally to us all, and makes us all equal when it comes." But I'll be damned if this is the case. Our cemeteries reveal where our values lie and how we lie about our values. Sacred places like Laurel Grove South, Brewer Hill, and Mount Zion/Female Union Band Society can point our compasses in a truer direction if we pay more attention to their stories. And place them rightfully on the map.

---

* According to the *Washington Post*.

Sleepy Hollow Cemetery was America's first natural conservation project—led by transcendentalist writer Ralph Waldo Emerson, who's buried on-site.

8. THE TONIC OF WILDNESS

How Emerson and Thoreau turned a new cemetery into the country's first conservation project

—

Sleepy Hollow Cemetery
Concord, Massachusetts
Established: 1855

MY HOMETOWN OF Bedford, Massachusetts, established Shawsheen Cemetery, its mini version of Mount Auburn, in 1849. Not to be outdone, Concord, the fancier town next door, opened Sleepy Hollow six years later. As a kid, I passed Sleepy Hollow countless times on the way to downtown Concord, a picture-perfect place that seems suspended in amber from 1775—but with BMWs and Audis parked on the street instead of horses.

I almost never went inside Sleepy Hollow because it seemed so impossibly old and haunted. Even the name creeped me out. Besides, I couldn't get myself to admire any part of Concord, which was the superior archrival to the more working-class Bedford.* It would have been like a nail looking upward to appreciate a hammer's fine wooden handle.

What I didn't realize at the time was that Sleepy Hollow is a national natural treasure. Before it became a graveyard, it was the outdoor playground for literary titans Louisa May Alcott, Nathaniel Hawthorne, Ralph Waldo Emerson, and Henry David Thoreau, who all ended up buried there. Its environs directly influenced the

---

* Back then. Hordes of Bimmers and Audis have invaded Bedford in recent years as well.

transcendental movement in America. Emerson, and to some extent Thoreau, led the effort to create the cemetery to forever protect the property's natural habitat from encroaching agriculture, deforestation, and development. In that way, Sleepy Hollow served as the country's first conservation land.

DURING THE EARLY and mid-nineteenth century, the seventeen-acre wooded tract on the edge of downtown Concord that houses the original footprint of the cemetery was surrounded by open farmlands. The property occupied a glacially formed ridge and a quiet hollow below it that looked, in Emerson's words, like it "lies in nature's hand."

Hawthorne described it as "a shallow space scooped out among the woods."

It was a popular leafy refuge and outdoor playground for locals. Emerson began spending time in the woods there in the early 1830s, when he moved into his grandfather's nearby old home on the Concord River, called the Old Manse. While writing his famed essay "Nature," he sought inspiration by losing himself among the property's thick groves of white oaks and pitch pines. The final product essentially became the founding document of transcendentalism, a literary and philosophical movement that laid the groundwork for the American environmental movement.

Transcendentalism emerged as a response to the Industrial Revolution, preaching that the most fundamental truths are found through individuality and intuition, not society and reason. It proposed that nature connects the human soul to God, joining them as one. A cemetery in the woods was the natural extension of this philosophy—here, a body would dissolve back into the soil, and the individual life was both marked and celebrated with a single stone.*

After "Nature" was published in 1836, Concord became the epicenter of the transcendental movement, and—for that matter—of American literature. Thoreau read "Nature" while studying at Harvard

---

* At this time, bodies were buried without being embalmed—either in a shroud or a simple wooden coffin—allowing for a faster, more natural decomposition process than what happens with the preservative-injected, tomb-encased corpses of today.

and was so inspired by the work that he moved to town. He joined a slew of other intellectuals in Emerson's orbit, like the famed feminist writer Margaret Fuller, who often stayed at Emerson's home, and Bronson Alcott, the muttonchopped freethinker whose views on communal living were a century ahead of their time. His daughter Louisa May published *Little Women* in 1868 based on her childhood experiences living in town.

Many of the transcendentalists who descended on Concord also sought refuge in the sleepy hollow that would become the cemetery. So did author Nathaniel Hawthorne, who was not a transcendentalist but as a writer was drawn to the town, regardless. He and his wife moved into the Old Manse—renting it from Emerson for $100 a year—upon their wedding in 1842. Thoreau planted them a vegetable garden in the backyard as a welcome gift.

The couple often meandered into the sleepy hollow to pass the time. Hawthorne described in his journal how, in its woods, the "sunshine glimmers through shadow, and shadow effaces sunshine, imaging that pleasant mood of mind where gayety and pensiveness intermingle." The couple imagined building a home for themselves on the property's ridgetop, overlooking the town.

Hawthorne wrote his famed collection of short stories *Mosses from an Old Manse* while living in Emerson's house, and it's believed that his wanderings at the sleepy hollow influenced details in many of his works, including a scene in the woods between Hester Prynne and her forbidden lover, Arthur Dimmesdale, in the classic *The Scarlet Letter*.

Then there's Thoreau, who also frequented the sleepy hollow. He wrote *Walden* from 1845 to 1847, about his two years living alone in the Concord woods beside Walden Pond (on Emerson's property, I might add). He famously wrote, "I went to the woods because I wished to live deliberately, to front only the essential facts of life, and see if I could not learn what it had to teach, and not, when I came to die, discover that I had not lived."

In *Walden*, he builds upon Emerson's views on nature—by describing how it connects us to our humanity and arguing for its preservation in an America where nature was regarded as something to be vanquished. "Our village life would stagnate if it were not for the unexplored forests and meadows which surround it. We need the tonic of wildness."

This philosophy, in my estimation, intertwines with the essence of a cemetery's ultimate role—to rejoin the human body with nature on the most elemental level. Rural-style burial grounds came closest to reaching the transcendental end state, but in time we've been diverted from it. The heavily watered, overfertilized, and carefully cut cemeteries we enjoy today return us to the vain projection of humans as all-powerful gods who can bend nature to our will—despite the overwhelming contrary evidence provided by the decaying bodies lying below the surface. Yet there are buds of hope, in the environmentally minded, all-natural burial grounds emerging across the United States.

By the time *Walden* was published in 1854, Concord had been stripped of 90 percent of its woodlands—and the only "tonic of wildness" accessible to the downtown was in fact the sleepy hollow, which Thoreau understood the need to protect. He once wrote in his journal, "Each town should have a park, or rather a primitive forest, of 500 or a thousand acres, where a stick should never be cut for fuel, a common possession forever, for instruction and recreation."

The best option to maintain a forest of this kind was a rural cemetery that would protect it for eternity. Encouraging human bodies to dissolve back into nature within it would be a feature, not a bug.

The construction of Sleepy Hollow Cemetery began in early 1855, and Emerson was elected by the townspeople as the chairman of Concord's five-person cemetery committee, created to oversee the project. Also on the committee was the local sheriff, who later served as a bodyguard for President Abraham Lincoln during the Gettysburg Address. Thoreau surveyed part of the property and designed a pond near the ridgetop. The overall site was designed to take advantage of its natural features by landscape architect Horace Cleveland, who later laid out the urban park system of Minneapolis and the hundreds of miles of boulevards and parkways of Omaha, Nebraska. The project foreman was a local attorney who wrote in his autobiography that he "saved as many trees as possible from cutting."

Emerson delivered the keynote address at Sleepy Hollow's opening ceremony in September 1855, describing how he saw the cemetery, open to all Concord residents, as an ideal union between humans—both living and dead—and nature, or "earth to earth." He praised the "irresistible democracy" of human bodies returning fully to the soil to sprout new life, and said he envisioned Sleepy Hollow's beauty maturing over time, as the trees and shrubs took deeper root, and "these acorns, that are falling at our feet" someday became "oaks over-shadowing our children in a remote century."

Being a small municipal cemetery, unlike privately operated ones like Mount Auburn and Green-Wood, Sleepy Hollow didn't have to rely on selling grave plots to pay for early operating expenses; they had no need to boost foot traffic by reinterring a famous body. Regardless, townspeople enthusiastically supported the new burial ground. The spring after its opening, on the anniversary of the start of the Revolutionary War at Concord's North Bridge, the cemetery committee organized a volunteer tree bee, as they named it, during which locals brought one hundred elms, pines, buttonwoods, and maples to plant on the property.

Intentionally protecting and cultivating nature on a patch of woods in this way was unprecedented for its time—and this milestone has been essentially overlooked in history. Although *Walden* is often credited for launching the conservation movement, the role of the Concord cemetery where its author's remains now reside has been forgotten, as so often happens to burial grounds. Instead, Yellowstone National Park, created by Congress in 1872 as the world's first national park, is widely considered the country's first protected natural space.

Within three decades of the cemetery's opening, Thoreau, Emerson, Louisa May Alcott, and Hawthorne all lay buried there, within a stone's throw of one another among a grove of mature pines on what's now called Author's Ridge. Hawthorne's dream of settling at the top of Sleepy Hollow's highest point eventually came true, in a way. His resting place is marked by a stone bearing simply his last name. Hawthorne's wife, Sophia, who died and was buried in England, was reinterred next to him in 2006. Louisa May Alcott's round headstone, located within

The grave of Louisa May Alcott, who died in 1888,
on Author's Ridge at Sleepy Hollow Cemetery

the Alcott family plot, is engraved with the humble initials L.M.A. and
the dates 1832–1888. A marker bearing her name lies flat in the ground
at the foot of her grave.

Thoreau is also surrounded by family. His granite stone barely
peeks above the roots and pine needles and contains just his first name,
HENRY. Emerson's resting place is by far the flashiest: A tall, teardrop-
shaped granite boulder bespeckled with quartz marks the spot, and a
bronze plaque is embedded into it, turned a deep green from age and
weather, bearing Emerson's name, his dates of birth and death, and a
line from his poem "The Problem," which reads: "The passive master
lent his hand / to the vast soul that o'er him planned."

Thousands of visitors each year make their way up the winding
paths that hug the contours of Sleepy Hollow that were so familiar to
the nineteenth-century authors who reside within the cemetery. People
leave pens, notes, and poems on the graves. The cemetery has expanded
over the years, and is home to more than 10,000 grave sites, including the resting place of the local legend Ephraim Bull, the creator of
the Concord grape; Daniel Chester French, who created the Abraham

The grave of Henry David Thoreau, who died in 1862,
on Author's Ridge at Sleepy Hollow Cemetery

Lincoln statue at the Lincoln Memorial; and Katherine Kennicott Davis, a local teacher who wrote the Christmas song "The Little Drummer Boy."

Sleepy Hollow's original heart still lies protected, serenely bringing humanity back to nature in the truest sense, as Emerson envisioned. All the while, the acorns that fell at the author's feet on the day of his convocation speech have in fact become the oaks that shadow him today.

The Imagine mosaic, which serves as a grave marker of sorts for John Lennon, near Strawberry Fields in New York's Central Park

9. A CEMETERY BY ANY OTHER NAME

Central Park, built on burial grounds, has become Manhattan's
most active repository for human remains

—

Central Park
New York, New York
Established: 1858

CEMETERIES ARE LOVELY places for a run. Their narrow roads are well paved, there's zero traffic, and the air is fresh, the scenery lush. The residents don't seem opposed to the company, either. When I worked in Boston, longer back than I'd like to admit, I belonged to a running club that met one evening each week at Holyhood Cemetery—a cozy burial ground that opened in 1857 and was modeled after Mount Auburn. We would run repeat sets of sprints, our heart rates pushed to the max, on a quarter-mile-long loop that threaded through the cemetery's winding, undulating roads. John F. Kennedy's parents are buried at Holyhood, and an adjacent grave was set aside for him after his death, but Jackie Kennedy decided Arlington National Cemetery was a more fitting resting place.

Years after my Boston stint, when I lived in the People's Republic of Vermont, I often jogged among the graves of board-flat, lawn-style Resurrection Park Cemetery, in the town of South Burlington. I almost never saw another living person there, and despite its name, I witnessed no resurrections. In Asheville, North Carolina, half of my workouts and one annual road race took me through Riverside Cemetery, an exquisitely Gothic, oak-filled resting ground built in a neighborhood of old Victorian homes on the slope of an ungodly steep hill that is home to writers O. Henry and Thomas Wolfe.

On Cape Cod—yes, I've moved a lot—I avoided the summer tourist traffic on runs by veering into Orleans Cemetery, where some of the faded slate gravestones date back nearly to the time of witch hunts. In Annapolis, Maryland, I ran several times a week through the Naval Academy's grassy cemetery.

However, my all-time favorite burial ground run is Central Park. Yes, Central Park. While living on the Upper West Side of Manhattan, I would escape to it, following roughly the same route every day, dodging cyclists and slow-walking pedestrians while passive-aggressively not letting faster runners pass me. All within a leafy tableau designed by legendary landscape architects 150 years ago.

You may not think of Central Park as a cemetery, but the facts—and I—beg to differ. Central Park was America's first true city park—and its design and creation were wholly inspired by cemeteries. It was built on top of at least a couple of burial grounds, with the bones never removed. In the last forty years, Central Park has enjoyed a rebirth as a repository for human remains, in becoming a popular spot to spread cremated ashes. Many other urban parks across the country are cemeteries in the same way, built atop graves and now popular for receiving cremated remains. Maybe even the one you happen to run in.

CEMETERIES, THROUGH NO fault of their own, are the ghosts of history—their importance to the course of events left unseen or ignored. There's no greater example of this than their unseen influence on the art and profession of landscape design. Most historical sources call New York native Andrew Jackson Downing, a horticulturalist born in 1815, the father of landscape design in America. He wrote *A Treatise on the Theory and Practice of Landscape Gardening*, which is considered the groundbreaking Book of Genesis for landscape architecture, in 1841.

But left on history's cutting room floor is the fact that Mount Auburn Cemetery in Massachusetts, the country's first true marvel in landscape architecture, opened a full decade before Downing's volume was published. If you leaf through academic journal articles like "Social

History and the History of Landscape Architecture," published by the Oxford University Press, you'll find ample references to Downing, but not a single mention of cemeteries.

A Treatise on the Theory and Practice of Landscape Gardening became an instant bestseller and turned Downing into an international celebrity. He published a handful of other books and articles on landscape design and used his fame to create a popular magazine with the scintillating title *The Horticulturist and Journal of Rural Art and Rural Taste*. Yet much of his early work built off prior achievements by the designers of rural cemeteries—a fact he openly admitted.

Downing was such a fan of rural cemeteries, and so fascinated by their popularity among the masses—especially Mount Auburn and Green-Wood—that he proposed in the early 1850s a revolutionary idea for New York City to build a similar public "pleasure-ground" in Manhattan, sans dead bodies. It would be a central park of sorts, festooned with trees and lawns and ponds and flowers and walkways. It would look as if it sprang naturally from the ground, unlike the city's smattering of crowded, dusty common areas open to the public. "What are called parks in New-York, are not even apologies for the thing," he wrote in complaint, "they are only squares, or paddocks."

The popularity of rural cemeteries was clear evidence, in his opinion, of the need for a sprawling, tree-filled oasis in Manhattan—the first of its kind, which he knew would inspire other cities to copy.

> Now, if hundreds of thousands of the inhabitants of cities, like New-York, will . . . incur the expense and trouble of going five or six miles to visit Greenwood [Cemetery in Brooklyn], we think it may be safely estimated that a much larger number would resort to a public garden, at once the finest park, the most charming drive, the most inviting pleasure-ground, and the most agreeable promenade within their reach.

Such a place, he continued, would "largely civilize and refine the national character, foster the love of rural beauty, and increase the knowledge of and taste for rare and beautiful trees and plants."

Similarly calling for a city park was William Cullen Bryant, editor of the *New-York Evening Post*, who wrote a series of passionate editorials on the subject. Though Downing died in a ferry accident at age thirty-five in 1852, the public support that he, Bryant, and others had stirred gained enough traction for the city government to finally act. Under the power of eminent domain, which allows a government to take over private land in the name of public use, the city bought 778 acres stretching from Fifty-Ninth Street north to the farmlands of 106th Street to build this "central park." Four years later, the city held a design competition to determine what the space would look like. The winning proposal among the thirty-three submissions came from landscape architects—and Downing disciples—Calvert Vaux and Frederick Law Olmsted.

Vaux was born in England and came to the United States in 1850, and collaborated with Downing to design part of the grounds surrounding the White House and Capitol in Washington, D.C. After Downing's death, Vaux teamed with the brilliant, ambitious, Connecticut-born Olmsted, who had been an engineer, magazine editor, and farmer, among other occupations, before becoming a landscape architect. Olmsted's name would become ubiquitous with nineteenth-century landscape design, and his works continue to influence the field, as he oversaw the construction of magnificent, enduring projects across the country—from Boston's Emerald Necklace of city parks, to Biltmore in Asheville, North Carolina, to the campuses of Stanford University and the University of Chicago.

Vaux and Olmsted's winning plan for Central Park drew heavily upon the design features unique to rural cemeteries at that time—but which now seem commonplace in city green spaces. It called for a landscape filled with ponds, paths, stone bridges and arches, promenades, formal gardens, meadows, green spaces, and the planting of hundreds of thousands of trees and shrubs. The park's natural grandeur under the plan was intended to match New York City's aspirations as the country's cultural nexus. Though the blueprints followed much of the site's natural contours, not a square inch of space would go untouched or unaccounted for. Construction began in spring 1858, and Olmsted stayed on with the Central Park project to oversee the work.

Much of the new park's land sat on undeveloped property, except for Seneca Village, then located between Eighty-Second and Eighty-Ninth Streets on the Upper West Side of Manhattan. The settlement was a rare haven of Black homeownership. Its population of 225 consisted mostly of African Americans, with some Irish and German immigrants, who bought their land from a local farmer. They worked downtown as laborers and in service jobs, and raised families and started a tight-knit community. Seneca Village included a few churches and shops, at least one school, some farm plots, and more than fifty homes. Since voting rights for African American men were only granted to property owners in New York, the settlement contained 10 percent of the city's Black voting population. It also housed two burial grounds containing dozens of bodies.

But, of course, Seneca Village stood no chance against the tidal wave of support for the park—interest in it had swelled among New York's political and economic elites, who envisioned luxury housing developments fringing its borders. The city evicted the devastated residents and compensated them with a paltry sum. Many refused to leave, knowing they would have almost no chance to own property in the city again, and they took their case against the eminent domain action to court.

Politicians and newspapers depicted Seneca Village as a place occupied by "miserable looking broken-down shanties" filled with "vagrants" and "scoundrels." The general public didn't show its residents much sympathy. In 1857, the Seneca Village residents lost their legal battle, and the city forcibly removed them. According to the *New York Times*, police "upheld" the law with their "bludgeons," resulting in "many broken heads and ensanguined eyes."

Quickly afterward, construction crews leveled the settlement, erasing all evidence of human life there. But the bodies in Seneca Village's graveyards were never exhumed; the park was simply built above them.

As was predicted at the outset of creating Central Park, real estate on its edges boomed. In 1881, the owner of the Singer sewing machine company built a nine-story-tall luxury apartment building, mimicking the style of a German Renaissance castle, across from the West

Seventy-Second Street entrance to the park, and called it the Dakota. Others like it arose as well. One *New York Times* article at the time observed, "It is the ambition of the New Yorker to live upon Fifth Avenue, to take his Airings in the park, and to sleep with his fathers in Green-Wood."

Despite displacing Seneca Village's residents to make way for the park, its success as a means of revitalizing the city was hard to deny. The masterpiece that is Central Park led to the proliferation of urban green spaces throughout the country. They were often built atop burial grounds for lack of other usable city real estate, and—like with Seneca Village—generally without the bodies being removed. New York City's Bryant Park, Union Square, Madison Square Park, and Washington Square Park all sit atop old graveyards. Chicago's Lincoln Park, the third-most-visited urban park in the country with 29 million visitors annually, was once the resting place for more than 35,000 people. Denver's Cheesman Park sits atop the graves of 2,000 people. San Diego's Mission Hills Park was home to at least eight hundred burial plots. And Philadelphia's Washington Square was built atop the mass graves of thousands of Revolutionary War dead and yellow fever victims.

In recent times, the injustice at Seneca Village has received more attention, and Central Park has erected educational placards where the settlement once stood to tell its story. Visitors can picture what once stood there and gain an inkling of what was lost. Central Park has now become a place not only built atop human remains, but also resting below them. With cremations exceeding burials across the country, urban green spaces have taken on a new role for mourning in America, as people spread the ashes of loved ones in them. Central Park might be the most famous cremation destination of all. And we have Yoko Ono to blame, or thank, for that.

ON THE EVENING of December 8, 1980, a gunman shot and killed John Lennon as the former Beatle stood outside the entrance to his longtime New York City home, the historic Dakota apartment building. The following day Lennon's wife, Yoko Ono, announced there would be no funeral. Instead, Lennon was cremated, and the family held a quiet, secret ceremony. It's believed that Ono spread his ashes in a two-acre triangle-shaped meadow in Central Park by the Seventy-Second Street entrance across from the Dakota, within view of the couple's apartment window.

The spot, like much of the park in the late twentieth century, suffered from neglect. So the spring after Lennon's death, Ono donated $1 million to improve the meadow and create a garden of peace where visitors from around the world could mourn and remember the music legend. In October 1985, the spot—revitalized with newly planted lawn space, decorative trees, and flower beds—was renamed Strawberry Fields in a dedication ceremony. Embedded into a path within it lay a round mosaic of black and white Italian tiles emblazoned with the word IMAGINE in the center. It now serves as his unofficial grave site for his admirers, and thousands of people pass it daily.

The notoriety of Strawberry Fields, and the rumors of Lennon's ashes spread atop it, put Central Park on the cremains map.* Scattering ashes wasn't legal in Central Park back then, but it is now, and in all New York City parks, as long as it's not done on athletic fields, or in playgrounds, bodies of water, or other restricted areas. Central Park has become so popular as a dust-dumping destination, there's even a long-distance ash-scattering service, called the Living Urn, that will spread people's remains there, for a fee. Photos and videos are taken, and the precise GPS coordinates of the scattering are provided. The company's promotional video shows one of its "trained professionals," as they're called, dumping an urn in the middle of Strawberry Fields. Because burials have been outlawed in Manhattan below Eighty-Sixth Street since 1852, Central Park is likely the borough's most active repository for human remains. Its lone competition is Trinity Church Cemetery, on Manhattan's far northern tip, the island's last active official cemetery, where burial costs range from $10,000 to $30,000, depending on location.

When I lived on the Upper West Side, I ran through Strawberry Fields and amid the former site of Seneca Village almost daily without

---

* Brilliantly, building a memorial park near the site of Lennon's death also diverted fans from gathering and placing flowers at the Dakota's entrance, which would have inconvenienced the residents and depressed the values of its posh apartments, which range from $5 to $20 million.

realizing the significance of its hallowed ground. I didn't think of Central Park as a cemetery in the way I understand it now. But on a recent Saturday afternoon jog with my wife, its status as a burial ground dominated my thoughts. I had recently read a story about the city's crematoria working overtime to meet the demands of the COVID crisis in the first wave, with state regulators allowing them to work twenty-four hours a day, seven days a week to keep up with the overwhelming toll. Lord knows how many of those freshly filled urns were carried by mask-wearing mourners into Central Park to mingle the ashes of the person they loved with the soil. How painful and beautiful.

The running route my wife and I took started at Seventy-Fourth and Broadway, and led us uptown to the Eighty-Fifth Street entrance to the park, where we descended past a playground into the heart of where Seneca Village once stood. We passed an educational display marking the location of the settlement's three churches.

"You know, this—"

She interrupted. "This is the location of where the cemeteries were. The bodies were never moved."

"Uh, yes," I said. She was listening to me after all.

We kept a steady pace, navigating around the walkers and runners who crowded the footpaths, making our way south. We skirted the Great Lawn and passed the Lake, which was a swamp before Vaux and Olmsted's plans transformed it into a place for ducks and swans, and romantic rides in rented rowboats. We veered onto the paved jogging lane on busy West Drive then took a sharp right into Strawberry Fields, climbing an oak-shaded path.

She spoke, clearly trying to mimic my voice but sounding like a walrus. (I am not the walrus.) "Yoko spread John's ashes somewhere in here," she said.

I didn't appreciate the humor.

We reached the Imagine mosaic, which someone had encircled with a wreath of fresh roses. A few people stood beside it, taking smiling selfies. A woman in her twenties, with long brown hair, sat on a nearby park bench, playing a guitar and singing Lennon's song "Across the Universe."

We kept moving, out of the park, the lyrics fading slowly behind us as we treaded toward the traffic of the city and the sight of the Dakota—a symbol of Seneca Village's shameful destruction to feed real estate greed, and the beauty that arose in the wake of Lennon's death. Central Park, America's first city park, has come full circle.

Numbered stones mark the Gettysburg National Cemetery burial places of 979 Union soldiers whose bodies were never identified after the Battle of Gettysburg.

10. FOUR SCORE AND SEVENTY-NINE
YEARS AGO

The Civil War opened the gates to the capitalism of corpses—
and death in America has never been the same

—

Gettysburg National Cemetery
Gettysburg, Pennsylvania
Established: 1863

ABRAHAM LINCOLN WAS no stranger to cemeteries. He worked
as a gravedigger for the Little Pigeon Baptist Church burial ground
near his home as a young teenager. He witnessed the burial of his two
siblings—an older sister and a younger brother—and two of his four
children during the span of his life. And as president, he delivered his
most famous speech, the Gettysburg Address, at a cemetery.

Still, there's another important connection between him and cemeteries, which history usually leaves out. Lincoln dramatically altered
the country's burial practices during the Civil War, leading to the emergence of the modern Death Industrial Complex. Consider it an unin-
tended consequence of politics and practicality that sprung from the
nation's bloodiest conflict.

The Civil War's unfathomable death toll brought with it the prob-
lem of burials. About 620,000 American service members—North and
South—died, more than ten times as many as in the entire Vietnam
War. As many African Americans died fighting for the Union—roughly
40,000—as the number of all Americans who died in the Korean War.
The body count from the ten bloodiest Civil War battles all individually
eclipsed the number of Allied casualties suffered on D-Day in World
War II. In total, more than 2 percent of the U.S. population perished

in the conflict to end slavery, either from combat or—in more cases—illness. Roughly 65,000 soldiers died from typhoid fever alone.

The majority of the dead were interred in hasty, anonymous mass ditches on battlefields or in local churchyards. Soldiers of the era didn't wear dog tags or carry official identification, so placing names to inert faces was nearly impossible when mass deaths occurred. There was no system for officially notifying next of kin of a loved one's death, leaving families in agonizing, prolonged limbo. Some parents, spouses, or siblings would travel to the battlefields themselves to search for answers or remains, or they'd hire undertakers to do so. Days or even weeks would pass after a battle, and bodies would often still be left lying, and decaying, waiting to be dropped into a resting place. Nearly half would never be identified.

Americans of the Civil War era predominantly believed a "good death" was necessary to ensure a soul would be saved.* The process, called the art of death, typically involved people making peace with God with their final words while passing away in the home surrounded by family. Afterward, the body of the deceased was to be bathed, groomed, and properly dressed in its churchgoing best, and placed in a part of the home called the parlor or death room, where mourners would visit to pay respects. A local carpenter or cabinetmaker would construct the simple wooden coffin and deliver it to the home for the funeral, and within forty-eight hours of death, the body would be carried by friends and family to a graveyard for interment.

The Civil War made good death almost impossible. Mass casualties prevented any semblance of ceremony, opting for efficiency in the form of anonymous graves at battlefields. This left families terrified for the ultimate spiritual destinations of their lost loved ones. Union soldiers on the verge of battle were equally distraught, unsure of their spiritual fate should they die—this damaged morale, as they desperately tried to find meaning in the carnage that surrounded them. Imagine fighting for a noble cause but thinking you'd go to hell for eternity if you're killed on the battlefield doing it.

---

* Drew Gilpin Faust, an American history specialist and the first woman president of Harvard University (serving from 2007 to 2018), wrote the definitive modern book on the "good death," entitled *This Republic of Suffering*, published in 2008.

Then came Abraham Lincoln's speech at the dedication of Gettysburg National Cemetery. Eyeing his flagging popularity, while anti-war sentiments grew, he used the new military burial ground to redefine to the nation a soldier's version of a good death—to reinforce commitment to the important cause. A good death didn't need to happen at home, in front of family, with one's last words memorialized. It could happen on the battlefield, in the name of justice.

By divorcing the act of proper mourning from these family-centered artisanal rituals, Lincoln opened the floodgates to the funeral industry and the capitalization of corpses. Death in America has never been the same.

BEFORE THE CAREFULLY designed creation of Gettysburg National Cemetery in 1863, American national cemeteries were largely just dumping grounds of the dead, born of necessity, and burial places of last resort. They were considered unconsecrated and unhallowed hellscapes. At the start of the hostilities, national cemeteries didn't even exist.

The first Union officer killed in the Civil War was twenty-four-year-old Colonel Elmer Ellsworth, a former clerk at Abraham Lincoln's law office, and a close friend of the president. In May 1861, he climbed the roof of an inn in newly Union-occupied Alexandria, Virginia, to remove a giant Confederate flag hanging atop it. The flag, as the story goes, was visible across the Potomac all the way to the White House—which, given that 1600 Pennsylvania Avenue was about five miles away, meant either the flag was incredibly huge, or someone was embellishing. On his descent, the innkeeper—a slavery sympathizer—shot and killed Ellsworth.

News of his death reverberated across the country, and a mournful and opportunistic Lincoln amplified the loss to stoke the necessary political and public support for the war. The president ordered the body to lay in state at the White House, then be transported with much fanfare for viewing in Ellsworth's home city of New York, with stops along the way.

Stepping from the shadow of Ellsworth's death was a surgeon named Thomas Holmes, who had been experimenting with embalming cadavers to preserve them for medical students and researchers to

Col. Elmer Ellsworth, considered the first Union casualty in the Civil War

dissect. His method involved flushing chemicals like mercury, alcohol, and arsenic through the arteries—in a process he borrowed from French doctors and using a pump he invented himself. At this time in America, bodies weren't embalmed; they were simply buried as quickly as possible. Sensing a possible business opportunity and marketing bonanza, he offered his services to President Lincoln to preserve Ellsworth, free of charge, to facilitate the dead hero's mini East Coast mourning tour.

The president accepted, and the embalming proved to be a success. The media coverage transformed Ellsworth into a national celebrity. Entrepreneurs hawked pro-war souvenirs carrying the image of his young face, graced by a thin black mustache, and topped with bushy black hair beneath a tilted U.S. Army cap. He was the all-American boy, dead. Songs about him were written. Rallying cries of "Remember Ellsworth!" echoed among the supportive throngs in political halls, in homes, and on the battlefields. Viewers were astonished by the deceased Ellsworth's lifelike features as he was paraded from place to place. A *New York Times* reporter who viewed Ellsworth at the glitzy Astor House hotel on the Upper East Side of Manhattan made note of the dead young colonel's vitality during the somber occasion. An estimated 10,000 people viewed Ellsworth there alone, with thousands of others standing outside. Near the hotel, a banner hung from a firehouse reading, ELLSWORTH, HIS BLOOD CRIES FOR VENGEANCE. Soon his blood would be far from the only one crying for vengeance.

The Civil War's first major engagement, the First Battle of Bull Run, occurred in late July 1861, leading to 460 Union soldiers and 387 Confederates dead. By April 1862 the multitudes of bodies strewn across battlefields were reaching such horrific proportions that the U.S. Army announced a set of standard burial procedures in order to place higher expectations, and a greater amount of responsibility, on field commanders to take care of their dead. Generals were required to create makeshift cemeteries after battles by designating a piece of ground "in some suitable spot near every battlefield, so soon as it may be in their power, and to cause the remains of those killed to be interred."

But the orders had limited effect. The army's resource-strapped commanders didn't have the power to seize private property for graveyards, nor did they have the appropriate time, equipment, or personnel for proper burials. So in July of that year, Congress, pressured by outraged constituents, took a further step by enabling President Lincoln to buy lands near battlefields, military training grounds, and medical facilities to repurpose them "to be used as a national cemetery for the soldiers who shall die in the service of the country." Like that, national cemeteries for the Union were born—no such places came into existence for Confederate casualties.

The first two national cemeteries arose in Alexandria, Virginia, and Annapolis, Maryland, to house the soldiers who died from illness and prolonged injury. The third was created in Sharpsburg, Maryland, where the Battle of Antietam took place on September 17, 1862, and more than 3,600 people died in the fighting.

Then came the Battle of Gettysburg, in July 1863. More than 7,000 soldiers, including roughly 3,100 fighting for the Union, died over three bloody days in southeastern Pennsylvania. An additional 33,000 were wounded and 10,000 captured or missing, overwhelming medical personnel and gravediggers. Doctors, inundated by the injured, cut off limbs and tossed them into massive discard piles that were then buried in limb pits. The battle would be Confederate general Robert E. Lee's last attempt to bring the fight north of the Mason-Dixon Line, in hope of forcing the U.S. government to concede defeat in the South. He failed.

When the fighting ended, Union forces quickly went in pursuit of the enemy, leaving the bulk of the burial tasks to locals. They raced against the ravages of the summer heat to dig shallow graves across the battlefield. Pennsylvania's governor, Andrew Curtin, devised plans to solve the massive corpse conundrum by establishing a grand Soldiers' National Cemetery that would commemorate the battle's victory and celebrate the war dead. A close personal ally of Lincoln, Curtin knew all too well about the American public's growing war fatigue, and how increasingly dim it left the president's reelection prospects in 1864. So there was both honor and an ulterior motive in establishing such a cemetery.

Curtin enlisted the support of governors from several Union states to help finance the project and purchase the land. To design the grounds, he hired a famed landscape botanist and architect, William Saunders, who designed Oak Ridge Cemetery in Illinois—where Lincoln would later be buried—and introduced the seedless naval orange to California. His blueprint called for the graves to collectively serve as a sort of sculpture, arranged in concentric semicircular rows and divided into sections by the home state of the dead. He was inspired by the picturesque rural cemeteries spreading across the country and recognized the growing importance Americans placed on memorializing the individual instead of depositing people in crowded churchyards. The new burial ground's creative layout of graves would set a design standard for national cemeteries, while its surrounding landscape doubled as an inspiring work of art in the vein of the classic American rural burial grounds.

To bring greater notoriety to the project, the governor planned a high-profile opening ceremony, modeled after the 1831 convocation of Mount Auburn. He invited America's most stirring orator, Edward

Everett—a former senator from Massachusetts and president of Harvard University—to deliver the keynote remarks. The governor was keen on extolling the virtues of those who died and rallying the Union around the war's cause.

Curtin also sent invitations to political leaders in Washington in the weeks leading up to the event, including Lincoln. The one the president received welcomed him to offer "a few appropriate remarks"—though according to scholars, no one, including Pennsylvania's governor, thought Lincoln would attend. Lincoln rarely ever left the capital during his time in office since his energies were consumed by the war. And up to that point in his presidency, he had never traveled outside Washington, D.C., to deliver a speech.*

But the election was looming, and Lincoln openly admitted the obvious to his aides: His chances at winning a second term were bleak. Giving a speech at Gettysburg would be politically advantageous, maybe even necessary—the state represented one quarter of all electoral votes, and his friend the governor held significant sway. Influential officials from Ohio and New York—the other two vital swing states—would also be in attendance, trailed by a sizable contingent of newspaper reporters from across the country.

So it was on November 19, 1863, that Lincoln went to Gettysburg, armed with a three-minute speech for the occasion. The ceremony took place while the cemetery was still under construction and crews were still completing the monthslong work of exhuming all the bodies from their temporary battlefield resting places. The keynote orator, Everett, spoke first, delivering a two-hour-long address, which—contrary to lore that it was a snoozer—was stirring enough, for a two-hour-long speech. Then, after a brief musical interlude, the president lumbered to the podium and delivered the Gettysburg Address.

Lincoln used words like *brought forth*, *conceived*, *birth*, and *live*, in striking contrast to the field of death that surrounded him. He told the crowd, "We cannot consecrate—we cannot hallow—this ground. The brave men, living and dead, who struggled here, have hallowed it, far above our poor power to add or detract."

---

* According to historian Martin P. Johnson in his book *Writing the Gettysburg Address*.

Lincoln was changing the narrative—assigning a holiness to Gettysburg National Cemetery's grounds, and salvation for those interred, that hadn't yet existed in the eyes of the American public for battleground burial places. He actually *was* consecrating and hallowing the grounds, and he vowed that the soldiers who died at Gettysburg "shall not have died in vain." They were words Americans were desperate to hear and accept. It was through his address that Lincoln redefined the good death as one that could take place outside the home.

According to an Ohio newspaper reporter covering the event, a Union officer in the crowd who had lost an arm in the battle "sobbed about while his manly frame shook with no unmanly emotion." The man exclaimed at the end, "God Almighty bless Abraham Lincoln!"

Americans soon began to regard burials in a national cemetery as an automatic get-a-good-death-free card. Drew Gilpin Faust wrote that the establishment of national cemeteries "became an ongoing national preoccupation." For families who wanted to bring the bodies of their fallen loved ones from the war to a home cemetery, the president commissioned Holmes, the embalmer, to teach and train a new legion of embalming surgeons. They set up embalming stations for Union dead, and the government paid embalmers a $30 fee to preserve an enlisted soldier, and an even higher bounty of $80 for officers to get the Elmer Ellsworth treatment.

A flash embalming industry emerged, with freelance embalmers—of varying skills and degrees of shadiness—suddenly stalking the battlefields before the engagements even ended. A good portion of them were the carpenters and cabinetmakers who had been plying their trade to make coffins and saw the opportunity for two-for-one fees by preserving the bodies. They set up tents and precharged some living soldiers for the privilege of being first in line for their services if death knocked. Some embalmers even preserved bodies without a family's permission, and then held the corpse until a ransom-like fee was paid by the helpless loved ones.

Holmes himself did a brisk business with the dead. The government was willing to pay him an even higher fee for his professional services, and he bragged that he embalmed 4,000 people during the war. He even opened two shops in the Washington, D.C., area, where he hung the preserved bodies of unknown soldiers in the front window to show off his handiwork, according to the National Museum of Civil War Medicine. And later, when Lincoln was assassinated, Mary Todd Lincoln enlisted Holmes to embalm him.

After the war, the U.S. government and charity organizations scoured the battlefields to dig up Union soldiers still lying in shallow temporary graves and properly bury them in national cemeteries. The Angel of the Battlefield, Clara Barton, opened the federal Missing Soldiers Office in 1865 to track down the missing killed in action. During the next three years, her office found the whereabouts of 22,000 dead soldiers, including 13,000 who died as prisoners of war at Andersonville Prison in Georgia. In 1867, Congress approved the National Cemetery Act, which funded the purchase of even more cemetery lands and improvements to existing national cemeteries.

Shortly after, landscape designer Frederick Law Olmsted was enlisted to advise the federal government on national cemetery design, to enhance their sanctity and allure. They were meant to be "studiously simple," he wrote in a letter to the army's quartermaster general. "The main object should be to establish permanent dignity and tranquility" so that the burial ground felt like "a sacred grove" of graves. He suggested planting decorative trees, shrubs, and flower beds, and adding statues and monuments throughout.

By 1871, more than 300,000 Union soldiers had been interred in seventy-four national cemeteries. At the end of the decade, Congress approved a uniform headstone design, and the wooden marker that stood at each grave was replaced with a permanent white marble one. The federal government generally didn't finance the identification or interment of the Confederate dead at that time, leaving the task largely in the hands of Southern charity organizations and states.

THE CIVIL WAR radically transformed the art of dying not only for soldiers, but for the American population at large. When the hostilities ended, the industry of full-service professionals who arose to build and sell coffins and embalm and prepare the dead looked for new customers among civilians in order to stay in business. These undertakers, as they were known, promoted the (highly profitable) idea that all people should be embalmed after death, arguing that it allowed mourners to travel from farther distances to see the deceased before burial. They began establishing parlors outside the home where funerals could be held, so a corpse wouldn't have to sit idly for longer periods in a family's death room.

They also changed the look and name of coffins. The word *coffin* comes from the old French word *cofin*, meaning "basket." Its English use, to mean a box for bodies, can be traced back to 1330, according to the *Oxford English Dictionary*. Coffins, usually made of wood and hexagonally shaped to be wider at the shoulders and narrower at the head and feet—like the ones movie vampires sleep in—were reserved for only the rich in England and North America until becoming more common for all burials in the 1700s.

Caskets, by contrast, are rectangular shaped—no longer reminding us of the human form kept inside them. The word arose in England in the 1600s to refer to a jewelry box until the nineteenth-century American funeral industry borrowed it to add marketing appeal to a new, higher-end coffin. Like a jewelry box, a casket is lined by silk, velvet, or fine cloth and has a hinged lid. But instead of being filled with precious gems, it's filled with a human corpse. One of the first mass-producing casket manufacturers to arise in the wake of the Civil War was Batesville, established in Indiana in 1884. Today, its annual revenue exceeds $772 million, cornering more than 40 percent of North America's market share for casket sales.

The burgeoning postwar funeral industry triggered the commodification of death just as American society in the late nineteenth century was becoming increasingly urbanized, secular, and capitalistic. Advances in medicine were changing the nature of how, when, and where people died, and cemeteries had untethered themselves from churchyards and family plots—they were becoming their own profit-making entities. Through the convergence of these conditions, the Death Industrial Complex that hovers above us—and eventually takes all of us as a customer—emerged.

The death care industry that blossomed in the early twentieth century secularized the good death, and customized burials and services to make every American's passing special and unique. Embalming became an act that's normal to us now but seems bizarre to nearly the rest of the world: The United States is one of only a tiny handful of countries, almost all exclusively English-speaking, where embalming the dead is common practice. In fact, in many places, culture and tradition forbid it, as do the Jewish and Muslim faiths.

In 1895, a movement arose in the funeral industry to coin a new title for the people responsible for preparing bodies for burial. Something less gloomy and more scientific, with Latin roots. The *Medical Herald*, a national monthly magazine "for the medical sciences," announced the consensus result in the News and Miscellany section of its December 1895 issue. "The New Name—An undertaker will no longer be known as an 'undertaker and embalmer.' In the future, he will be known as a mortician."

Later it would be changed again, to *funeral director*. New, modern morticians became full-service. They upsold expensive metal caskets with polished handles for pallbearer carrying, and turned customers away from the simple wooden coffin. They coordinated floral arrangements, obituary postings, and a permanent stone monument to be placed at the grave site—most of which were new customary practices, largely untethered to religious tradition. The use of flowers at graves, for instance—though common in ancient cultures—wasn't a part of American practices before that time.* Morticians convinced mourners of the need for concrete vaults—with personalized options and varying levels of protection—to preserve the caskets underground. They provided transportation of the body from the funeral parlor to the church and cemetery.

And almost overnight, the act of displaying the loved one at home was out. In 1910, an article in *Ladies' Home Journal* recommended people start calling the old death room in their homes by a new, more pleasant and appropriate-sounding name: the living room. It stuck. By 1920, nearly 25,000 funeral homes were operating across the country, a figure that grew annually. The rising Death Industrial Complex was offering Americans the good death in a box, and we were buying it at a premium. We still do. Thanks, Abe.

---

* America's first florist shop, Butz Flowers, opened in 1895 in New Castle, Pennsylvania, and is still in operation today.

A lone bugler from the U.S. Army Band stands within a
sea of graves at Arlington National Cemetery.

11. SWEET AND FITTING TO DIE FOR ONE'S COUNTRY

How Arlington National Cemetery's success as a monument to war made Americans too eager to fill it

—

Arlington National Cemetery
Arlington, Virginia
Established: 1864

CHAPERONING A THREE-DAY elementary school trip to Washington, D.C., is my very definition of hell. The cheap buffet restaurants for dinner; the hotel way, way outside of town; the constant yelling and screaming—which was mostly done by me, I must say, at the pint-size monsters from my daughter's fifth-grade class who were under my supervision. I volunteered to chaperone for selfish reasons: I wanted to make my daughter love me a little bit more. I had returned home from serving in Afghanistan for the navy a few months earlier, and felt I had some making up to do.

Our tour bus left Asheville, North Carolina, on a cold March morning at some ungodly hour for the eight-hour drive to our nation's capital. The action-crammed itinerary ensured we would be sleep-deprived throughout, so that—as one of the teachers informed us—the kids would "keep out of trouble." Worst of all, it became clear from the start that my daughter would not love me more for being there, despite the awesome arsenal of dad jokes I came armed with for the trip.

For example: *What did the ocean say to the beach? Nothing, it just waved!*

And: *I lost my job at a cemetery yesterday. I made a grave mistake.*

On the subject of cemeteries, it should be noted that the visit we made across the Potomac River to Arlington National Cemetery was by far the highlight of the entire trip. (For me, at least.)

We visited the cemetery early on our final morning. The almost gale-force Arctic winds that had been torturing us throughout subsided, the clouds parted, and for once—thank the lord—we were in a place where our bus didn't have to double-park in the middle of traffic for our entry and exit. At Arlington, there was space. Even though more than three million people visit the cemetery each year, its 639 hilly, grass-covered acres can more than handle the crowds.

The early part of our walking tour took us past the iconic mansion known as Arlington House, which was the former home of Robert E. Lee. From there, we stopped at the eternal flame by the grave site of President John F. Kennedy, then visited the broad, marble Memorial Amphitheater, where American presidents have given speeches on Memorial Day for the past century. Adjacent to this commanding structure is the neoclassical Tomb of the Unknown Soldier, where we watched the ceremonial changing of the guard.

After the ceremony, we rested, briefly—and my daughter and I took a seat alone on some steps. She was having friend drama, and her glasses had just broken, which frustrated her, and she was as exhausted as I was. Maybe for the first time since we had left Asheville, she seemed like she actually wanted to hang out with just me, instead of those feral, sugar-demented elementary school deviants. I was delighted.

We sat in silence for a little while, until I suddenly waved my arms at the expanse of cemetery around us. "You know how many dead people there are in a cemetery?" I asked her.

"No. How many?"

"All of them! Ha! Get it?" I was trying to lighten the mood. Grave mistake.

She looked up at me, pools of tears filling her eyes. "No, Dad. You promised, no more dad jokes."

"Okay," I lied. "No more dad jokes."

My daughter shuffled off to join her pals, who were discussing how and where they could score their next Red Bull–and–Twizzlers fix.

"All" the dead people, I would have explained had she stayed, totaled around 400,000. Roughly twenty-five burials for American military veterans take place on Arlington's hallowed grounds daily. Burial rights at the cemetery are granted almost exclusively to people killed in action, or who earned a combat award like the Medal of Honor or Purple Heart, or who served a full career in the military and retired honorably. I could have said to her that Arlington, as the country's biggest and premier national cemetery, is still a military installation. Because it hosts so many official ceremonies and high-profile visits from foreign heads of state, it's run by the U.S. Army, as opposed to nearly all other national cemeteries, which fall under the U.S. Department of Veterans Affairs.

Finally, I could have pointed out to her the words, only a stone's throw from us, that define this place. They're etched atop the entrance to the cemetery's Memorial Amphitheater, written originally by the Roman poet Horace: "*Dulce et decorum est pro patria mori,*" or, "It is sweet and fitting to die for one's country."

Arlington, with its buzz-cut fields and board-straight rows of starch-white marble headstones—all the same shape and size for generals and privates alike to create a sense of equity in death—is as breathtaking in person as it is in its many famous photographs. It has transformed over the years from its origins on the site of Robert E. Lee's former plantation, as a symbolic act of defiance aimed at the Confederate general and the South, to the country's centerpiece national cemetery. Arlington has become America's temple to the god of war, its inhabitants our offerings. To be buried in its soil is to be instantly and forever mythologized—for right or wrong. It is one of our biggest military recruiting tools, and the subject of songs and poems. Its success as a symbol has made Americans all too eager to fill it.

Arlington, a human creation as flawed under the surface as it is beautiful above, is now running out of room for all our sacrifices.

ARLINGTON NATIONAL CEMETERY sits upon a rolling, fertile swath of northern Virginia where the coastal plain collides with the foothills of the Blue Ridge Mountains, along the southern bank of the Potomac River. Shaped like a giant oval, most of its grassy, rolling expanses are decorated as far as the eye can see with tight rows and columns of perfectly spaced, nearly identical white marble headstones. It seems almost like if you toppled the right one, you could send them all down like an elaborate domino creation stretching three-quarters of the size of New York's Central Park. At the cemetery's center juts a 220-foot-tall hill that peers unimpeded across the Potomac toward the National Mall, the monuments, the White House, and the Capitol.

No wonder President John F. Kennedy remarked to his brother Robert in 1963, as the two surveyed D.C. from Arlington, "It's so beautiful, I could stay here forever."*

No wonder also that John Parke Custis, son of Martha Washington and adopted son of George Washington, was inspired to originally purchase the 1,100 acres that now house the cemetery in the late 1700s, while the nation's capital was being built. Custis died in the early 1800s, and his son inherited the land and constructed a mansion at the hill's crest. The structure was fronted with eight Doric columns that made it look like it belonged on the Acropolis in Greece. The home was called Arlington House, and the plantation around it Arlington. Hundreds of enslaved people worked its broad, sun-drenched fields, and what wasn't being farmed was covered by the Park—an Edenic forest of towering centuries-old oaks, chestnuts, elms, and walnuts.

Next to inherit the property was Mary Custis Lee, Washington's great-granddaughter and wife of an ambitious West Point graduate named Robert E. Lee. The two were married in the mansion's parlor and lived in the home for the better part of three decades. It was there, on April 19, 1861, less than a week after the hostilities at Fort Sumter sparked the Civil War, that Lee decided to take up arms against the United States and lead Virginia's military forces in rebellion. Three days afterward, he left the plantation, where "my affections and attachments are more strongly placed than at any other place in the world," he wrote.

U.S. Army leaders understood the strategic importance of the Lee family's beloved plantation, given its direct vantage above Washington,

---

* According to author Robert M. Poole in his definitive and impressively researched history, *On Hallowed Ground: The Story of Arlington National Cemetery.*

D.C. They also realized its profound symbolic meaning. A month after General Lee left Arlington, army forces seized and occupied it, forcing Mary to flee with what prized family possessions she could carry.

The Union immediately emancipated the African Americans living on the plantation and turned Arlington House into the Army of the Potomac's headquarters. They built a tent city, and chopped down trees to construct artillery positions, fortifications, and barracks. The following year, in 1863, the army built a town of wood-framed homes for newly freed and runaway enslaved people on a corner of the estate, named Freedman's Village. The effort to humiliate and demoralize Lee—who had become the name and face of the proslavery position to many Americans—on the property was innovative and unrelenting.

An article in the Washington *Daily Morning Chronicle* headlined "Gen. Lee's Lands Appropriately Confiscated" described the "happy thought" of establishing Freedman's Village, which over the years would grow to include schools, churches, and farm plots, and become the home to thousands of emancipated Americans. But it was only meant to be temporary, and was vacated at the turn of the twentieth century.

By early 1864, nearing the end of the Civil War, army planners turned their attention to the Lee plantation for another purpose: a graveyard. Washington, D.C., was running short on burial space, and there, across the Potomac at Arlington, stood vast, fertile, and easily accessible lands, ripe for receiving the dead. The army buried its first 1,000 soldiers alongside an African American graveyard next to Freedman's Village, about a half mile from the mansion. The area, now Section 27 of Arlington, became the Lower Cemetery. Months later, military leaders went one step further and ordered the army's quartermaster general, Montgomery Meigs, to find two hundred acres on the property to establish a national cemetery, in the wake of the growing popularity of national cemeteries after Lincoln's Gettysburg Address.

The quartermaster general responded by recommending that the burial ground be placed directly surrounding the mansion, because the area was "admirably adapted to such a use." Yes, it was a gorgeous and fitting resting spot for those who gave their lives to their country, but Meigs also knew that filling the house's front and backyards with tens of thousands of dead bodies would make the place permanently uninhabitable to the Lees, no matter what the outcome of the war might be. A West Point graduate like Lee, Meigs wanted Arlington to become a giant, symbolic middle finger, flipped directly at the Confederate general—and the federal government gave its approval.

The first twenty-six graves —all occupied by officers—were planted at the foot of Mary Lee's rose garden, and burial sites adjacent to the mansion spread like ivy from there. Soon, the quartermaster general ordered a Civil War Unknowns Monument to be built nearby, with a tomb containing the unidentified remains of 2,111 American soldiers, putting the final nail in the coffin for the Lee house ever being a home again.

Once designated as a national cemetery site, Arlington, like Gettysburg, was designed to be a work of art in the tradition of rural cemeteries—something like an American Elysian Fields, where the souls of those who died for their country were rewarded with immortality for their virtue and righteousness.* The Greek Revival–style mansion at its center fit perfectly with the mythical ideals. Graves in the new cemetery were placed in rows with order and military precision and marked with wooden headboards bearing either a name or, for the anonymous dead, an identification number. They were sectioned off by officers and enlisted personnel, and segregated by Black and white. The Lower Cemetery became designated specifically for troops from Black regiments, as well as formerly enslaved people who died while living in federally constructed Freedman's Villages around the capital. Arlington grew, and grew, and grew.

By the end of the Civil War, the national cemetery contained 16,000 graves. Lee quietly fought in vain to regain his former plantation, and after his death in 1870, wife Mary took up the cause. Meanwhile, the army's determined quartermaster general continued directing its expansion and beautification, cementing the foundation of the grounds we now recognize. Mary died in 1873, after which her son, George Washington Custis Lee, regained the property for a stint by way of a lawsuit decided by the Supreme Court in 1882. But with almost no

---

* The Elysian Fields were a paradise in Greek lore, reserved for heroes killed in battle.

other inheritance to his name, and in need of cash, he sold it in 1883 for $150,000 to the U.S. government, which kept it as a burial ground. Since Arlington was administered by the army, the official who finalized the agreement with the son of the late Robert E. Lee was Secretary of War Robert Todd Lincoln—the son of the late Abraham Lincoln.

MASS OBSERVANCES COMMEMORATING the Union dead arose in national cemeteries and across the country following Lee's unconditional surrender to General Ulysses S. Grant at Appomattox Court House, Virginia, on April 9, 1865. Perhaps the earliest was one held by formerly enslaved people in May of that year in Charleston, South Carolina. Many of the gatherings involved decorating soldiers' graves with flowers—a practice borrowed from the ancient Greeks, who did the same for their fallen warriors. In 1868, the commander in chief of the largest Civil War veteran's organization called for designating May 30 as Decoration Day—during a time of year when the most flowers would be in bloom. Decades later the holiday would become Memorial Day, and from that point forward, floral arrangements would increasingly become an element of all American funerals.

On the first Decoration Day in 1868, General James Garfield delivered a speech at Arlington National Cemetery, while thousands of volunteers placed flowers on every grave. President Andrew Johnson gave federal employees the day off to attend. By this time, the War Department had replaced all wooden grave markers in national cemeteries with the permanent marble ones containing a recessed shield engraved with the name—if known—rank, and home state of the soldier beneath it.

Decoration Day turned into an official national holiday in 1871, and at that year's ceremony, statesman and former enslaved person Frederick Douglass gave remarks at Arlington dedicated to the "Unknown Loyal Dead." His words received almost no press, and have largely been overlooked, even though they're exceptional in their beauty and power. Douglass, standing before President Ulysses S. Grant, alluded to ancient warriors and the Christian good death. He referred to the crowd gathered there as making an "offering" and "tribute." He called the fallen buried at Arlington the nation's "greatest benefactors," who "imperiled all for country and freedom," and whose "whitened bones have been piously gathered here."

Most poignantly, Douglass made an impassioned appeal. He said the growing movement "in the name of patriotism" to rewrite history and deny "the dark and vengeful spirit of slavery" as the war's cause, or to give "equal admiration" to the Confederacy, which "struck at the nation's life" to defend slavery, would be to "forget the merits of this fearful struggle" and betray the "noble cause" for which so many Americans fought, sacrificed, and died. Douglass concluded:

> We must never forget that victory to the rebellion meant death to the republic. We must never forget that the loyal soldiers who rest beneath this sod flung themselves between the nation and the nation's destroyers. If today we have a country not boiling in an agony of blood . . . if now we have a united country, no longer cursed by the hell-black system of human bondage, if the American name is no longer a by-word and a hissing to a mocking earth, if the star-spangled banner floats only over free American citizens in every quarter of the land, and our country has before it a long and glorious career of justice, liberty, and civilization, we are indebted to the unselfish devotion of the noble army who rest in these honored graves all around us.

The growing importance and popularity of Arlington's annual Decoration Day ceremonies led to the need for a dignified, permanent place to hold them. So the cemetery, on limited funds, built a simple, open-air, turf-carpeted amphitheater by Arlington House in 1873. It was encircled by wooden columns with a trellis roof. By the twentieth century, it became too small for the ever-expanding crowds, leading to the ground-breaking for Arlington's resplendent Memorial Amphitheater in 1915. Construction crews finished in 1920, two years after the end of World War I, which brought 2,100 new residents to the cemetery.

The classical-style open-air amphitheater contains curved rows of benches sufficient to seat a crowd of four thousand people, facing

Arlington National Cemetery's neoclassical Memorial Amphitheater,
completed in 1920 and made of Vermont marble

a towering semioval stage where you could almost imagine a Roman emperor standing. This is where, every year on Memorial Day, presidents deliver their remarks paying respects to the military dead. The amphitheater is encircled by a two-story-tall white marble colonnade of Ionic columns. To step through one of its entryways is almost to feel what it must have been like to walk inside the Colosseum or Circus Maximus. And this is by design: Horace's Latin words, about how it is sweet and fitting to die for one's country, *Dulce et decorum est pro patria mori*, are inscribed above the western arched entrance, which hung overhead as my daughter and I sat during our brief tour break.

What I didn't say to her then, as I spouted dad jokes, was how devastatingly ironic I found—and still find—those words. I had just been so freshly removed from my navy deployment to a war zone.* I was attached to a small, active combat unit that experienced all-too-frequent tragedies, including while I served in it. And I can say without

---

* Firing weapons wasn't my job over there, and if it had been, given my aim, I would have posed a greater threat to my foot or the ground than any enemy.

equivocation that there's nothing sweet or fitting about dying on the battlefield. Living to fight another day is infinitely better.

Around the time the amphitheater was being dedicated at the national cemetery in 1920, the classic poem "Dulce et Decorum Est" by Wilfred Owen, a British soldier killed one week before World War I ended, was being published posthumously in England. In it, Owen describes the horrors of watching a comrade die during a gas attack in the trenches. "In all my dreams before my helpless sight, / He plunges at me, guttering, choking, drowning."

The poem ends with these words:

> If you could hear, at every jolt, the blood
> Come gargling from the froth-corrupted lungs,
> Obscene as cancer, bitter as the cud
> Of vile, incurable sores on innocent tongues,—
> My friend, you would not tell with such high zest
> To children ardent for some desperate glory,
> The old Lie: *Dulce et decorum est*
> *Pro patria mori.*

It's often said that honest war literature is, by its nature, anti-war literature. Owen's poem is honest, and it calls out the "old Lie" that now hangs, in high zest, at Arlington's Memorial Amphitheater. Its irony isn't lost on many who pass beneath it.

Still, I understand that it hangs there with good reason, surrounded by the trappings of myths. We need people ardent for some desperate glory—as the cemetery's planners have always known. We need Arlington to be the temple to the god of war it has become, dressed in faux classical architecture connecting the world's ancient, storied empires with its modern one. We need it not just to pay respect to those who have died or to offer comfort to their loved ones, but to glamorize the ultimate sacrifice for those who might someday see battle, to tell them they'll be mythologized like Odysseus and Achilles. We need the members of our all-volunteer military to be willing, excited even, to ride into the valley of death and when there, not to reason why. We need them to know that when they die, they'll be buried flag draped, with guns firing into the air, in an immortal, green field of glory alongside the other righteous.

Through Arlington, Uncle Sam is selling not just a good death, but an awesome death, on a plate—and it works with devastating effectiveness. In every corner filled by the dead at the national cemetery, the old Lie lives.

On the opposite end of the Memorial Amphitheater, at its eastern plaza, lies the Tomb of the Unknown Soldier. In 1921, the body of an unidentified American who died fighting in World War I was exhumed from a graveyard in France and buried in a simple tomb made from a marble slab built into the steps of the amphitheater. It became so popular with tourists paying homage to that antiquated American notion of anonymous sacrifice in the name of the greater good that soldiers were assigned to stand guard during daylight hours in 1926. Six years later, a seventy-ton sarcophagus of white marble, taken from the mountains of Colorado, was installed atop it. On the east-facing side of the sarcophagus, sculptors carved three classic, Greek-looking figures—two women and one man—representing peace (a figure holding a dove), victory (a figure extending an olive branch), and valor (a figure carrying a broken sword). Decorating the north and south sides are laurel wreaths, the ancient symbols of military triumph. On the west side an inscription reads, HERE RESTS IN HONORED GLORY AN AMERICAN SOLDIER KNOWN BUT TO GOD. Spaces beneath it now contain the remains from Americans lost in World War II, Korea, and Vietnam.

Since 1937, the tomb has been under guard around the clock—at first to keep crowds from climbing on it, but then more as a symbolic unending vigil for all missing and unknown Americans who gave their lives at war. An elaborate three-soldier public changing of the guard ceremony occurs at the top of every hour in the winter, and half hour in the summer, with the duties performed by elite members of the 3rd U.S. Infantry Regiment—who don't look like they've ever eaten a donut or Big Mac in their lives. Intimidatingly stone-faced and clad in razor-sharp dress uniforms, they execute intricate movements that involve lots of straight-backed marching and white-gloved examinations of bayoneted rifles. In many ways, they're the face of the army, and the U.S. military itself, to the American public and the world. In early October 2021, one lucky crowd of spectators was fortunate enough to witness the first all-woman changing of the guard ceremony.

AS SURE AS sunrises, taxes, and death, white gravestones continue to spread across Arlington's fields, marking each war and conflict, and the passing of veterans who have earned their rightful place there through prior service. Arlington and other national cemeteries, despite their egalitarian facade, didn't admit women until the late nineteenth century. They remained segregated, and many barred African American veterans altogether, until 1948, when President Truman integrated the military and national cemeteries with it after World War II.

In the 1950s, the U.S. government, under the American Battle Monuments Commission, constructed fifteen Arlington-like satellite cemeteries overseas to house the American World War II dead. Built from Tunisia to the Philippines but clustered mostly in Europe, they contain the remains of 92,000 service members whose families preferred they be buried near where they fell instead of being shipped home.

Unlike the World War II burial grounds constructed by other countries, which were essentially simple graveyards, the U.S. ones were deliberately landscaped and decorated as artistic and architectural spectacles in the same vein as Arlington. Their purpose stretched far beyond simply serving as resting places, intended as symbolic outposts to remind the world of America's newly established dominance as a superpower—and stand as dramatic backdrops for U.S. presidents to deliver speeches. In fact, the five American military cemeteries built in France in the 1950s are considered the first cultural battlegrounds in the Cold War between the United States and Soviet Union.*

The French Communist Party enjoyed significant public support and political clout at this time, and the country was considered a vital front in the contest of ideas. The verdant grounds of the U.S. military cemeteries in France were intended to counter communism by

---

* Historian Kate Clarke Lemay, of the National Portrait Gallery, fully illuminates this topic in her authoritative 2017 book, *Triumph of the Dead: American World War II Cemeteries, Monuments, and Diplomacy in France.*

projecting awe-inspiring images and slogans of the holy trinity of God, democracy, and the American Way. The Normandy American Cemetery and Memorial, the world's most visited foreign military cemetery, is one stirring example. Dedicated in 1956 on a cliff above the famed D-Day landing site Omaha Beach, it's the resting place of nearly 10,000 American troops.

The cemetery's centerpiece is a semicircular classical-style colonnade bearing the inscription THIS EMBATTLED SHORE, PORTAL OF FREEDOM, IS FOREVER HALLOWED BY THE IDEALS, THE VALOR AND THE SACRIFICES OF OUR FELLOW COUNTRYMEN. In it stands a bronze, twenty-two-foot-tall nude statue of a young man, representing all American soldiers who gave their lives nearby, rising from sea waves at his feet. Etched into the pedestal below him are the opening lines to the "Battle Hymn of the Republic": MINE EYES HAVE SEEN THE GLORY OF THE COMING OF THE LORD.

All but 151 of the white marble grave markers that spread in straight rows and columns across the Normandy cemetery's flat 174 acres are shaped as crosses. They're divided into sections by two wide main walkways that intersect to form the shape of a giant cross. At their meeting point rests a circular, classical-style granite-and-limestone chapel. The black marble altar inside is engraved with a line from John 10:28, I GIVE THEM ETERNAL LIFE, AND THEY WILL NEVER PERISH.

Back at Arlington, one of the most publicized and symbolically meaningful burials on its grounds came in 1963 with the interment of thirty-seven-year-old World War II veteran and civil rights leader Medgar Evers, who was shot and killed by a white supremacist in June of that year. Evers served in the army in England and France and was interred at Section 36, grave 1431, with full military honors in front of a crowd of 3,000 people, including Attorney General Robert F. Kennedy.

Evers's wife, Myrlie, said after the service, "For the first time in my life, I had a sense of pride in being a real American and not merely a second-class citizen."*

On November 22 that same year, President John F. Kennedy died from an assassin's bullet and became the second president buried at

---

* According to the book *The Politics of Mourning: Death and Honor in Arlington National Cemetery*, by Micki McElya.

Arlington, after William Howard Taft. The army immediately set aside a 3.2-acre tract for his grave site on a slope directly below Arlington House. Jackie Kennedy envisioned a grand grave site there, open to the public, where an eternal flame would perpetually burn to keep his spirit and memory alive. Eternal flames have been a symbol of purity since antiquity, like the legendary one at the Temple of Apollo at Delphi in ancient Greece—in keeping with the national cemetery's motif.* She intended this one to flicker as brightly in the American consciousness as the presidential monuments on the other side of the Potomac.

Establishing a kind of national memorial for Kennedy at Arlington was an elegant, brilliant idea. The approval process to build a monument on the National Mall is time-consuming and complicated—and it involves a vote by Congress, reviews by various government commissions and agencies, and a large dose of politics. The Washington Monument and Lincoln Memorial weren't built until a half century after their namesakes died; and the Jefferson Memorial didn't take shape until a whole century after Thomas Jefferson's passing.

So instead, Jackie circumvented the process. At Arlington National Cemetery, she only needed the go-ahead from her husband's vice president and successor, Lyndon Johnson, and the secretary of defense for the construction of a John F. Kennedy memorial. The two men agreed. Because the planning and construction for the permanent grave site would take time, President Kennedy was buried after his funeral in a temporary resting place at the cemetery on the hill below Arlington House, and the flame placed in a temporary base. Millions of people flocked to the site in the year after his death. Through Kennedy, Arlington became even more mythical. Like at other cemeteries, from Père-Lachaise and Green-Wood to ones throughout Hollywood, a high-profile celebrity's grave led others to follow. After Kennedy's internment, requests by veterans to be buried at the cemetery skyrocketed to unprecedented highs.

Kennedy's permanent grave site, bankrolled by the Kennedy family, was completed in March 1967. It consists of a plaza of granite cobblestones carved into the hillside. The president's gravestone is a

---

* Of course, the eternal flame at Delphi wasn't so eternal, was it?

simple piece of gray polished slate, lying flat among the cobblestones, and engraved with his name, a cross, and his dates of birth and death. Jutting above it is the eternal flame, housed within a single five-foot circular stone taken from a granite quarry on Cape Cod, near the Kennedy summer home. The flame forms a straight geographic line with the Lincoln Memorial and Washington Monument.

Kennedy's brother Robert, assassinated the year after the memorial's completion, was buried nearby in the family's section at Arlington. Jackie took her place beside her husband in 1994. Kennedy's brother Ted, the longtime Massachusetts senator, was placed next to Robert in 2009.

In the decades after Kennedy's death, Arlington's fields became the resting place of so many Americans who served that it began running out of space. The cemetery took over surrounding federally owned lands to expand its boundaries in the 1990s, and in 2013—with the threat of reaching capacity by the early 2020s—it targeted clearing the final twelve acres of the property's old-growth forest, the Park, until the plans became public and local activists intervened, forcing a compromise. Around the same time, a damning Inspector General investigation of the cemetery revealed ongoing mistreatment of the dead. Hundreds of recent graves had been given the wrong marker, or contained the remains of multiple people, or no people, or were mislabeled on cemetery maps. Some cremated remains received by the cemetery were being emptied from their urns into a nearby landfill, and headstones were found dumped in a stream.

Somehow, at some point, perhaps efforts at promoting the "old Lie," that it is sweet and fitting to die for one's country, became too successful. Suddenly, it stopped mattering at Arlington who was buried where, or even if the right gravestone was used to identify the correct person. The bodies became space fillers within a larger symbol for our temple to the god of war.

Not helping matters is the country's growing civilian-military divide. Less than 10 percent of the American population has served in the military, and about .4 percent are serving actively. Military recruits increasingly come from concentrated areas of the country, and almost 80 percent of those who serve are members of a larger military family, meaning the country is drawing from an ever-shrinking pool of candidates. As a result, it's easier for many to root for others to find their place in Arlington, to promote the "old Lie," without feeling any personal sacrifice—and sometimes even to profit from it.

Case in point: The country artist Trace Adkins released a song in 2005 in tribute to a fallen marine called "Arlington." The lyrics are sung from the perspective of someone killed in war who's thrilled to be buried at the national cemetery, near where his granddad lies. The narrator repeats four times in the song, "I'm one of the chosen ones, I made it to Arlington," like he's just won a VIP pass to Disney World. He ends, speaking for all American heroes killed in battle, with "We made it to Arlington, yeah dust to dust / Don't cry for us, we made it to Arlington."

The song climbed into the Top 20 in the country music charts. Adkins recorded a video for it, too, which mostly shows him sitting on a chair with images of eagles, the word *freedom*, and fields of graves at Arlington flashing on a screen behind him. Halfway through, the video cuts to him taking off his cowboy hat and laying a wreath in front of the Tomb of the Unknown Soldier. America loved "Arlington," of course. Except for some families of troops stationed in Iraq. They protested, saying that making it to a graveyard, however beautiful, wasn't actually the goal for their loved ones. So Adkins stopped promoting the song but not performing or monetizing it. Its download is still available for $1.29 on iTunes. God bless the U.S.A.

Still, it's easy to understand the cemetery's siren song, and why an average of twenty-five burials are performed there each day. Arlington now has 85,000 spaces remaining, but—given America's many military entanglements over the past sixty years—there are 22 million living people eligible to be buried there someday. To make sure the cemetery doesn't run out of room this century, the army is considering restricting burials only to war "heroes," whatever that means, along with troops who die in battle and VIPs. Retired veterans who didn't serve in combat would be left out. The action would strip Arlington of its foundational everyone-is-equal-among-gravestones ideal. Veterans' groups are opposed.

The time I toured Arlington with my daughter and her school group, I felt profound sadness, thinking of the names etched into the rows of white marble of people who would never grow older than eighteen, or twenty-two, or whatever their age when they died, their life stories so prematurely ended. People who were not myths.

The last stop for our school group before climbing back onto the tour bus was the Military Women's Memorial, completed in 1997 near the cemetery's entrance. It's a round granite-stoned courtyard halfway enclosed by a semicircular, arch-filled, thirty-foot-tall wall. At its center sits a wide reflecting pool, placed in perfect alignment with the Kennedy, Lincoln, and Washington memorials. In keeping with the rest of Arlington, it looks like it was stolen from Olympus. If given the time, I would have lingered longer, to consider the 152 female American military members killed during the country's two wars in the twenty-first century—leaving spouses, parents, siblings, and children behind. But we had exhausting miles to go before we'd sleep. So I shifted emotional gears and scooted up to my daughter as the group started making its way toward the tour bus.

"You know why they have fences around cemeteries?" I asked.
"Why?"
"Because people are dying to get in!"
Dad jokes never die.

A stone sphinx guards the Woolworth Mausoleum at Woodlawn Cemetery.

12. KEEPING UP WITH THE CORPSES

The way cemeteries set the mold for
America's suburban subdivisions

—

Woodlawn Cemetery
Bronx, New York
Established: 1863

NOTHING MAKES STOPPING by a graveyard more inviting than
the offer of a free hot dog. Not that it was the only reason I visited
Woodlawn Cemetery in the Bronx that day. But it helped. The free hot
dogs, with potato chips, were part of Woodlawn's Earth Day celebration,
held on a Saturday in late April 2021. Also headlining the event was a
tree-carving exhibition, free coloring books, yoga among the graves, and
trolley tours. I peeled into Woodlawn just after three in the afternoon,
excited for the sights and running on fumes with an empty stomach.

I had spent much of my jam-packed early afternoon in midtown
Manhattan with plenty of opportunity to grab something to eat, but I
declined, knowing I'd be able to enjoy a leisurely hot dog at the cemetery
later. Did I mention the hot dogs were free? But time got away from me,
tragically, and I started for Woodlawn much later than planned, arriving
just as the Earth Day volunteers were packing up the tents and tables
and the events had ended. I searched everywhere for the hot dog truck
until I asked a pleasant volunteer for help.

"The hot dog truck? Oh, that left already."

The horror!

Hangry is no way to tour a cemetery. Yet there I was, hangry, on my
first-ever visit to one of America's most famous and fanciest graveyards.

So I toured. It didn't take long for the sensory overload of its memorials to make me forget my starvation.

If Green-Wood Cemetery in Brooklyn is stately in design, and old, and blended with nature, Woodlawn Cemetery in the Bronx is its opposite. Promoting itself as "a popular final resting place for the famous and powerful," it's flashy and audacious, and somewhat flatter in spots and much more wide open. It boasts the country's largest collection of cottage-size mausoleums, which steal your breath with their artistic craftsmanship and faux ancient Greek, Egyptian, and Roman flourishes—and with the thought of their staggering price tags. The cemetery leaves you unsure if you should feel proud or guilty for admiring its uniquely American brand of well-manicured gorgeous excess. Which is probably the point.

There's even more to Woodlawn's four hundred acres than overwhelms the eye. It stands as America's first true suburban subdivision, and it paved the way for the first planned communities designed for the living that sprouted across the country in places like Levittown, New York, nearly eighty years after its opening. Woodlawn is also the shining, and perhaps earliest, example of how the new American cemeteries of the late nineteenth and much of the twentieth centuries were initially founded as real estate schemes that secondarily performed a public service—a fact that has largely been buried. The creative and well-managed ones among them, despite their nonprofit status, continue to be revenue makers. In fact, Woodlawn's financial endowment exceeds in dollar value the gross domestic product of some small island nations.

But like with modern planned communities for the living, an exclusive cemetery's clean-cut grass, perfectly trimmed hedges, and hot dog socials represent more of an American ideal than reality, leaving behind the less fortunate as if they don't exist.

WHEN YOU ENTER Woodlawn Cemetery through the main western gate and travel down its Central Avenue, you're transported into what can only be described as Rodeo Drive for the dead. The street is lined with opulent-mausoleums, made from gleaming marble or granite, styled in Classic Revival designs. The members of New York's elite from the last two centuries who have taken eternal residence in them clearly understood that although we can't bring riches with us to the afterlife, we can deposit them at the final departure station in the cemetery. The mausoleums are surrounded by trees and shrubs, on grounds carpeted by interconnecting lawns, making the work easier for the landscaping crews while providing a rolling, more uninterrupted feel.

When I visited, the layout and spread of the cemetery's mausoleum-filled avenues reminded me of streets on my own idyllic subdivided neighborhood, where, as my wife puts it, "everyone takes care of their lawn like it's an Olympic event."

I half expected an old-timey kid wearing knickerbockers to ride by on a bike, tossing newspapers at each mausoleum's front stoop. Or maybe to see a Peloton truck parked outside one for a delivery, or hordes of kids in Halloween costumes jumping from parked minivans to go trick-or-treating door-to-door. Woodlawn's sales materials refer to the burial plots as "property" and "lots," in keeping with the look, as if you're considering plans for a six-bed, four-bath Colonial.

Despite their compact dimensions, the gobsmacking opulence of these McMansions for the nevermore is heart-stopping. If the one to your left seems like a pint-size edition of the Jefferson Memorial in Washington, D.C., that's because it was probably designed by the same architect. If the one on your right looks exactly like a mini version of that church in France designed by Da Vinci, down to the gargoyles, that's because it is. If the one in front of you is bedazzled with windows that you think might be Tiffany stained glass, it's most certainly bedazzled with windows that are Tiffany stained glass.

I found the most spellbinding of the stately corpse castles at Woodlawn to be the Woolworth mausoleum, built in 1921 for the founder of the chain of five-and-dime stores that bore his name. Designed by architect John Russell Pope, the creative genius behind the National Archives building in D.C., it's made of massive Vermont granite blocks, and looks like the stone pool cabana of an ancient Egyptian palace, in keeping with the popular architecture of the time. Two sphinxes guard its broad front steps, which lead up to a portico supported by a pair of round columns marked with hieroglyphics. The heavy bronze front door is a work of art unto itself, and the coarse exterior walls have the feel of fine-grit sandpaper, inviting you to run your fingertips along them.

There are more than 1,300 mausoleums at Woodlawn, showing off a more impressive variety and bigger volume of architectural masterpieces among its buildings than most American cities do. The ages vary, with some born in the Gilded Age of the nineteenth century while others have been built in present days, or somewhere in between. One of the most frequently visited domiciles for the dearly departed is a boxy, white-marble neoclassical one surrounded by fragrant perennial flower beds built as the forever home of salsa queen Celia Cruz, who died in 2003.

Not that all of Woodlawn's residents are sealed in mausoleums. Far from it. Veer onto the cemetery's side roads and paths, and you'll find a majority of the roughly 300,000 buried there were placed in traditional graves marked by traditional monuments—including scores of the cemetery's most famous tenants. The resting spot for famed journalist Nellie Bly, who died in 1922, lies at the foot of an ordinary tombstone donated by her admirers from the New York Press Club in 1978. Jazz great Miles Davis boasts a wide polished-granite marker engraved with bars of musical notes. Duke Ellington is remembered with a simple stone embedded in the ground, barely bigger than a piece of sheet music. Newspaper titan Joseph Pulitzer's grave marker is similarly modest, but just behind it towers a monument containing a life-size statue of him. Herman Melville's gravestone carries a carved blank scroll. (Love that guy's last name.)

Woodlawn is a sight, and it's meant to be seen. It's a designated National Historic Landmark, and an artistic national treasure. Which would come as a pleasant surprise to its founders, who started the cemetery in order to make cash while filling an urgent need.

PROPERTY SHORTAGES BECAME a problem in Upper Manhattan in the second half of the 1800s. After Central Park (that popular cemetery of today) was established, construction spread like kudzu uptown on either side of it, as developers and speculators snatched all the existing and available open land. The brownstone era of development began on the West Side and moved east, as townhomes, Queen Anne–style brick homes, apartment buildings, and mansions like the Carnegie home on Fifth Avenue and Ninety-First Street sprouted from the former farmlands.

Harlem, more affordably located above the park, attracted a large population of immigrants, followed by an influx of Black Americans fleeing the Jim Crow South during the Great Migration, looking for work and a brighter future. The city's grid of streets spread north, as did the railway lines, and the population exploded exponentially. Real estate on the island became scarcer and scarcer. Finally, in 1852, New York banned the creation of new cemeteries below Eighty-Sixth Street to maximize room for the living over the dead.

This edict posed significant and immediate problems—primarily, there was nowhere to dump the city's poor, diseased, or imprisoned dead. And New York's well-heeled residents along and above the park found it inconvenient to make the long journey to Green-Wood in Brooklyn to bury and visit their loved ones. New cemeteries were needed, but they couldn't occupy prime real estate.

The issues for the rich were solved first, thanks to Reverend Absalom Peters, a poet, philosopher, and Congregational minister who graduated from Dartmouth College. In 1853, he laid the groundwork for Woodlawn Cemetery, located at that time within the southern boundaries of Westchester County, and later annexed into the Bronx. Most historical accounts portray Peters as a pious problem solver, who simply wanted to find a quiet, beautiful spot where the deceased—regardless of denomination—could find the eternal peace they deserved. New York's Historic Districts Council asserts this well-respected man of God was motivated simply by "civic pride." But, of course, it's more complicated.

To enact his plan, Peters enlisted a dozen reputable members of the Bronx community to form a board of trustees for a nonprofit cemetery corporation. Together, they found a patch of 313 fertile acres that would become Woodlawn, which sloped down a rock ridge that was formed billions of years ago and spilled into the narrow Bronx River. Peters's enthusiasm for the project was "infectious," according to an official history published by the cemetery in the late twentieth century.

The plan called for an even more impressive rural-style cemetery than Green-Wood, with meandering roads and paths hugging the property's natural contours, and scores of decorative trees and shrubs planted to accentuate its garden-like beauty.

This is where things got shady. The members of the Woodlawn board then quietly bought the land themselves—not through the cemetery corporation. Peters was the biggest investor, purchasing 224 acres of the site. Taking advantage of a loophole in New York State cemetery regulations, they then sold the property to the cemetery corporation, under the condition that they, as individuals, receive 49 percent of the proceeds from every grave plot sold. This arrangement allowed them to silently reap massive profits on land that was owned by a nonprofit organization and exempt from property taxes. They were providing a civic service and taking advantage of an opportunity.

This plot sales skimming scheme wasn't made public until the city sued Woodlawn in 1883 over a municipal drainpipe issue, and the trustees were forced to admit their actions "for the first time" under oath, according to a *New York Times* reporter who was there, in an article headlined "Fortunes in a Cemetery; Profits and Demands of the Owners of Woodlawn."

Not that they were alone. It's likely that most of the nonprofit burial grounds created during that time to form the Queens-Brooklyn Cemetery Belt worked on a similar model with their founders, who also generally consisted of clergy and highly esteemed civic leaders. This explains why the cemeteries there sprung up so quickly and occupied the maximum size the state allowed. Their profit-centric establishment contrasted to the creation of Green-Wood, which its founder (who was a rich real estate developer) said was intended as "a Public Institution, unconnected with any purposes of profit or gain to any individual whatever."

Although Woodlawn and the area's other new cemeteries were nonprofits, there's a difference, of course, between a nonprofit and a charity. And although they accepted donations, they were not charities. By the early 1870s, the only cemetery in the New York area, besides the state-run potter's field at Hart Island, that would bury the poor free of charge was Calvary Cemetery in Queens. As a *New York Times* article from 1872 described the situation regarding the city's nonprofit burial grounds, specifically mentioning Woodlawn and Green-Wood, "most of the cemeteries are allowed by law to accept gifts for the purpose of renewing improvements on lots, and embellishing the grounds generally; but so far not a dollar has been bequeathed for the purpose of free ground."

Not much is different with cemeteries across the country today, though state and federal oversight are much stricter. Almost none of them sets aside spots for the homeless and poor—unless compelled by the municipality or state—and grave sales don't work on a sliding scale for those who can't afford them. Cemeteries aren't established by people or organizations who want to break even or lose money for their time and effort. Quite the opposite.

By the late nineteenth century and into the early part of the twentieth century, the real estate profit model that lay at the foundation of Woodlawn and other new New York burial grounds was adopted by cemetery developers across America, transferring more money from mourners' pockets to the burgeoning Death Industrial Complex. Grave plot profiteers made a killing, yet their methods were hardly unearthed. One exception came in 1938, when a court case revealed that the purveyors of Kensico Cemetery, located fifteen miles north of the Bronx in Westchester County, had pocketed a whopping $1.2 million during a thirty-five-year span starting in 1889 using the grave sales skimming method. In the 1940s, after a series of highly publicized investigative newspaper and magazine articles uncovering the subject, cemetery laws changed dramatically in America, giving rise to much greater regulation—but not deterring the profit-minded ambitions of cemetery operators.

Success was not guaranteed for Woodlawn, of course. The venture required ambition, extensive earthmoving work, creative sales and marketing strategies, and sound financial decision-making. In 1867, only a few years into the project, the trustees radically changed Woodlawn's landscape plan, tearing up the rural cemetery blueprints and enacting a new lawn-style cemetery design. The shift transformed the budding cemetery's popularity and profitability—and maybe in some small way changed the future look and layout of America's suburbs with it.

The newfangled lawn-style cemetery design was developed less than a decade earlier by landscape architect Adolph Strauch in 1859, when he remodeled the down-on-its-luck, rural-style Spring Grove Cemetery in Cincinnati, Ohio. He eliminated hedgerows, fences, and individual flower beds surrounding the plots. He leveled the ground to a flatter surface and planted long, broad expanses of grass. He removed flamboyant statues and gravestones, and set size standards for markers and memorials. He carefully planted groves of ornamental trees and dredged swamplands into lakes, and connected it all with paved walking paths. The result was a 166-acre, turf-carpeted marvel—and original style of burial ground—that captured the attention of landscape architects and cemetery designers around the world.

Strauch's lawn plan at Spring Grove offered a wide-open appeal and a sense of order, as well as an infinitely more economical layout. It crammed grave sites closer together, generating the potential for monumentally higher revenue per acre, and the grounds were much easier to maintain than at a rural-style one, thanks to its sprawling, level lawn space (and the invention of the power mower a few years earlier). The public loved how Spring Grove mimicked the greens of a European estate or around the U.S. Capitol, and they flocked by the thousands to visit and linger. Frederick Law Olmsted paid close attention. He said it was the "best" cemetery in America, "from a landscape gardening point of view." Spring Grove Cemetery, through its massive influx of notoriety and burials, was practically growing money.

Woodlawn's trustees took note of Spring Grove's success, and after visiting it, they wisely changed their cemetery's entire landscaping plans to follow Strauch's lawn style. Nearly all new cemeteries in America would soon do the same—and even Mount Auburn, Green-Wood, and the other well-established rural-style cemeteries would adopt the lawn style in their newer sections.

But Woodlawn's layout took Spring Grove's one new, revolutionary step further. It called for several long, looping streets, where the open lawn spaces lining them could be subdivided into parcels to house opulent cottages for the dead. The lots would be sold at a premium to well-to-do families looking for a quiet escape, still within an easy train commute from Manhattan. It was, in essence and action, America's first suburban subdivision.

One of Woodlawn's most grandiose and earliest mausoleums is the Gould Mausoleum, built in 1884 on the cemetery's highest spot and largest plot—about two-thirds of an acre. It was owned by Jay Gould, the corrupt railroad tycoon and financial market manipulator nicknamed the Skunk of Wall Street. His rectangular, unmarked granite temple to himself is wreathed by columns, in a look that mimics the Parthenon. Inside, the walls consist of pink polished marble, illuminated by the sunlight that beams through its six-foot-tall stained glass window. Gould was deposited at the mausoleum in 1892, his resting nook soldered shut to protect from grave robbers. His edifice sparked a suburban-style keeping-up-with-the-Joneses competition of corpse cottage construction among the other Gilded Age moguls who owned subdivided lots at Woodlawn, which led to the grandeur of the cemetery's main thoroughfares that I witnessed during my visit—grandeur that stood in stark contrast to the graves at nearby Hart Island, also in the Bronx area codes.

At the same time that I toured the grounds, prison inmates at Hart Island were no doubt busy at work, digging graves in the sprawling potter's field there. It was still catching up to its recent spike in new residents, from the early stages of the pandemic. An overwhelmed New York City unloaded one in ten of its COVID deaths, predominantly poor and elderly, into the island's mass burial ditches.

Woodlawn and Hart Island are disparate in every way possible, but they were both founded around the same time to answer the same need, and arose out of real estate greed. Which is so typically New York. It's impossible to tell the full story of Woodlawn without including its less affluent neighbor.

A POTTER'S FIELD can generally be defined as a burial place for the neglected, ostracized, and forgotten. It's often kept hidden from public view, to avoid confronting how we, as a society, failed its occupants. Its name is derived from the barren field in Jerusalem scarred by potters digging for clay, mentioned in the Book of Matthew, chapter 27. After Judas throws the silver pieces he received for betraying Jesus into the temple, the high priests use the blood money—in the words of the King James Bible—to buy "the potter's field, to bury strangers in. Wherefore that field was called the field of blood unto this day."

"The field of blood" is still a pretty accurate term for these types of burial grounds, including the one on Hart Island.

Hart Island, a mile long and shaped like a stag's hind leg, peeks barely above Long Island Sound about a mile from the Bronx shore. The smattering of old, decrepit brick buildings and clusters of trees that huddle on its narrow expanse look especially desperate in winter, when their bare, gray branches blend with the drab sky. The rebirth of spring and the verdant vibrancy of summer don't make the place look much cheerier.

The State of New York bought the island in 1869 as a much-needed mass burial ground for the poor, criminals, and victims of disease—the island being in one of the least desirable, most obscure locations. (The wretched refuse of our teeming shore, if you will.) The two potter's fields in Manhattan were closed shortly after the prohibition on burials and were turned into city parks; Hart Island would replace them. The state stationed prison convicts to live beside it and work as gravediggers. A steamer grimly named *Hope* owned by the Department of Public Charities and Correction ferried people to and from the shore.

The potter's field originally shared Hart Island with a hospital for yellow fever victims, which was replaced in the 1870s by a facility for tuberculosis patients, and then a psychiatric hospital and industrial school for indigent children—who apparently needed to be taught the restorative value of forced labor. The *New York Times* noted that the "little boys and girls" at the "school," when "they have behaved themselves well through the week, and the weather is fine, the teachers let them have a half-holiday on Saturday afternoons, and go out and play among the graves."

A newspaper article from the late 1800s described the burial process at the potter's field: "Here bodies are deposited in trenches, one above the other, and once buried, can never again be identified." All "unknown" people were photographed before interment, with the album of their images kept by the reform school warden to aid people who later came searching for vanished loved ones.

Hart Island continued its brisk burial business throughout the twentieth century, and still does today. The city's child labor facility there eventually closed, followed by the mental institution. In the 1980s, the city—out of the ever-constructive combination of ignorance, fear, and bigotry—carved out an isolated section for AIDS victims on the far southern end. Roughly 100,000 New Yorkers died from complications of the disease during the epidemic's peak in the late twentieth century, with the city's gay community disproportionately devastated. Many local funeral homes and cemeteries refused to accept the victims, leaving no alternative for the remains of the thousands killed by AIDS but to be transported to the mass pits dug for them by prisoners from Rikers Island at Hart Island. The spot is considered the largest AIDS burial ground in the world.

Hart Island captured the national spotlight during the early stages of the COVID crisis in 2020 with viral drone footage of inmates dressed in white hazmat suits tightly packing pine boxes into shallow pits, shoveling dirt on top of them. During the disease's peak spread in the city, overwhelmed funeral homes couldn't handle the volume of bodies, and mobile morgues were set up for hospitals that ran out of storage for the dead. The city medical examiner's office reduced the amount of time for someone to claim a loved one's body before disposal from thirty days to fifteen. And families were struggling financially due to the economic crisis COVID caused. This confluence of factors led to a massive influx of bodies at Hart Island. An analysis published by the Columbia Journalism School Toni Stabile Center calculated that one in ten of the city's 24,000 COVID victims were buried there.

Hart Island and its 101-acre cemetery of necessity and last resort house the remains of more than 1 million people, its population expanding daily. Although it's the country's largest potter's field, it's not unique. Across the United States, the responsibility for the poor, vulnerable, and unclaimed dead usually falls upon state, county, or municipal governments. Some maintain their own potter's fields, or publicly funded cemeteries. Others resort to creative alternatives. One day every year Los Angeles holds a mass interment, with a public memorial service, for the cremated remains of roughly 1,500 unclaimed human beings. King County in Washington does the same every two years, for about 150 people. Sullivan County in Tennessee donates the indigent and unclaimed dead to science and medical schools. Massachusetts is one of about twenty states that provides indigent burial subsidies to low-income families. It also sets the rates funeral homes can charge for services to the poor, though the cemeteries still receive close to their full cash cut for a burial. One funeral home in Boston provides no-cost services for 150 homeless people a year, who are then buried in a municipal cemetery with help from volunteer pallbearers from a local high school. Not the kind of scene you'll find at a typical nonprofit cemetery like Woodlawn.

I SPENT A couple of hours walking down Woodlawn's mausoleum-lined streets during my Earth Day visit, exploring its hidden corners, and marveling at its beauty. Although its lawn plan is much sunnier than rural-style Green-Wood, it's still decorated with more than 3,500 carefully placed ornamental and shade trees among the graves, like white pines, weeping beeches, white oaks, and dogwoods. I can only imagine how impressed the cemetery's founders would be with the mature landscape it possesses.

To deny the sway of cemetery design on the layout of American suburban residential neighborhoods is to deny the obvious. In 1868, one year after Woodlawn changed its development blueprints to follow the lawn style, Frederick Law Olmsted drew up the plans for the village of Riverside, a town ten miles outside of Chicago that is called the country's first planned community. Much like he did when drafting plans for Central Park, he took significant inspiration from traditional rural-style cemeteries. (Olmsted eventually designed a rural cemetery of his own, Mountain View in Oakland, California, in 1863.)

Riverside, located on the Chicago, Burlington and Quincy Railroad along the winding Des Plaines River, followed a design that hugged the terrain's natural contours and blended with the landscape. Half of its land area was covered by trees, and its streets took long bends and curves but never formed cul-de-sacs or square corners. There was no uniformity to the individual property parcels, and what was constructed on them was up to the discretion of the wealthy buyers—who hired the likes of architects Frank Lloyd Wright and Louis Sullivan to design their luxurious homes. Olmsted also barred fences on the properties, to maintain its wide-open appeal—and in keeping with his mentor Andrew Jackson Downing, who reportedly called them "an abomination among the fresh fields, of which no person of taste could be found guilty."* Drive down the shaded, old residential streets of Riverside today, and it's reminiscent of a spacious Green-Wood or Mount Auburn, but for the living.

The sun-bathed, perfectly coiffed modern suburban yard draws clear influences from the lawn cemetery, which had proliferated across the country in the early twentieth century. The first modern American cookie-cutter suburb, Levittown, on Long Island in New York, was built shortly after World War II by the Levitt & Sons real estate firm and set the prototype for today's suburbia. Its founder, Abraham Levitt, was a horticulturist and lawyer. Each of the 17,000 houses the company mass-produced followed his core principle that "no single feature of a suburban residential community contributes as much to the charm and beauty of the individual home and the locality as well-kept lawns." It, too, prohibited fences from yards at first.

This "charm and beauty" of uniform, tightly interconnected, turf-covered plots promoted by Levitt is identical to the clean aesthetic, economy of design, and ease of upkeep that lawn-style cemeteries had been perfecting for seventy-five years prior to Levittown. And famed Woodlawn, considered New York's prettiest cemetery, had been subdividing its mausoleum properties for nearly as long. It seems likely that the Brooklyn-born Levitt, an expert in landscape architecture and New York real estate law, drew elements of lawn cemeteries in general, and Woodlawn Cemetery in particular, when creating his new, idyllic community. Yet Levitt gets all the credit, as if his ideas were completely original—in another example of American burial grounds being overlooked or forgotten in history.

---

* I found this quote in an April 2019 *Smithsonian Magazine* article, "How Did the White Picket Fence Become a Symbol of the Suburbs?," by Michael Dolan. I couldn't verify it for myself.

The neoclassical Ehret Mausoleum in the Bronx's Woodlawn Cemetery was designed in 1900 for beer baron George Ehret, who died twenty-seven years later. Two granite lions flank the structure's iron doors, which open to reveal a set of Tiffany stained-glass windows on the opposite wall. Woodlawn contains the country's largest collection of mausoleums, more than 1,300 in all.

The timelessness of Woodlawn's all-American appeal hasn't dulled in the least, as it remains a financial success story. According to its tax filings in 2019, it brought in $29 million in revenue for the prior year, $18 million of it in investment income from its perpetual care fund. Its total assets were priced at a whopping $203 million, nearly all of it in publicly traded securities. But as we know, nonprofits do not necessarily act as charities. This is not a place for the poor. That designation belongs to the crammed, anonymous, government-funded mass pits of Hart Island, dug by prison inmates.

I must admit, it was pleasant to finally see Woodlawn, even if I arrived too late for the free Earth Day hot dogs. I can understand its idyllic, exclusive allure as a final resting place, just as I can understand the appeal of buying a mansion in a high-end suburb. I enjoyed mingling with the remains of the rich, and powerful, and famous—even if I had no desire to keep up with them.

The grave of a woman known only as "Mrs. Ah Lum" and "China Mary" in the Chinese section of Tombstone's Boot Hill

13. LASTING IMPRESSIONS

Tombstones in old boot hill graveyards keep alive
the lost story of Chinese immigrants
in the nineteenth-century American West

—

Boothill Graveyard
Tombstone, Arizona
Established: 1878

POOR OLD LESTER Moore. According to the story spun over the generations in the town of Tombstone, Arizona, he worked as an agent at a Wells Fargo outpost in the days of the Old West. His was a dangerous job back then, considering all the valuables that passed through those stations, and the criminals who roamed on horseback looking to rob them. One fateful afternoon, a scoundrel walked through the outpost's front door to pick up a package. A disagreement arose, as they often did. The next thing you know, this being the Old West and all, the man and Lester Moore drew their six-shooters and . . . *bang-bang-bang-bang* . . . *bang.*

As wisps of smoke rose through the air, witnesses could see that the scoundrel had plugged four fatal slugs of lead into poor old Lester Moore's chest. Yet before the final breaths escaped the Wells Fargo agent's lungs, as he fell to the floor, he managed to fire one shot in return, which sailed true and found its mark in the man's cold, murderous heart. As Scripture tells us, "But let justice roll down like waters, and righteousness like an ever-flowing stream."

Poor Moore's remains now lie at Boothill Graveyard in Tombstone, beneath a wooden marker bearing the epitaph HERE LIES LESTER MOORE, FOUR SLUGS FROM A .44. NO LES NO MORE.

Old "boot hills" like the one in Tombstone are strewn throughout what remains of the frontier settlements, from Dodge City, Kansas, to Deadwood, South Dakota. These small, dusty graveyards received the nickname because so many people buried within them died suddenly, violently, with their boots on. The epitaphs on the graves can be grimly amusing, and the narrow scope of end dates on them reflect the length of the town's brief boom cycle.

Nowadays, boot hills lend authenticity to a locale's nostalgic, touristy Old West flair and heritage: Here lie the actual bodies of real sheriff's deputies, and bandits, and bank tellers, and saloonkeepers, all laid to rest in pine boxes some 150 years ago.

Beyond Moore's grave in Tombstone lie the much-visited resting places of outlaws Billy Clanton and the McLaury brothers—Tom and Frank—who were killed nearby in 1881 by Wyatt Earp and Doc Holliday in the gunfight at the O.K. Corral. There are also local characters like Dutch Annie, known as the queen of the red-light district during the town's coal-mining heyday, whose burial 1,000 people attended.

Yet what goes unrealized by nearly all the 150,000 annual tourists who pay the cemetery's $3 entry fee to walk among the graves is the evidence the grounds contain, in clear sight, of another important piece of Tombstone's history—and the history of the entire frontier era. It's something not captured in the shoot-'em-up reenactments, or displayed among the period-era saloons and storefronts. It's the essential contributions made by Chinese immigrants in building the American West.

Starting in the late 1850s, a wave of Chinese immigrants arrived on the West Coast looking for new opportunities. They worked in the gold and silver mines, taking up labor-intensive jobs that no one else would. They made up nearly the entire workforce that completed the western portion of the transcontinental railroad in 1869, which made America bicoastal and transformed the economy.

These immigrants became vital members of Old West communities and were often buried in the segregated Chinese sections of the boot hills—the plague of segregation as common on this coast as the East. That is, until fervent anti-Chinese sentiment and violence drove them out, to the cities of California or back across the Pacific, toward the end of the century. Once gone, their contributions were largely, deliberately, erased from history and folklore of the frontier, while the legends of people like Lester Moore were embellished, amplified, and glorified. Nearly all that's left as reminders of the Chinese American presence and experience—and to mark the immigrant's story—in Tombstone and across much of the Old West are a scattering of graves in the boot hills.

BOOTHILL GRAVEYARD IS an appealing appetizer for tourists to get them in the Old West spirit before proceeding onward to the gunfight site at the O.K. Corral or sidling up to the long, wooden bar at the Crystal Palace Saloon where patrons like Wyatt Earp and Doc Holliday once stood. The burial ground entryway's wooden shed eases you through time as you walk down its planks and into the frontier past.

The graveyard opened in 1878, a year or so after the area's first silver claim was discovered, which led to the boomtown rise of rough-and-tumble Tombstone. Boothill's gravediggers were kept constantly busy. They shoveled out shallow plots in the property's parched, hard-packed Arizona clay, deposited new residents, then piled a mound of rocks atop them to keep animals from unearthing them. Within five or six years, the burial ground's three acres were filled to capacity with about 250 graves—neatly arranged in west-facing rows, in Christian tradition, surrounded by cactuses and scraggly mesquite, overlooking the 7,400-foot Dragoon Mountains way off in the distance.

I visited on a sun-bleached late-summer afternoon, and for a while found myself as the lone soul within the graveyard, which is probably a rarity, given its volume of yearly visitors. The well-kept condition of its dusty grounds surprised me, but shouldn't have. Although Boothill fell into disrepair in the early twentieth century after the local silver boom went bust, it was restored in the late 1920s with the rise of western movies and dime novels, which revitalized the frontier tourism trade; it has been a well-maintained cornerstone of the town ever since.

I walked, stones crunching underfoot, among the white-painted crosses and wooden markers, and spied Les Moore's grave almost immediately. His isn't the only eye-catching epitaph, I should note. There are others, like HERE LIES GEORGE JOHNSON, HANGED BY MISTAKE. HE WAS RIGHT, WE WAS WRONG, BUT WE STRUNG HIM UP AND NOW HE'S GONE, and JOHN HEATH,

TAKEN FROM COUNTY JAIL AND LYNCHED BY BISBEE MOB IN TOMBSTONE and the succinct JOSEPH ZIEGLER, MURDERED.

But the most compelling portion of the graveyard lies in its two westernmost rows, a spot known as the Chinese section: seven marked graves belonging to people of Chinese descent who lived and died in

The grave of George Johnson, who bought a stolen horse by mistake and fell victim to frontier justice, at Tombstone's Boot Hill

Tombstone during the Wyatt Earp era. Several of the unmarked graves around them are believed to house Chinese immigrants, as well. The two most prominent resting places belong to a woman nicknamed China Mary, who was known as an employment broker, shopkeeper, and opium dealer; and a man named Quong Gu Kee, who owned the popular Can Can Restaurant downtown until he sold it in 1886.

Quong died in 1938 and per his wishes was permitted to be buried in Boothill, even though the cemetery had closed decades earlier. He was a fixture in Tombstone's sizable, bustling Chinese immigrant community in the late nineteenth century, but when he died, he was the last person of Chinese descent living in the town.

The obituary writer waxed poetically about him. "The life of Quong Kee was also a story of the West, the saga of the boom towns, the tough and roaring rail camps, the clinking of chips, the roar of guns in the mining and cow towns, and now, the men of the boom towns sleep the sleep of ages on Boothill."

Yes, Quong's story was a story of the West, all right. But not nearly in the way the obituary writer tried to portray it.

CHINA IN THE mid-nineteenth century faced massive conflict. Internally, its citizens suffered from widespread famine and extreme poverty, which led to civil unrest against the corrupt Qing Dynasty government; externally, the country was fending off the hostile imperial aspirations of the European powers and Japan. Some of its citizens saw the California Gold Rush of 1849 as maybe the only opportunity to lift themselves and their families out of abject suffering. These early immigrants, almost exclusively men, borrowed money for making the journey across the Pacific from Chinese-run "benevolent associations" based in California, and couldn't book a return trip home until their debt was paid in full.

The organizations, known as the Six Companies, served as safety nets, bankers, medical providers, employment brokers, and a collective lobbying voice for Chinese people in the halls of power. They also shipped the bodies of immigrants who died in America back to their homeland for a traditional burial—a responsibility they went to surprising lengths to uphold.

The Six Companies would generally collect a Chinese immigrant's remains after they were buried for six or seven years to allow for full decomposition before packing them into boxes for shipping back to China. The people employed to do the work were called bone scrapers, and would accompany the deceased on the journey across the Pacific, where loved ones on the other end would receive and rebury them in a family grave plot or tomb at home.

From the start, Chinese immigrants faced significant resistance. California began levying onerous taxes on Chinese prospectors, and only allowed them to work in mines that were already exhausted and abandoned by white miners. Chinese people were not permitted to testify in court, which meant crimes committed against them—from robbery to murder—went unpunished. And crimes were regularly committed against them.

A young Mark Twain offered a graphic account of the violent attacks against Chinese people in San Francisco in his 1872 travel memoir *Roughing It*. When describing their lack of legal rights, he wrote, derisively, "Ours is the 'land of the free'—nobody denies that—nobody challenges it. [Maybe it is because we don't let other people testify.]"

Yet the immigrant wave continued. By 1860, some 30,000 Chinese-born people were living and working in the United States. That number doubled in the following decade and reached more than 100,000 by 1880. Twain called the people who committed acts of hate against Chinese immigrants "the scum of the population." This too often included, "naturally and consistently, the policemen and politicians."

Maybe the worst among the politicians in the West was wealthy industrialist Leland Stanford, founder of Stanford University. He based his successful campaign for California governor in 1862 on stirring up public hatred and fear of the Chinese. In his inaugural address he called Asians an "inferior race" and complained that China "send[s] to our shores the dregs of her population."

Systemic discrimination against the Chinese trickled down to burial rights. Los Angeles and San Francisco barred them from access to local cemeteries, forcing them to pay for interments in the municipal potter's fields—where the white poor, homeless, and criminals were interred for free. Other communities in the West forced Chinese immigrants to form their own graveyards outside of town, or relegated them to segregated sections of burial grounds. Not that their bodies stayed there forever, because they were ultimately shipped back to China.

The extensive efforts of the Six Companies, combined with real estate development that eventually swallowed urban potter's fields, have left almost no visible remnant of nineteenth-century Chinese graves in places like San Francisco and Los Angeles. However, the bone scrapers weren't quite as successful at reaching the remains left in the boot hills of the Western mining outposts or railroad towns.

IN 1863, A grim but rare work opportunity presented itself to Quong. Central Pacific, the company contracted to build the Western portion of the transcontinental railroad, couldn't find workers. Perhaps this was understandable, as the job required dangerous, back-breaking labor: laying seven hundred miles of train tracks from Sacramento through the treacherous mountain passes of the Sierra Nevada and across the deserts of Nevada and Utah. So the company hired 20,000 Chinese-born laborers, at a well-below-market wage of $24 a month. They comprised 90 percent of the workforce.

The president of Central Pacific happened to be Leland Stanford, the race-baiting governor. Even he admitted, during testimony in Washington, D.C., in 1865, that without Chinese laborers, "it would be impossible to complete the western portion of this great national enterprise within the time required by the Acts of Congress."

An estimated 1,200 of Quong's fellow Chinese railroad workers died and were buried somewhere alongside the Central Pacific tracks in unmarked graves before its completion on May 10, 1869. At a ceremony in Promontory Summit, Utah, on that date, Stanford symbolically joined the rails connecting East and West by tapping a final spike, made of 17.6-karat gold, into a wooden tie. The journey across the country was instantly shortened from six months to four days.

The iconic image from the event shows two engineers surrounded by a mass of celebrating men in work clothes, all standing in front of two train engines that meet, front grille to front grille, at the joining point. Quong can't be found in the photo, nor can any other Chinese laborers. They were excluded—and for much of the next century would be largely erased from the narrative and nearly forgotten. For instance, at the 1969 centennial celebration of the transcontinental railroad's completion, the U.S. transportation secretary boasted, "Who else but Americans could drill ten tunnels in mountains thirty feet deep in snow? Who else but Americans could chisel through miles of solid granite? Who else but Americans could have laid ten miles of track in twelve hours?"

The Chinese Historical Society of America had been scheduled five minutes to address the crowd during the event—but was ultimately skipped, due to time limitations. Yes, Quong's story was one of the West. It was a story of omission.

DESPITE THE WEST'S explosive population growth and new railroad connection to the East, it faced constant economic struggles in the late 1800s. The Long Depression gripped the entire post–Civil War country in the 1870s, followed by a deep recession in the 1880s. Chinese immigrants, even though they made up a relatively small percentage of the Western population, bore the brunt of the blame for driving down wages and job opportunities. Aiming mindless rage at so-called outsiders is much easier than looking inward for answers to problems, as we know.

In October 1871 in Los Angeles, a mob of 10 percent of the city's population attacked Chinese immigrants living in its Chinatown district, looting shops and homes, and killing nineteen of its 190 residents. The victims were buried in the Chinese section of the city's public cemetery at Fort Moore Hill, but there's no lingering evidence of their burial sites or the tragedy, and the land is now a public school for the arts.

Four years later, about 150 white miners stormed the Chinese section of Rock Springs, Wyoming, torching homes and killing at least twenty-eight Chinese miners—some burned alive—while wounding fifteen others and driving the rest from town. The burial site for the dead is unknown, and no markers can be found.

Then, in 1877, about 8,000 people marching in San Francisco in an anti-Chinese rally stormed the city's Chinatown, destroying and looting property and killing four residents. The dead were believed to be buried in the Chinese section of the city potter's field that now lies under the municipal Lincoln Park Golf Course. But again, their grave markers—and most likely their bones—are gone, leaving no visible record of what occurred.

During this same period, Congress passed the Chinese Exclusion Act, which prohibited the immigration of Chinese laborers, and barred those already in the United States or their American-born children from becoming citizens. This was the first law aimed at excluding a specific group of people from coming to the country, and wasn't repealed until the cusp of World War II, when America needed China as an ally against Japan.

Meanwhile, in Tombstone, the influx of Chinese-born residents began not long after the town was founded in 1879, and quickly reached a peak population of more than five hundred (the overall population was roughly ten thousand). The Chinese traveled to the smaller towns of the Arizona Territory in hope of finding havens from the increasing racial violence. Quong was among them. Their hopes were short-lived; even though the segregated Chinese section of Tombstone played a vital role in the local economy, local whites began holding their first John Chinaman Must Go! rallies in the early 1880s.

In 1886, Tacoma, Washington, rounded up all seven hundred of its Chinese residents and forced them out of town, inspiring other Western cities to follow the Tacoma method of ethnic cleansing, Tombstone's homegrown Anti-Chinese League ratcheted up its rhetoric and threats. At one of its regular Saturday meetings, which attracted crowds of about five hundred people, they hired a brass band to march through town and "serenade" the business owners who had fired their Chinese employees. At another, it called for boycotting all Chinese-owned businesses, and published lists of white residents known to be their customers.

As a result, the Chinese population began to shrink noticeably. Quong sold his successful restaurant, the Can Can, at the height of

Nearly all of the roughly 250 graves filling Tombstone, Arizona's Boothill Graveyard were dug during the height of the town's silver boom, between 1878 and 1884. The locals in that era were no strangers to violence and untimely death.

tensions in 1886. Not long afterward, the mining companies in Tombstone laid off half of their miners, as the price of silver suddenly plummeted, and the local veins tapped out.

Almost overnight, Tombstone faced bigger worries than fabricated threats from immigrants. By 1890, the town was bust. More than 90 percent of its entire population, so dependent on the silver mine's fortunes, disappeared in a matter of a few years, leaving the Western-style storefronts and saloons, and the O.K. Corral, and the Bird Cage Theater to collect desert dust. One of the few to remain was Quong. He died at age eighty-seven in the county hospital in 1938. He was swiftly interred in a potter's field before friends had him exhumed and brought to Tombstone's Boothill. He was laid to rest beneath a placard that reads, A FRIEND TO ALL. His obituary said that with his death, there were no other Chinese-born people living in Tombstone.

After I visited his grave and the others at Boothill, I drove into Tombstone to stop at its shops in the old Western buildings, so well-preserved they look like they were from a movie set. The town's kitsch isn't new—even at the time of Quong's death, Tombstone had already become a tourist attraction. It offered a real-life morsel of the romantic narrative arising out of the Old West, which hasn't changed much since. It tells of brave pioneers vanquishing nature; cowboys, and sheriffs, and bandits, and saloonkeepers, and Western Union station agents. It leads people to the popular graves at Boothill in search of gunslingers like the McLaury brothers, or poor old Lester Moore.

It leaves out Chinese Americans—their contributions and persecution—quite deliberately. Yet the remnants of their stories are still there. They're told by the markers, and what's buried beneath them, in Boothill at Tombstone, and in similar Chinese sections of boot hills that can still be found in former Old West outposts like Deadwood, South Dakota; Idaho City, Idaho; and El Paso, Texas. These are the places where the Six Companies didn't collect all of the bones. They still bear witness. And this is one reason why I love cemeteries. They leave bread-crumb trails to truths too often buried and forgotten.

The Memorial Court of Honor, decorated by a thirty-foot-long
stained-glass replica of Leonardo DaVinci's *The Last Supper*,
inside Forest Lawn's Great Mausoleum

14. THE DISNEYLAND OF GRAVEYARDS

How a Los Angeles cemetery corporatized mourning in America

—

Forest Lawn Memorial-Park
Glendale, California
Established: 1917

OTHER THAN GETTING a ticket to the Oscars or crashing one of its after-parties, the best way to place yourself within a crowd of Hollywood celebrities is to go to Forest Lawn Memorial-Park in Glendale, California. The cemetery's grounds probably contain more stars per square foot than any zip code in Los Angeles. The problem is that their graves can be so hard to find.

More than 350,000 people lie buried within Forest Lawn's three-hundred-plus acres. The grounds cling to the steep slope of the Verdugo Mountains, and the grave markers are embedded flat in the ground, making it hard to single out any one person. The property's scattering of aboveground tombs don't offer much relief, either, as they're mostly hidden within a maze of gardens and courtyards. And don't bother asking the people who work there for directions to a celebrity grave—out of respect for the dead's privacy, they won't help. Instead, you're left to the devices of your devices to locate a star's resting place.

Forest Lawn's flat, open layout, known as the lawn-park design, was the invention of its founder, Hubert Eaton, who established the cemetery in its present form in 1917. At eye level, you can barely see the horizontal markers, obscured by a sea of green grass. It's the model of organization and efficiency—and one that would be copied countless times over by other U.S. cemeteries. But viewing Forest Lawn from overhead, the sight of thousands upon thousands of distinctly visible graves all crammed together is astonishing—and utterly creepy.

During the first half of the twentieth century, Eaton turned the property into more than a cemetery. It doubled as a spectacle of art, Christianity, architecture, and the Red, White, and Blue—a theme park of good old American everlasting life, if you will—drawing millions of visitors annually, and millions of dollars into his pockets. In doing so, Eaton established Forest Lawn as a groundbreaking success that changed the face of cemeteries across the country; it corporatized mourning in America in a way never seen before, opening the door to aggressive sales and marketing and a tsunami of revenues for the modern Death Industrial Complex.

EVEN THOUGH FOREST Lawn is filled with people who became wealthy off their fame, one of the reasons celebrities choose to be buried there is for the anonymity it provides after death. There are five other Forest Lawn Memorial-Parks in the Los Angeles area using the same model. The one in Glendale, about seven miles north of downtown, is the first and oldest, populated mostly with classic stars from the silver screen like Jimmy Stewart, Elizabeth Taylor, and Humphrey Bogart. The Forest Lawn in Hollywood Hills is a hipper resting place for the modern celebrity crowd, among them Carrie Fisher from *Star Wars*, Paul Walker of the *Fast & Furious* movies, and rapper Nipsey Hussle. The others—Long Beach, Covina Hills, Cypress, Cathedral City—are populated by a tiny smattering of B- and C-list celebrities.

My mission as I drove to Glendale's Forest Lawn one glorious late-September afternoon not too long ago—besides to take in the mythical grandeur of the grounds—was to find the resting place of Walt Disney. His name and company represent everything commercial, contrived, prepackaged, cynically capitalistic, and completely awesome. Disney is America.

Turning into Forest Lawn's front drive, I passed its immense wrought iron front gates, which were—successfully—designed to stand bigger and more ostentatiously than the ones at Buckingham Palace.

Beyond them, I was surprised how immaculate the cemetery looked. Nothing was out of place, not even a blade of grass, and no gravestones peeked above the ground anywhere.

Forest Lawn seemed more like a country club or theme park than a cemetery—which is by design. Nearly all the property's thousands of trees and shrubs stay green year-round so the place will look the same every time you visit, which, given that the cemetery lies in the desert, you can regard either as an irrigation marvel or an environmental abomination. Or maybe both.

Forest Lawn is divided into sections with dreamy, inviting names like Dawn of Tomorrow, Memory Slope, Whispering Pines, Babyland, and Slumberland. It offers an artificial but impressive air of international culture, displaying eye-popping replicas of world-famous art, like a Goliath-size version of Michelangelo's *David* statue. The cemetery's themed attractions are meant to transport visitors to a cartoonish time and place, like its fake seventeenth-century Scottish stone chapel called Wee Kirk o' the Heather, which looks stolen from the movie *Snow White and the Seven Dwarfs*. Even the trash cans are camouflaged as fake logs, so the magical experience won't be broken. And the focal point of the property is a tower-filled palace, known as the Great Mausoleum.

There's no wonder so many architectural critics and journalists refer to it as the Disneyland of cemeteries. But they actually have it backward. Disneyland, which opened in 1955, is more accurately a Forest Lawn without the graves.

BALDING, BESPECTACLED HUBERT Eaton didn't lack self-esteem. He went by the godlike nickname the Builder, and in the early days of his cemetery, he crafted a mission statement that sounded more like a set of holy commandments than a business plan. He had the Builder's Creed etched onto a giant stone tablet that still stands in front of Forest Lawn's Great Mausoleum.

The Creed demeans traditional cemeteries as "unsightly stoneyards full of inartistic symbols and depressing customs," and promises all who read it that the Builder would offer a better place for people to go after their deaths. His Forest Lawn is "as unlike other cemeteries as sunshine is to darkness, as eternal life is unlike death."

The Builder envisioned the cemetery as a garden temple, "filled with towering trees, sweeping lawns, splashing fountains, singing birds, beautiful statuary, cheerful flowers, noble architecture with interiors full of light and color and redolent of the world's best history and romances."

His temple would also flow with money. The Creed piously concludes by commanding that Forest Lawn shalt be a place "protected by an immense Endowment Care Fund."

Directly in front of the tablet stands a statue of two young children with a puppy by their side. Even though neither of them looks old enough to read, they're craning their necks upward to behold the Builder's words, their faces filled with awe and joy.

Eaton was born in 1881 in Liberty, Missouri, and moved west after earning his degree in chemistry, hoping to make his riches in silver mines. Things didn't work out as planned, and in 1911, he moved to Los Angeles, where he took a job selling grave plots on commission to mourners at a new cemetery in what is now Glendale.

While others saw little more than a forlorn, sun-parched hillside burial ground in the suburbs, Eaton, always with a Disney-like eye to the future, pictured a real estate bonanza on a parcel soon to be enveloped by the city. Los Angeles was on the verge of completing the 233-mile-long Aqueduct that would supply it with endless amounts of water from the fertile Owens Valley, high in the Eastern Sierra, and entirely transform its fortunes. By the 1920s, it would occupy America's largest metropolitan area.

And he was right about a well-placed cemetery's potential. Consider the math: A typical grave takes up about thirty square feet of space, meaning that more than 1,300 graves can easily be crammed into a single acre. The potential cash return on a cheaply bought piece of land like the one where Eaton worked—even if a plot sold for a paltry $10—was immense. The problem that his cemetery, and so many others, faced was that it could take a long time to fill the grave plots. More people needed to die to see much of a reward. And young, newly transplanted professionals landing in Los Angeles weren't likely to die in profitable numbers.

But there was another way. Eaton devised an aggressive presale program aimed at the healthy and living, not the mourning or dead. Although the concept of presale, or preneed, had been used in other places, Eaton took it to a creative new level. He pitched people on security for their family if the unfortunate happened. He sold them everlasting life, not death, on a patch of sacred land where they could find immortal rest after their earthly terms ended. He wasn't selling a grave plot, he was selling spiritual, and physical, peace of mind. Still, the cemetery was floundering in debt. The owners, losing faith in the venture, didn't see the future potential that Eaton did.

At the end of 1916, Eaton, through a set of aggressive financial maneuverings, and with the partial financial backing of close relatives and the legendary Los Angeles real estate speculator William Irving Hollingsworth, purchased a majority stake in the burial ground and became its director. On January 1, 1917, it became Forest Lawn Memorial-Park. He called the property a memorial park because it had a happier ring to it than cemetery.

To maximize his personal profits, he set up a real estate arrangement like Woodlawn's in the Bronx. In it, he created a private real estate company to buy the undeveloped portions of the cemetery land. Then the company sold it, plot by plot, to the nonprofit memorial park, skimming off 50 percent of the proceeds from each grave sale and 60 percent from all crypt and mausoleum spaces. He also paid himself a sizable annual salary, and bonuses, as cemetery director. This is how Forest Lawn—and Eaton's fortunes—came to be. And it was good.

The Builder's first act as cemetery director and owner was to get rid of all traditional gravestones that jutted above the ground. They announced too loudly, "A dead person lives here," took up too much space, and made maintaining the grounds too time-consuming and costly. Instead, burial spaces at his cemetery would be marked by bronze plaques embedded flat in the earth, carpeted by vast lawns that an industrial tractor mower could quickly speed over. He called this blueprint the Memorial-Park plan. Within a couple of decades, it became the predominant landscape design in America for new cemeteries, and was adopted in newer sections of many existing ones, as well. The Builder gave birth to a cemetery landscape revolution.

The Builder's sales and marketing strategies were as equally groundbreaking as his landscape design. He printed splashy advertisements in newspapers, which until then, cemeteries had never done. He ran ads on billboards pitching Forest Lawn as a place with "beauty that comforts," and as an exciting attraction where the whole family could visit for fun. The cemetery employed a force of salespeople, deployed to go door-to-door selling prospective customers on Forest Lawn as their home for eternity. No need for people to see the grave site in person; a picture would do. Door-to-door presale became standard throughout the cemetery industry in America, and often lent itself to predatory practices and scams by fly-by-night outfits.

All the while, the Builder was turning Forest Lawn into a destination like none other, tapping into the American cultural psyche. He collected original sculptures from around the world and commissioned replicas of famous religious and patriotic artworks that would outshine the originals for display throughout. But unlike at other cemeteries, most of the art wasn't attached to a grave. It stood on display separately. The property became a magical kingdom divided into themed sections, bursting with flowers, greenery, and statues. He constructed fairy-tale chapels for not only funerals, but weddings. Before long, tourists from around the world lined up to spend the day at Forest Lawn, buying postcards and souvenirs at the gift shops. He created an experience and destination both.

A theme park, as opposed to an amusement park, is an outdoor area intended for entertainment and centered around a specific theme or divided into sections of different themes. By definition, Forest Lawn was the nation's first theme park, established thirteen years before Knott's Berry Farm in Southern California—which is generally credited with the title.

If imitation is the sincerest form of flattery, then Walt Disney was very flattering to his close friend Eaton. When he opened his first theme park, Disneyland, in Anaheim in 1955, Forest Lawn had already been California's most popular tourist stop for almost four decades. He clearly borrowed a great deal from the cemetery's layout and business model in designing his namesake attraction. It's fitting that Disney chose to be buried at Forest Lawn.

The cemetery's popularity as a destination for the living drove up the demand, and prices, for burial spaces. A burial at Forest Lawn was marketed as a privilege, accessible only to the upper middle class and the elite. Like a five-star resort, Eaton offered different levels of luxury and accommodation based on price and location. The lawn park's palace, the Grand Mausoleum, which opened in 1920 and houses the Builder's Creed tablet out front, is the most exclusive spot. Inside it, Eaton created a Memorial Court of Honor, where its occupants are buried in the floor, like at Westminster Abbey. You can't just buy a spot there. You need to be selected as an "immortal" by a secret committee from Forest Lawn to gain access.

The resting places in the Memorial Court of Honor lie directly beneath a thirty-foot-tall stained glass reproduction of Leonardo da Vinci's *The Last Supper*. Unlike at Westminster Abbey, which houses the remains of British queens and kings, not to mention Charles Darwin, Geoffrey Chaucer, and Charles Dickens, I didn't recognize any of the so-called immortals buried in the Memorial Court of Honor. Except, of course, for the Builder himself.

IT'S PROBABLY NO coincidence that Eaton was laying out Forest Lawn and devising its membership structure at a time when country clubs were gaining a foothold in suburban America.

The nation's first country club was established in Brookline, Massachusetts, in 1882, more than three decades before Forest Lawn, and the concept of sprawling, turf-filled pleasure grounds for the well-to-do quickly spread. Like country clubs, Forest Lawn's membership was rooted in bigotry. The cemetery barred the interment of Jews and minorities on its grounds until 1959. Also like country clubs, Forest Lawn was an immensely successful wedding venue. Its chapels hosted tens of thousands of marriage ceremonies by the mid-1950s, and they continue to be popular today. The cemetery is a more appealing place to get married than you might think. Entering through the regal front gates can make you feel like royalty, and on the tree-lined limo drive to the ceremony, all you'll see are flat, expansive lawns carpeting the hillside. Not a single gravestone shows its face to break the spell on this magical journey, nor is there a single sign on the property that uses the word *cemetery*.

Ronald Reagan famously married his first wife, Jane Wyman, at Forest Lawn's Wee Kirk o' the Heather chapel in 1940. None of the many press reports I found even mentioned that it took place inside a graveyard. That same year, Forest Lawn welcomed 1.6 million tourists through its gates and sold twice as many burial plots as any cemetery in the country.

But the Builder wasn't done building. He acquired and displayed the seventeen-foot-tall *David* statue, and a thirteen-foot-tall statue of George Washington originally meant to stand in the rotunda of the U.S. Capitol building. He hung the world's largest religious painting—an original portrayal of the crucifixion of Jesus, which stretches nearly two hundred feet long—in the cathedral-like Hall of Crucifixion-Resurrection. It's found within an auditorium room like the Hall of Presidents at Florida's Disney World. Aside from flashy decorations, Forest Lawn turned itself into a one-stop funeral shop, elbowing out local funeral homes by housing its own mortuary and florist on-site. The cemetery began hawking caskets, memorial markers, and even life insurance. The Builder then expanded his empire across Los Angeles County by opening other Forest Lawn Memorial-Parks in the area under the same model. He showed the immense, untapped potential for profit in the business of selling graves, and the rest of America's funeral industry took note—and followed his example.

Part of Forest Lawn's success was surely Eaton's marketing and innovation, but it was also the benefit of good timing. This template for corporate efficiency and a revenue-driven approach to mourning in America came when people sought to separate themselves from reminders of death and their own inevitable expiration dates. Life expectancy was up and infant mortality down, people were dying in greater numbers in hospitals, and the death room in American homes had fully become the living room. Americans were more than willing to hire other people to handle the unpleasant needs of the deceased.

These conditions sent the Death Industrial Complex into expansion overdrive, like adding manure to a mushroom field. By 1950, nearly 20,000 funeral homes had opened, and seven hundred different casket manufacturers operated nationwide. Cemeteries around the country followed Forest Lawn's aggressive grave sale methods. And insurance companies—not to be outdone—began knocking on front doors offering a slight variation, called burial insurance, which charged people low monthly payments to buy a specific grave, or as the premium on a one-time cash payout upon death for cemetery expenses. During the first half of the twentieth century, three-quarters of life insurance policies in America were sold in the form of burial insurance. Not until the 1970s did the more lucrative term life insurance that we know today overtake burial insurance in sales.

There was an understandable sense of security that burial insurance gave customers, even if it made more financial sense for them to set aside the money each month in a savings account. People knew that upon their passing, a sum of cash would be passed to their loved ones, with no strings attached, to cover ever-ballooning funeral costs. During the height of discriminatory real estate lending practices, otherwise known as redlining, home ownership was made impossible for a large percentage of people of color. For instance, in 1960, only 38 percent of Black families owned a home compared to 65 percent of white families. A grave, on the other hand, was seen as an attainable slice of the American Dream, even if only realized after death.

Former U.S. poet laureate Natasha Trethewey, born in Gulfport, Mississippi, in 1966, captures this notion in her poem "Collection Day." It takes place in the country on a Sunday morning in 1969 and is told through the perspective of a child.

The narrator's family is looking forward to the arrival of the burial insurance man from the Everlast Interment Company who, in the living room, will "pull out photos of our tiny plot" before collecting the premium. The mother always keeps her payment card in her Bible at the ready, the narrator says at the end of the poem, and each month the salesman stamps PAID in green letters, "putting us / one step closer to what we'll own, / something to last: patch of earth, / view of sky."

In the early 2000s, nearly one hundred insurance companies settled sixteen major court cases for overcharging Black Americans for burial insurance over an eighty-year period. The litigation encompassed 14.8 million policies that charged 30 percent higher rates to Black people. The companies agreed to pay more than $556 million in restitution, fines, legal costs, and charitable donations. The second-largest payment came from Metropolitan Life Insurance, better known as MetLife, which doled out $157 million. MetLife originally built its business, according to the Associated Press, "largely on the profits from burial insurance." Now it's one of the hundred largest companies in America, reaping $67 billion in revenues in 2020.

As the second half of the twentieth century carried on, more cemeteries started following the Forest Lawn model of offering the full slate of funeral and mortuary services; funeral home corporations did the opposite, swallowing up cemeteries, while consolidating businesses and killing the competition. These shifts left grieving families with fewer options and an ever-growing array of unforeseen and unnecessary charges, add-ons, and upsells.

In 1963, British investigative journalist Jessica Mitford published a book called *The American Way of Death* that uncovered the unseemly underbelly of the funeral industry and its exploitative practices. Her book sold millions of copies and led to new federal oversight on transparency and predatory practices, including the Federal Trade Commission's Funeral Rule, which forces funeral homes to provide written price lists to anyone who asks. But the Death Industrial Complex kept amassing profit and power, with corporations extinguishing mom-and-pop operations and larger pieces of the pie falling into fewer and fewer hands.

Today, one manufacturing company, Hillenbrand Inc., produces 45 percent of all caskets in the United States, and brings in $2.5 billion in annual revenue. A single American mortuary company, Service Corporation International (SCI), owns 1,500 funeral homes and 480 cemeteries, raking in about sixteen cents out of every dollar Americans pay for funeral expenses. Recently, a comprehensive report by two consumer organizations claimed that SCI charges as much as 72 percent more for funeral services than other funeral homes. The U.S. Death Industrial Complex as a whole now generates a whopping $20 billion in annual sales. (By comparison, the American sneaker industry sells $16 billion of products a year.)

How does this translate to the American mourner? On average, a funeral and burial costs $9,135, and a cremation $6,645—unexpected prices that are beyond the reach of many people already maxed out on credit from health-care and living costs. Early in the COVID outbreak, Congress allocated as much as $9,000 in funeral assistance to people in need. It was the first sweeping federal program to address burial poverty in U.S. history. All it took was a mass casualty event.

As for Forest Lawn, it has turned into a burial behemoth, its network now consisting of its six cemeteries, five mortuaries, and sales offices across Southern California. It sits on assets that exceed $900 million, including $630 million in securities investments, and real estate and buildings worth $26 million, according to its most recent available tax filing. Forest Lawn pays its CEO, who started working at the cemetery in 1984 as an apprentice embalmer and climbed through the ranks, $1.5 million a year in salary and bonuses, and gives each member of its board of directors a compensation of about $100,000 annually. The chairman of the board and former CEO is Eaton's great-nephew.

The Builder died in 1966. His funeral was one you'd expect for someone exceedingly rich and not lacking in self-esteem. Forest Lawn was decorated with ostentatious Christian imagery befitting the death of a pope or a saint, like a cross made from 11,000 white carnations and 5,000 red roses. During the services, a chorale sang a booming version of the "Hallelujah Chorus" from Handel's *Messiah*—like is performed at the Washington National Cathedral every Christmas season—and the guest list included the West Coast's most powerful and famous people, including Reagan. The Builder's friend Walt Disney was named an honorary pallbearer but couldn't attend due to his battle with cancer. Former vice president (and future president) Richard Nixon also received an invitation but was a no-show. The ceremony concluded with the Builder being declared an immortal by the former governor of California, then entombed in the floor of the Memorial Court of Honor. Today, Forest Lawn continues to find creative ways to reach the public and sell them on spending the ever after on its grounds, in the spirit of the Builder.

Most recently, it opened kiosks at five Southern California shopping malls selling grave plots and funeral services.

DISNEY WOULD PASS away three months after the Builder, his cremated remains deposited in a quiet garden nook at Forest Lawn. A not-so-easy-to-find quiet garden nook, I should add—I spent about an hour searching for his burial spot, wandering in and out of other garden nooks, and began wondering if maybe the urban legend was true, that Disney was actually cryogenically frozen and stored beneath the Pirates of the Caribbean at Disneyland.

To reach Disney's grave, I drove up Forest Lawn's twisting Cathedral Drive—the steep main avenue that ascends the mountainside— and, just before Arlington Road, parked at the Freedom Mausoleum. The overlap between Arlington, Freedom, and Cathedral is no accident. Throughout the property, Forest Lawn interweaves Christianity with the Stars and Stripes.

Once I reached the tan, mid-century modern structure near the ridgetop that is the Freedom Mausoleum, I continued my quest on foot. I knew Disney's spot lay around here somewhere. But where? Climbing a set of steps toward the mausoleum, I kept on the lookout for members of the cemetery's ever-present security force, who shoo people away from the celebrity graves that are off-limits to the public. I wasn't sure if that included Disney's.

Standing in a broad courtyard behind me was the mausoleum's glass front entrance, and in front of me spread a lush, close-cropped lawn, filled by eight long, tight rows of flat gravestones. On the far side stood the bronze statue of what looked like an American soldier in a World War I uniform. Above him hung the words COURT OF FREEDOM. I walked in his direction and noticed three cozy little walled-in gardens, each one accessed by a waist-high swinging iron gate door. No Disney.

I then passed the soldier statue and entered an even longer, grass-carpeted courtyard. On my immediate left stood a massive bronze George Washington, posed like he was leading a boat across the Delaware River. He was staring across the green expanse at the statue of someone dressed in a toga at the other end. I strode down the cement path running along the right side of the courtyard until I reached a side plaza, about halfway down. I caught an astonishing sight here, of a three-story-tall copy of the famous *Declaration of Independence* painting, portraying the signers in Independence Hall, that's shown in every high school history book.

This version looms several times bigger than the original and is composed of 700,000 shards of Venetian stained glass. It's gaudy, mesmerizing, and magnificent. Prying my eyes from it took some effort, but I had to keep moving. I passed through an entryway to its right, which led me into a statue-filled terrace called the Garden of Honor, which led to more terraces, and more hidden garden nooks, and more graves.

I wish I could say that this was when some magical good fortune led me to the correct spot. Like maybe Tinker Bell, or Olaf the goofy snowman, or a cartoon bluebird appeared and showed me the way. But instead, nothing. At last, I stood in front of the Freedom Mausoleum, where my hunt began, and grabbed my phone. Through the wizardry of the Internet, a guy in a YouTube video showed me the exact directions—about ten steps from my location. Disney's garden burial place hides adjacent to the mausoleum building itself. I made the quick journey, pushed open the garden's hinged gate, and walked in, half expecting to be jumped by security hiding behind the shrubbery.

I found myself standing on a square, perfectly cut bed of grass surrounded by a broad frame of flowers and ornamental trees and plants. Kneeling among the blooms was a pint-size bronze statue of a young girl. It looked like the famous, and much larger, *The Little Mermaid* statue in Copenhagen, but this girl was much younger. Fresh pink lilies and roses had been recently left in her lap. I looked up and there, behind her on the ivy-covered brick wall, hung a metal plaque containing four names, with the top one reading WALTER ELIAS DISNEY.

This spot was refreshingly understated and tasteful relative to Forest Lawn's overwhelming chintz and gaudiness. I was disappointed there was no bench or anywhere else to sit to enjoy the warm sun. It was easy, for a moment, to forget I stood in the presence of Disney. He shaped how the entertainment business influences our lives; how fitting that he should lie in Forest Lawn for eternity: the place that shaped how the funeral business influences our lives—and afterlives—for better or worse.

Natural sunlight bathes the statues, plants, and book-shaped
cremation urns at the Chapel of the Chimes.

15. WE DIDN'T START THE FIRE

Cremation now outnumbers burials in America and has surprisingly led some dying cemeteries to rise from the ashes

—

Chapel of the Chimes
Oakland, California
Established: 1929

IT'S ONE THING to walk into a nearly empty cemetery alone and wander among the graves. It's another to walk into a giant, empty mausoleum alone. Footsteps on the stone floors echo off the walls—*clack, clack, clack*—and the odor of damp mustiness permeates the air, as if in a dungeon. And if it's not brightly lit, well, keep an eye on the tombs and make sure none are suddenly sliding open. Mausoleums, to put it mildly, can be creepy when you're solo.

Which is probably why the Chapel of Chimes in Oakland, California—arguably America's largest indoor cemetery—boasts so many chambers illuminated by vaulted glass ceilings, which invite you to look skyward and bathe in the sun's soft, life-giving rays. Otherwise, the act of browsing its rows and stacks of 30,000-plus urns filled with cremated remains, along with its handful of full-body tombs, could be a little anxiety inducing.

I took a self-guided tour while crashing for a couple of days at the house of an old college friend in nearby Palo Alto, home to Stanford University. The evening before, I asked him to join me on the expedition, but he laughed as if I had just told the funniest joke ever, and gave me a firm "hell no."

Not only did he have no time or desire to tour a cemetery— "important conference call first thing in the morning, couldn't get around it, even if I wanted to"—but he asked me not to mention my little mission in front of his family. There was "no reason to disturb the kids," he said. Teenaged kids, mind you.

I complied and tried my best to hide my crazy from his wife and children. When one of the kids asked me at the (vegan) dinner table where I was headed the next morning, I said I was visiting a beautiful old chapel, and left it at that—stifling the urge to add, with an evil laugh, "Filled with tens of thousands of dead people, mwah-ha-ha-ha!"

If, in some alternate universe, my college friend had given me permission to speak freely at the dinner table, I would have told his family, with great gusto, how the Chapel of the Chimes is one of the Bay Area's most important pieces of historic architecture, although it's too often overlooked. I would have said it was designed about one hundred years ago by Julia Morgan, the first woman to be a licensed architect in California.

I would have also explained, in between asking for someone to pass me the gluten-free rolls or tofu meat loaf, how at the beginning of the twentieth century, almost no one in America was cremated. But a growing movement of people arose who envisioned cremation as a more affordable and ecologically friendly method of body disposal. They began a pro-cremation movement.

Then the Chapel of the Chimes, Morgan's masterpiece, arrived. It quickly became the most successful memorial space for displaying funeral urns in the country, and an innovator and leader in the cremation business. Today cremations outnumber traditional burials in America, and the Chapel of the Chimes played a pivotal role in shifting public attitudes and bringing about this transition. Ironically, its efficient, attractive, high-volume method of storing human remains also revolutionized and ultimately rescued American urban cemeteries, which were running out of space, from extinction. But alas, I kept this all to myself.

I ARRIVED AT the Chapel of the Chimes right as it opened, but lingered for a moment in its small parking lot. The building lies on sleepy Piedmont Avenue in northeastern Oakland, just past a Pilates studio and a gym where I glimpsed people pedaling hard on exercise bikes on an outside patio.

I texted my friend: *This is your last chance. About to head in*

His reply came fast for someone on an important conference call: *Still a no!*

I stepped out of the car and headed toward the stately stucco Chapel of the Chimes. Topped by a terra-cotta roof, it looked like an ancient Spanish village church, complete with bell tower. Inscribed in block letters above its arched front entryway hung the word MAU-SOLEUM. Another name for it would be columbarium, which is what a structure—indoor or outdoor—intended to hold and memorialize funeral urns is generally called. But mausoleum works fine, given that it also houses some tombs. Po-tay-to, po-tah-to.

I pulled at the thick, wooden front doors, but they didn't budge. Peeking through the glass panes, I spied the pews and altar of a formal-looking chapel—the chapel that gives the place its name—lit by stained glass windows, on the other side. I figured this area was locked in prepa-ration for an upcoming funeral.

A smaller entrance several paces to the right was open, I found, and it led me into a small, empty anteroom with a tiled floor. I didn't see another living soul—no reception area or greeters. A draft carrying the damp chill of the bay filled the air and added a sense of foreboding. I knew it was okay to wander, but still, it felt a little like I was intruding.

I climbed a few steps and entered a chamber called the Garden of Memories, which fills an area maybe about the size of a volleyball court. It's decorated with potted palm plants and other tropical greenery, as well as a bubbling fountain designed by Morgan, and a polished-granite bench. I turned my head upward to see a second-story balcony above, framing the skylight. Despite the pleasant, sunny setting, it still would have been nice to have a friend with me.

Bookshelves line much of the Garden of Memory's walls, their square, glassed-in nooks containing what look like books, if you squint. Up close you can see they're book-shaped urns that vary in shape and size. Their spines are engraved with the names and dates of the deceased—each set of ashes containing a unique life's story. The book symbolism is undeniably clever, and their sight is imminently more comforting than a room filled with traditional urns. The books are also a much more compact storage method, allowing more sets of ashes to be stacked closely together.

Straight beyond me, through a wide entrance, I spied another courtyard, followed by what looked like another courtyard, followed, I think, by another. Through some trick of time and space—or simply brilliant architectural design—the place seems so much bigger on the inside than it looks from the street. The book-urn shelves that decorate the spaces are separated by stretches of wall that hold larger niches sealed by flat marble panels marked by the names of their residents.

The Chapel of the Chimes's interior, through Morgan's artistry, is clearly supposed to make you think you've been transported into a vast, elegant monastery library from the Renaissance. In fact, it keeps on display illuminated manuscripts of Bibles dating back to the sixteenth century, and a page from an original Gutenberg Bible, printed in 1453. The effect works. Cremation proponents have long fought organized religions for the practice's acceptance. This place makes it seem steeped in old Christian tradition.

Without a specific destination in mind, I took a few rights and lefts, winding my way into and out of different cloisters and chambers and chapels. I soon realized there aren't any corridors in the mausoleum, only interconnecting spaces. Which can be confusing, I must say. The deeper you go inside, the more it becomes like a labyrinth of the no-longer-living, a corn maze of the ever after. Suddenly, I couldn't find my bearings. I felt like I was trapped in an Edgar Allan Poe story.

Relax, I told myself with a sharp inhale, *and go with the flow. Enjoy the journey. Ignore the tens of thousands of dead people who fill the walls!*

I took a moment to sit and consider my surroundings, allowing my runaway heart rate to slow. The building, it became clear, isn't meant to disorient. It's meant to disconnect visitors from the outside world, and deliver them into a more contemplative realm. Morgan's choice of combining the imagery of books and learning with religion was brilliant. She was targeting an intellectual audience for her work during a time in America when cremation was considered, at best, an oddball option and, at worst, heresy.

JULIA MORGAN HAD her hands full in 1926. At fifty-four years old, she found herself nearly a decade into overseeing what would be a twenty-eight-year effort to design and build the 60,000-square-foot Hearst Castle for newspaper magnate William Randolph Hearst. The mansion, as it took shape, mimicked the look of a Spanish Renaissance cathedral, and stood atop a forested hill that spilled into the San Luis Obispo coast. The estate surrounding it stretched half the size of Rhode Island, midway between San Francisco and Los Angeles.

As the home's construction progressed, bit by bit, and its expansive rooms filled with more and more pieces of priceless art and furniture collected from around the world, it gained renown as the exclusive gathering place of presidents and prime ministers, movie stars and multimillionaires, all of them seeking an audience with the powerful, bombastic media baron. Hearst Castle became maybe the most famous active residence in America excluding the White House, a place where names and careers could be made or broken.

The unassuming Morgan navigated deftly among the rich and famous as she went about her work. The daughter of a mining engineer, she grew up in Oakland, and became the first woman to earn a B.S. in civil engineering from the University of California, Berkeley, and to study architecture at the renowned École des Beaux-Arts in Paris. Each day, she went to work dressed in a tie and suit coat, her belongings stuffed in the pockets, above a long skirt.

Not much of a self-promoter, she had nonetheless cultivated a devout following in the Golden State for her sturdy, magnificent, poured concrete, and practically earthquake-proof creations—including Hearst Castle. All the while, the male architects of her time, like Frank Lloyd Wright, became national celebrities.

It was in 1926 that Morgan was approached by a former casket salesman in Oakland named Lawrence Moore who ran a columbarium and crematory and wanted to enlist her services. Then, cremation was a niche afterlife option among a small portion of Americans but was starting to catch fire. He envisioned a resplendent columbarium—the grander the space, the more appealing cremation might be to the general public. It would include a chapel, where religious services could be booked on-site, removing cremation's atheist stigma. Growth potential in this untapped segment of the funeral market seemed limitless—the country's population continued to grow, and available urban real estate continued to shrink. Plus the profit potential seemed greater than burials—the number of people who could be deposited per square foot of land in a two- or three-story-tall indoor columbarium was exponentially higher than in a traditional cemetery.

The building Morgan was being asked to renovate and expand had served as the California Columbarium since 1909 and was once a trolley station. It sat on a quiet street that dead-ended into the front gates of Mountain View Cemetery, a 226-acre, rural-style burial ground and popular tourist spot designed in 1863 by none other than Frederick Law Olmsted of Central Park fame.*

Morgan accepted the job. She took three years, while still working on Hearst Castle, to transform the building into the Chapel of the Chimes. She loosely based the exterior on the Alhambra, the wondrous palace in southern Spain where Queen Isabella and King Ferdinand ruled when they dispatched Columbus to sail the ocean blue. The result was a resplendent structure with an all-too-ideal location next to Mountain View Cemetery. From a sales perspective, Morgan's columbarium gave the crowds passing the chapel each day, as they entered and exited Mountain View, a new, warmer alternative to burial.

IT'S IMPOSSIBLE TO pin exactly when humans began turning bodies to ash as a funeral custom. The earliest discovered cremated remains belonged to a woman who died 20,000 years ago in Australia. Archaeologists believe people in Europe began using the practice sometime around 3000 B.C.E., though not commonly. When the Trojan War took place around 1200 B.C.E. during the Bronze Age, most people were likely buried, despite the descriptions of the massive funeral pyres in *The Iliad* and *The Odyssey*. The practice didn't become more widespread in Greece until four centuries later, around the time when Homer—if he was a real person—spun his epic tales.

---

* Mountain View was the only cemetery Olmsted ever designed, although he did consult on the construction of Arlington National Cemetery.

Cremation was difficult in ancient times. The human body is 60 percent water, and about 1,000 pounds of wood is needed to produce enough heat: about 2,000 degrees Fahrenheit to turn one person into ashes. Cremation was difficult, if not impossible, in regions without heavy tree cover—and where there was enough timber, cutting and hauling the wood required was no small task. Even today, in India, where about 84 percent of people are cremated in a traditional Hindu funeral pyre, about 50 to 60 million trees need to be cut down annually for the job.

The Romans began cremating around 1000 B.C.E., although it never fully replaced burial. Ambitious entrepreneurs and burial societies in the empire constructed ornate—and profitable—columbaria where the upper middle class, who couldn't quite afford massive monuments, paid for their urns to be placed and displayed. One of the most famous ones still preserved is the Columbaria of Vigna Codini in Rome. Used during the first couple of centuries C.E. and discovered in the 1800s, it consists of three buildings containing hundreds of rounded niches carved into marble slabs for holding urns.

Meanwhile, Jewish tradition of the era required burial—the body was seen as a sacred vessel belonging to God, which needed to be placed in the ground intact in order to rise when the messiah came. These views have evolved somewhat today, as cremation has gained acceptance and popularity in many reform congregations, but not among orthodox ones.

Cremation in the Roman Empire dwindled around 300 C.E. when Constantine declared Catholicism as the empire's primary religion— and the Christians largely followed Jewish burial traditions, rejecting pagan ones. The Church didn't outright forbid the practice, however, until the eighth century, when Charlemagne declared that the Saxons and the other Germanic tribes he conquered must convert and abandon their cremation customs. Anyone who helped perform a cremation would be put to death; the act of burning a body and turning it to dust was seen as a rejection of God and the Second Coming of Jesus. Its use would be reserved only for punishing the worst sinners in the eyes of the Church, making their salvation and resurrection impossible.

As a result, Europe kept relatively cremation free, except in times of plague, until the latter half of the nineteenth century. It was then that urban burial grounds stretched beyond capacity and concerns arose over dead bodies spreading diseases through the air, soil, and water. In Germany in the 1860s—and again a century later in another study—higher case numbers of typhoid fever were recorded in populations who drank water from wells near cemeteries. In 1879, the French Society for Hospital Hygiene noticed similar connections with typhoid sufferers and burial grounds in Paris. Physicians led the movement, promoting cremation as a preferable public health option. The first modern crematoria—built with newly invented, industrial, high-temperature furnaces—opened in Europe in the 1870s. The United States followed around the same time, sparked by the activism and promotion of a Pennsylvania doctor, F. Julius LeMoyne. Concerned over cemeteries contaminating drinking water with disease and chemicals from the new trend of embalming, he was inspired by the cremation movement across the Atlantic.

By the turn of the century, twenty crematoria were operating across America, mostly in major cities and predominantly run by cremation societies, which were small organizations committed to ensuring the cremation of their members and promoting the practice as a better alternative to burial. California's Bay Area was particularly ripe for the cremation movement at that time. San Francisco, desperately strapped for real estate space, banned burials in the city limits in 1900, and later ordered the removal of thousands of graves from its four largest downtown cemeteries and replanted in the nearby suburb of Colma. This would become the primary destination for new burials, as well—up to this day.

The San Francisco Columbarium, located north of Golden Gate Park, because it wasn't a cemetery, kept its doors open for cremating and storing cremated remains. A domed, bank-like building adorned with Greco-Roman flourishes inside and out, it's built in a style that could alternately be called Pagan Revival. Being San Francisco's lone active resting place, it motivated locals to at least consider the possibility of cremation.

Then, in 1910, the city also banned the practice of cremation—though not the storage of ashes—within its boundaries, and the columbarium's revenues essentially dried up. The building slowly fell into disrepair until in 1980 a cremation society bought it, refurbished it to its former glory, and began accepting new remains to be deposited within its walls once again.* The columbarium's interior is a sight worth seeing—a confluence of art, architecture, and craft, with stained glass windows, and mosaic tile floors, and intricately carved woodwork.

The building was commissioned by the nonsectarian Independent Order of Odd Fellows and consists of an open atrium at its center, encircled by three stories of balconies, each one packed with rounded, glassed-in niches displaying urns inside them, reminiscent of the ones at the Columbaria of Vigna Codini. The columbarium contains the remains of 8,500 people dating back more than a century, and to see so many urns lining the walls is to feel a bit like you're in ancient Rome, for sure.

Yet there's something overwhelming about the place, death being so omnipresent. Its atmosphere contrasts the light-filled, life-affirming design and decor and mortality-obscuring, book-shaped ash containers of the Chapel of the Chimes, or really what you'll find at any modern columbaria, which are generally designed to hide the contents of their urn lockers behind marble or granite covers.

If the San Francisco Columbarium lit a spark toward cremations within the Bay Area in the early twentieth century, the Chapel of the Chimes turned it into a roaring blaze. Morgan's masterful architectural work put the building on the map, and business boomed, turning it into "the most successful crematory and columbarium in the country."

All the while, the man who ran the business, Moore, continually innovated to make the economics of cremation more efficient and profitable. He served as the cremation industry's most vocal advocate for promoting the idea that cremated remains should be stored and memorialized—for a price—like buried ones, rather than scattered to the winds. He was the first crematory operator to place a metal identifying disc in every cremation to mark the ashes. His operation was the first to deposit remains in a cardboard urn after cremation to upsell mourning loved ones on pricier and fancier alternatives.

---

* The cremations themselves take place outside of the city, because San Francisco's ban on them still stands.

By 1934, the Chapel of the Chimes had performed nearly 24,000 cremations, with the ashes from more than half of them retained for eternity in one of its niches, far above the norm. (Today, about 30 percent of cremated remains in America are placed in a cemetery or columbarium; the rest are scattered or kept in a loved one's home.) The Chapel of the Chimes confirmed Moore's notion that Americans would buy memorial space for cremated remains in an attractive repository—thanks to the elegance, immense talent, and aesthetic touch lent by architect Morgan.

The impressionist painter Edgar Degas once said, "Art is not what you see, but what you make others see." Morgan, through her breathtaking masterpiece, made others see a marriage of cremation and religion, stealing the process of turning a body to ashes from atheism or agnosticism. Her building mimicked Catholic architecture, design, and iconography. It was, as the word *chapel* in its name was intended to suggest, a resoundingly pious-feeling place, home to legendary religious texts, where cremation was successfully depicted as a sacred act, not the revival of a pagan tradition. She created art.

Chapel of the Chimes led a major marketing and philosophy shift among American columbaria that would alter the public attitude toward cremation in a positive direction. Its effect on the funeral business was monumental.

Throughout the twentieth century, the popularity of cremations versus traditional burials in the United States grew steadily. In 1960, 3 percent of deaths resulted in cremations. By 1970, the number rose to 5 percent. By 1995, the number was up to 20 percent nationally—and in the Bay Area, 60 percent. Americans drifted toward cremation partly in response to the growing costs that the Death Industrial Complex influenced. People were eager for a simpler, more affordable option. With cremations, embalming wasn't required, nor was a high-priced casket. And if the loved ones planned to scatter the ashes, neither was a fancy headstone, or flowers, or a church, or a hearse. As we approached the twenty-first century, Americans more aggressively and thoughtfully questioned the environmental impact of burials, and grew increasingly concerned over responsible land use.

To keep up with the trends, Christian denominations started reexamining, and abandoning, their prohibitions on cremation. What was once considered a defiant act against God slowly turned into an accepted part of religious rituals. The Vatican came around in 1963, lifting its thousand-year-old cremation ban if a funeral was held with the full body intact, inside a Catholic church, first. Then in 1997, it allowed cremation to take place before the funeral. It clarified in 2016 that cremated remains had to be deposited in a cemetery and were not allowed to be scattered or stored at home. Some religious experts have speculated that the Catholic Church's acceptance of the practice emerged largely out of fear of losing followers in Asian countries with near-universal cremation rates—in Japan, 99.8 percent of people are cremated.

The Death Industrial Complex initially tried to resist these developments through its powerful corporate muscle. It successfully lobbied to create laws in many states that all but force mourners to pay for the services of funeral homes and cemeteries—even when cremation is the chosen option. For instance, in Delaware, a body must be embalmed within twenty-four hours of death if it's not rushed to cremation or placed in refrigeration by that time. And several states and cities prohibit ash scattering in public spaces and implement inconvenient bureaucratic hurdles for people who decide not to deposit a loved one's ashes in a cemetery or columbarium. In South Dakota, mourners are required by law to file paperwork with the local register of deeds before getting permission to receive the remains.

Yet in 2005, the percentage of deaths in the United States resulting in cremations jumped to thirty-two. In 2015, the number rose to 45 percent. And in 2020, it reached 56 percent, far outpacing traditional burials. The National Funeral Directors Association estimates that in 2030, 70 percent of Americans will opt for cremation.

As cremation's popularity overtook burial's in the last decade, surprising the funeral industry, it managed to save the American cemetery. Near the start of the twenty-first century, many admired American burial grounds faced the looming prospect of running out of space, and without a steady flow of money coming in, they feared insolvency. The famed Mount Auburn Cemetery initially projected it would be filled to capacity by 2001. Green-Wood in Brooklyn foresaw the same for itself by 2015. Arlington National Cemetery thought it would have to close its doors to burials by 2040.

But as the demand for burials has fallen off a proverbial cliff, cemeteries have embraced columbaria. The cost for a columbarium receptacle, more commonly called a niche, at Green-Wood starts at $2,250 and goes up to $19,000. At Forest Lawn in Glendale, California, niches start at $11,900.

Suddenly the same cemeteries that, not long ago, faced the prospect of extinction now expect to be welcoming residents into the next century. And some that had even been filled for years are opening to new business again. The Los Angeles National Cemetery—which closed to burials in 1978—unveiled an expansive new columbarium in 2019 with enough room for 10,000 people, and it plans to add another 80,000 urn lockers in the coming years.

Yet not all the news is positive with cremation. There's a growing awareness that the practice isn't *as* environmentally friendly as we would like to believe—due to its energy use and emissions. During the height of the first COVID wave in 2020, cities like New York and Los Angeles made the grim decision to relax the daily limits on cremations to handle the overwhelming demand, despite the emissions. Residents in some communities complained about the resulting pollution choking their neighborhoods. Crematoria are often powered by natural gas, and one cremation is estimated to create somewhere around 550 pounds of carbon dioxide, or the equivalent of driving a car seven hundred miles. Cremations also account for 5.5 percent of America's mercury emissions, due to the burning of dental fillings.

One earth-friendly alternative to cremation that's gaining attention and some popularity is alkaline hydrolysis, or Aquamation. In it, a body is placed in a chamber filled with water and lye. The liquid is heated to a few hundred degrees, and within hours the flesh is fully decomposed so that all that's left are bones, which are then crushed into dust. The process is low emission and consumes one-eighth the amount of energy of cremation. It's legal in only twenty states, however, and has met fierce lobbying opposition—particularly from the casket-making industry, because the process doesn't necessitate caskets. U.S. Catholic Church bishops have also strongly opposed it, saying it violates the sanctity of the human body. This is the exact language churches used against cremation a century ago. Until the Chapel of the Chimes came along.

ALONE AND SLIGHTLY lost, with my college friend offering me no text support, I wandered through the chapel's hallways and chambers until finding a concrete stairwell. I climbed its cavernous steps and emerged on the second floor, which is similar in styling to the ground floor, but smaller in size, and its balconies that overlook the first-floor garden rooms offer a better perspective on location.

My breathing calmed as I explored, taking occasional snapshots of the giant urn bookshelves. Then I backtracked to the stairwell and climbed to the third floor, which was smaller, and brightly lit by windows. The niches here were newer, and mostly decorated with marble covers. I entered into an area on the westernmost side aptly called the Chapel of Light, where the full-body tombs lie. It even has a celebrity section. The two resting places there that caught my eye belonged to blues great John Lee Hooker, who passed away in 2001, and Al Davis, the former owner of the Oakland Raiders, who died in 2011. Each gleaming marble tomb displays the occupant's autograph, drawn in giant metal script above a three-foot-tall portrait of the person in livelier times.

I took selfies in front of both and sent them to my friend, then made my way down two floors and out of the Chapel of the Chimes. As I crossed Piedmont Avenue toward the car, a young couple, dressed in black, walked through the iron front gates of Mountain View Cemetery. Julia Morgan, architect of the Chapel of the Chimes and Hearst Castle, and more than seven hundred other buildings, actually resides there now, beside her four siblings and both parents in a family plot. She died in 1957 in her San Francisco apartment, and her grave on a grassy hill that overlooks San Francisco Bay offers a prominent view of the Chapel of the Chimes.

Recently, Morgan's prolific work has finally started to receive some of the appreciation and recognition that escaped her while she lived. In 2014, the American Institute of Architects awarded her with its prestigious Gold Medal—making her the first woman ever to receive the

Architect Julia Morgan designed Chapel of the Chimes—Oakland's famed crematorium and storage vault for cremated remains—in the 1920s to resemble a Spanish palace and lend a sense of history and piety to the practice of cremation.

honor. In 2019, the *New York Times*, which printed the news of Frank Lloyd Wright's death on the top fold of its front page in 1959, ran her obituary for the first time on its pages as part of its Overlooked No More series, lauding her "sterling reputation . . . now known around the world."

It's notable that she chose not to be cremated and memorialized in her masterpiece—considering how profoundly her work there influenced American burial culture. It's even more notable that the structure is her one work that sits within perpetual view of her resting place. But for her, designing the Chapel of the Chimes was probably more of a commission than a personal mission. She was paid to make art that gave others a new perspective, and not necessarily one that changed her own on cremation versus burial. I planned to make these points to my friend and his family—including the kids—at dinner that night. Forget hiding my crazy.

Inside the front entrance to Hollywood Forever Cemetery, under the iconic Hollywood sign's watchful gaze

16. LEVERAGING BURIED ASSETS

Facing an existential threat from Digital Immortality, cemeteries are staging a gritty fight for survival

—

Hollywood Forever Cemetery
Los Angeles, California
Established: 1998

TO WHISTLE PAST the graveyard, as the saying goes, is to pretend you're calm when you're actually terrified. Because graveyards are scary, right? Hollywood Forever Cemetery in Los Angeles is meant to be the opposite of scary—all implausibly tall palm trees, and eclectic art and architecture, and joggers running down its paths, and a big lake filled with ducks, geese, and turtles who circle around a bubbling fountain. It's even home to a pack of peacocks, who strut among the graves of an awe-striking lineup of La-La Land legends, from actress Judy Garland to Soundgarden lead vocalist Chris Cornell.*

If you stare straight out of Hollywood Forever's front entrance across Santa Monica Boulevard, you can't miss the famous Hollywood sign beaming back at you from the hilltop in the distance. Turn in the opposite direction, and you'll see the iconic, white water tower of Paramount Pictures next door, looming over the cemetery's rear wall.

Hollywood Forever is even welcoming at night—thanks to its packed schedule of everything from concerts and movie screenings to author events and cultural celebrations. I mean, how terrifying can a place be that puts on after-sunset outdoor showings of *The Breakfast Club* on its lawn to a crowd of four thousand people?

---

* Or, formally, an ostentation of peacocks.

The cemetery's most popular occasion is its Día de Los Muertos celebration—hands down the city's biggest—every fall. It attracts tens of thousands who come dressed in costumes to see the performances held on three separate stages, to sample the offerings from local food vendors, and to wander among the art exhibitions and arts-and-crafts stalls.

Hollywood Forever Cemetery holds the largest
Día de los Muertos celebration in Los Angeles every fall.

The original cemetery, established more than a century ago as Hollywood Cemetery, was on the brink of crumbling ruin in 1998 when a new owner rescued it from bankruptcy, and renamed, rebranded, and revitalized it.* The new, improved Hollywood Forever that rose from the ashes was designed to appeal not just to tourists but, more importantly, to locals as a welcoming community space where they could exercise, or come to read a book on a bench beneath the Southern California sun, or take a date to see a movie. The underlying strategy was to get people emotionally attached to the place, so they might be more eager to reserve a permanent spot for themselves on its grounds, between the stars.

Cemeteries these days need brilliant marketing concepts like this because they're not just competing against one another; they're now competing with the metaverse. In a world where social media preserves a person's existence with infinitely more power, reach, and data than an etched piece of granite planted in the ground, and where artificial intelligence is redefining the word *afterlife*, cemeteries are scrambling for creative ways to stay relevant, and solvent. Hollywood Forever embodies—and in many respects, leads—this existential struggle against the encroachment of Digital Immortality. By leveraging its buried assets, it's creatively welcoming members of its local living community to whistle *into* the graveyard, not past it.

DESIGN-WISE, HOLLYWOOD FOREVER is a hot mess. A beautiful hot mess. It's a mix of modern and old, kitsch and classical, all blended within a combination of landscaping styles—from influences of the early-nineteenth-century rural design like Mount Auburn and Green-Wood that conforms to the property's natural features, to the open memorial park model inspired by nearby Forest Lawn, with tombstones embedded flat in the ground. The sculptures that litter its grounds include a stone mini grand piano shellacked a shiny black; a rocking-out, life-size, greened-with-age bronze Johnny Ramone, the

---

* It was later named Hollywood Memorial Park Cemetery, in the mold of Forest Lawn Memorial-Park in Glendale.

punk rock pioneer buried on-site in 2004; along with many blissful sculpted stone angels and an occasional Virgin Mary. The evening before I visited, the cemetery held a celebration to unveil a life-size, cowboy-hat-wearing bronze bust of actor Burt Reynolds, as pristine as a new penny, anchored atop a marble pedestal next to his burial spot.

The bronze statue marking punk rocker Johnny Ramone's grave at Hollywood Forever Cemetery

Does it look out of place a bit on the grassy slope where it stands? Absolutely. The cemetery's lack of uniformity is what gives it harmony.

Upon passing through Hollywood Forever's wrought-iron gates, I entered into what looks like a garden oasis of palm trees. I had to step on the gas of my rental car slightly to pass a couple of joggers moving with surprising speed through the cemetery on their morning workout, then pulled over just past the domed Chapel Columbarium, built in 1928—and where niches cost $17,000—to begin my exploration of the property on foot. Hollywood Forever is compact, manageable, and full of character. To tour it by car would be a sin.

I walked south down the street aptly called West Avenue, which follows Hollywood Forever's western border. To my right stretched an ivy-covered mausoleum, fringing the cemetery's outer bounds. Sunlight beamed through the long building's arched glass ceilings and lit its tomb-filled, marble-walled rooms.

To my left spread the cemetery's expanse. The graves closest to the edge of the street were new and packed together. Nearly all consisted of granite tabletop vaults that jutted slightly above the grass, marked by polished gravestones of all shapes, sizes, and colors. Each featured a laser-etched, high-resolution image of the smiling person it memorialized.

One of the most appealing aspects of Hollywood Forever is the freedom it grants to people in choosing how they want to be remembered. The burial ground has become permanent home to eighty thousand residents since it first opened in 1899 as Hollywood Cemetery, with almost none of its aboveground graves looking exactly like another. In 1937 the property was bought by a convicted swindler named Jules Roth who spent the next six decades dipping into its endowment funds to maintain his own lavish lifestyle at the expense of maintaining the grounds. He installed a wet bar in his office, and cruised around in a yacht bought by the cemetery that he told the IRS was for scattering cremated ashes in the ocean. At first, the property's slow deterioration didn't dissuade Hollywood's celebrities, like actor Douglas Fairbanks and director Cecil B. DeMille, from being buried there. But then in 1974 the cemetery stopped performing cremations after its furnace collapsed while the remains of famed singer Mama Cass Elliot were in it. By the late 1990s, the dilapidated cemetery was reportedly bringing in more money from people paying to *remove* the remains of loved ones than to bury them.

Roth died in 1997, and a year later a young entrepreneur named Tyler Cassity, who came from a midwestern family entrenched in the funeral business, bought the property for $375,000. He renamed it Hollywood Forever and immediately sunk millions into restoring the buildings and graves and revitalizing the landscape. His vision for the cemetery appeared to be twofold: First, turn the property into a cultural hub for members of the community—who would then be more enthusiastic about buying burial plots or columbarium niches there. Hollywood Forever already had a powerful natural draw: its celebrity residents, which cemeteries have used to lure customers for centuries. Second, and more ambitious, was to create a parallel digital forever cemetery by producing electronic biographies and slideshows, known as LifeStories, of Hollywood Forever's permanent residents—new and old—and posting them online. A person's page would contain an array of videos, photos, and content from emails and voice mails, and include comments from friends and loved ones.

Sound like a familiar social media setup? Back then, it was visionary—Mark Zuckerberg wouldn't launch Facebook in his Harvard dorm room for another seven years. *The Atlantic* magazine featured Hollywood Forever in a 2001 article, calling it the American trailblazer in "digital immortality." The cemetery charged between $400 and $4,000 for the service, depending on the level of content on a person's page, and billed itself as the Internet's most expansive memory keeper, with a catalog of profiles in the thousands.

The LifeStories-producing arm was run as a separate side business to Hollywood Forever, led by Cassity's brother. By late 2003, still before Facebook, the two men had expanded the social network's services beyond cemeteries, and onto the campuses of twelve colleges, hoping students would want to connect with one another through it. They also eyed college alumni associations as possible customer bases. "They want to be the digital custodians of their clients' narratives, voices, and images, and they want to do it on a grand scale," a *Money* magazine profile said. They even envisioned creating an app for mobile devices someday, they told *St. Louis* magazine, allowing someone to "whip out a BlackBerry and download LifeStories." (The iPhone wouldn't debut until 2007.)

But in August 2003, a Los Angeles–based tech start-up launched a powerful, and free, web-based social network called MySpace, which gained instant popularity. Then a few months later, Facebook rolled along. By the end of 2005, Facebook boasted six million members, and today the number exceeds 2.9 billion active users globally. So much for the cemetery's social network that preceded it.

Hollywood Forever's vision as a source of Digital Immortality suffered perhaps its fatal blow in 2010 when Cassity's brother and father were indicted by federal prosecutors for allegedly scamming roughly $500 million from customers who bought funeral insurance from a company they ran. (Tyler Cassity was not connected to the scandal.) They were accused of running a Ponzi scheme wherein they took cash from 97,000 customers and used it to purchase real estate, cover personal expenses, and invest in other businesses. The company collapsed under its own weight in 2008, as state investigators started looking at the books. The father received a nine-year prison sentence, the brother five years, and the two men and three other defendants were ordered to pay $435 million in restitution.

Digital Immortality now rests firmly in the domain of tech companies, leaving Hollywood Forever, and the entire Death Industrial Complex, for that matter, in its dust. If a cemetery can be defined as the resting place for the essences of people's lives, then Facebook is by far the world's biggest cemetery. Zuckerberg's metaverse preserves and displays the profiles of more than 30 million of its members who have passed away, and that number grows every minute. In fact, estimates say that within fifty years, Facebook's population of dead account holders will outnumber its living ones. Talk about a virtual graveyard. But that's just the start.

Through artificial intelligence, Silicon Valley is redefining the concept of the afterlife. While it will forever be a spiritual mystery whether our souls linger in the clouds after we pass, it's a concrete fact that our electronic souls linger in the cloud. Consider that the average American spends about seventeen hours a week on social media. Then think about how the metaverse is spreading its roots through all our interconnected gadgets—tracking our locations, heart rates, daily calorie intakes, sleep patterns, driving speeds, exercise routines (or lack thereof), TV binge watches, groceries, and what thermostat settings we like to keep at home. Not to mention all our actions, reactions, interactions, and transactions made in the ever-expanding virtual reality realm.

Scores of different start-ups are using the data from these extensive digital footprints to market AI versions of ourselves—and even people who have already passed. Some companies already offer chatbots that allow the living to direct message with digital approximations of a deceased loved one. One, called Eternime, is developing an app it claims will generate lifelike animated avatars of deceased friends and loved ones that will speak back and forth with you in what sounds like their voice—as if you're having a FaceTime call with the dead.

Chillingly, you don't even need permission to make an AI version of someone else, since there are few set legal restrictions—beyond trademark laws for celebrities—for Digital Immortality, and there are no commonly agreed upon ethical standards. Meaning, you can use the technology not just to bring grandma back to life, but to generate a copy of the still-living ex-partner who dumped you last year and moved to Seattle. Or you can create a new BFF who looks and sounds an awful lot like Beyoncé. As for what's on the horizon: Transhumanists, or those who believe that someday all our thoughts and memories will be uploaded to computer chips, claim we're only decades away, tech-wise, from going full *Black Mirror* by creating artificial bodies that allow us to outlive our biological ones.

Then there's Facebook, and the mountain of internal data it stores on nearly all of us. As it becomes a bigger and bigger graveyard, it could inevitably weaponize Digital Immortality. What's to stop the company from using all my data it owns—including my direct messages—to sell an AI version of me for my descendants to interact with a century from now? What's to stop the company from doing the same with celebrities, thinkers, artists, and world leaders? Think the Madame Tussauds wax museums, or Disney's animatronic Hall of Presidents, but with infinitely more detail and accuracy. We can only imagine the possibilities. Then what about Twitter? LinkedIn? TikTok? Tinder? Apple? Google? Amazon?

Meanwhile members of the traditional death industry are still try-ing to beat Silicon Valley at its own game. You can imagine how badly that's going. Recently some cemeteries have started selling QR codes for gravestones that can lead smartphone users to a web profile of the grave's occupant. But given mobile technology's changing fast pace, QR codes will likely be obsolete sooner rather than later.* Even the U.S. Department of Veterans Affairs has launched a digital national cem-etery called the Veterans Legacy Memorial. It features profile pages of 4.2 million veterans buried at national cemeteries, allowing people to visit a veteran's grave from an electronic device. Heaven knows how many of our tax dollars went to that venture. It's a slick setup, but a simple Google search of the deceased generally provides a mountain of more substantial, meaningful, and emotionally driven data than the VA's virtual graveyard database, or any actual cemetery gravestone, can.

There's no way around the uncomfortable truth: The rise of Digital Immortality poses an existential threat to cemeteries. Now that crema-tion outpaces interments at a higher rate every year, and social media—and other technologies on the horizon—memorialize people far better than a gravestone can, the need for a dedicated physical space to store your remains grows less and less relevant. But not all is lost.

THE SOLUTION TO cemetery survival might be through the embrace of the organic human community like at Hollywood Forever. Make people plant roots in a burial ground while they're living, and they'll be more inclined to be kept there when they're dead. My visit to Hollywood Forever lasted a few hours—I had some time to kill, so I strolled at my own pace, assessing its appeal. Eventually I made my way over to the easternmost section, where an oval pond, about the size of a soccer field, is the centerpiece. It's surrounded by grass where most, but not all, markers lie flat in the ground. I came upon the newly installed Burt Reynolds bust, staring straight across the water, to an island in the middle, filled by a tall, slim mausoleum of white Georgia

---

* Although QR codes were taken off life support by the COVID pandemic, for restaurant menus, retail shopping, and other contactless and socially distanced interactions.

marble designed to look like an Athenian temple. Past it, guarding the pond's opposite shore, I could spot the guitar-clutching statue of Johnny Ramone. Its unveiling ceremony attracted a crowd of 1,000 spectators.

Hollywood Forever hosts an annual tribute to the late punk rocker organized by Ramone's widow, which includes a public screening of a different one of his favorite movies—like cult classics *The Warriors*, *Barbarella*, *Buffalo '66*, and *Rock 'n' Roll High School*. The cemetery's calendar is constantly filled with events like this. If I had stayed later that day, I could have caught a concert by Josh Ritter, considered one of the best living American songwriters, in the property's century-old Masonic Lodge. If I had arrived the prior evening, I could have watched a preview of the documentary film *I Am Burt Reynolds* shown before his bust's dedication.

Leaving my spot next to Reynolds, I strolled around the pond to the Ramone statue, where a couple of professional photographers had set up tripods to snap pictures. I slid my phone out of my pocket and stood alongside them, mimicking their shooting angles and perspectives to include in the background the temple floating on the pond behind him.

Nearly every cemetery has a superpower—whether it's the location, history, view, occupants, architecture, or something else. Hollywood Forever's is, of course, its stars. You can't swing a dead cat without hitting a celebrity's memorial—like that of steamy black-and-white film star Rudolph Valentino and the voice of Bugs Bunny and other Warner Bros. characters, Mel Blanc, along with film noir star Peter Lorre, gangster Bugsy Siegel, and campy actress Maila Nurmi, better known as Vampira. The celebrity residents bring in the tourist traffic, and customers wanting to be buried—or have their ashes placed—next to greatness. Graves within the proximity of a famous person can go for as much as $250,000. I checked the secondary grave market online—which is a thing—and found a spot on the property near B-list sitcom actress Estelle Getty, who starred in the sitcom *The Golden Girls* and died in 2008, listed for $26,000. Grave sites are sold throughout the country on Craigslist, eBay, and specific grave-selling sites. Most of the time the sales are made by people who have prebought a plot, maybe next to a loved one or near their home, but suddenly need to relocate far away, or they simply want to be cremated or buried elsewhere. Sometimes, with cemeteries that boast a lot of famous people—like Hollywood Forever—grave plot speculation does take place. The price to be in Getty's proximity pales in comparison to the mausoleum space directly above Marilyn Monroe at Westwood Village Memorial Park in Los Angeles, which sold for $4.6 million on eBay in 2009.

While Hollywood Forever's star power gives it notoriety, and real estate cachet to some of its burial plots, the meat of the cemetery's business comes from the surrounding community. They're the ones who will fill most of the columbarium niches and remaining burial spots out of sight of the celebrity resting places. They're the ones who need to be convinced that a cemetery is more appealing and fun as a resting place than simply having their ashes scattered in Santa Monica Bay or in Yosemite National Park, with Facebook serving as their electronic grave markers.

Since Hollywood Forever began its community-oriented approach with its rebranding two decades ago, many other cemeteries have done the same, leveraging their own superpowers. Nearby Evergreen Cemetery in Los Angeles took advantage of its size and proximity to a young, health-conscious population to create a 1.4-mile-long jogging path that has become immensely popular. Congressional Cemetery in Washington, D.C., now derives one-third of its income from charging an annual membership fee that allows the mass of dog owners in its surrounding neighborhood to let their pets off leash among the graves in its thirty-five acres of completely fenced-in grounds. The Woodlands cemetery in Philadelphia, a national historic landmark built in the 1840s that doubles as an arboretum, started a Grave Gardener program that invites people to adopt a grave and maintain a mini garden atop it filled with Victorian-era flowers.

In many ways, this civic-minded approach is a return to the roots of the original rural American cemeteries of the nineteenth century—like Mount Auburn and Green-Wood—which were meant to serve as gathering and recreation places before the creation of urban parks. What's old is new again.

Once I finished snapping my pictures of Johnny Ramone, I found a gravestone that doubles as a bench alongside the pond and sat,

The larger-than-life bust of Burt Reynolds, who died in 2018, stands above the actor's grave, gazing toward the reflecting pool in the Garden of Legends section of Hollywood Forever Cemetery in Los Angeles.

stretching out my legs. Amid the chatter of passersby talking and the occasional squawk from a goose, the sounds from the outside neighborhood drifted over the ivy-covered eastern wall into the cemetery. I heard a car's honk. The buzz of saws from construction work at an apartment building next door. The cacophony of life.

Hollywood Forever and others now find themselves in a death match with the tech world over what it means for a person to be forever memorialized. But I do believe the embrace of flesh-and-blood community can lead to their salvation. No combination of ones and zeros can match the emotional connection we carbon-based life-forms can make with a sense of place, a feeling of belonging to a patch of earth. Yes, for cemeteries, the future is analog.

The bike path entrance to West Laurel Hill Cemetery,
home to the 3.5-acre Nature's Sanctuary, considered
America's greenest natural burial site

17. BACK TO NATURE

Green cemeteries return America's burial practices
to the country's earliest days

—

Nature's Sanctuary, West Laurel Hill Cemetery
Philadelphia, Pennsylvania
Established: 2008

DESPITE WHAT POP culture says, it's not always sunny in Philadelphia. On a particular late-November Saturday morning, a veil of thick clouds draped itself over bare treetops as my wife, Ann Marie, and I jogged past a tiny Victorian-era train station on the edge of town and onto the paved Cynwyd Heritage Trail bike path. The smell of damp woodsmoke whooshed through the air whenever riders pedaled past us.

We set a steady pace on the path, aided by a downhill slope, flanked by the backyards of century-old homes—many built from stones taken from the surrounding landscape. We veered around dog walkers, and well-bundled families out for a stroll. I hoped the exercise would eventually start to warm me up, and maybe burn off a few excess Thanksgiving calories. About a mile into the run, a long stone retaining wall, reminiscent of a castle turret, emerged to our right, the words WEST LAUREL HILL CEMETERY etched into it.

"Ooh, would you look at that!" I said.

Ann Marie deadpanned, "A cemetery. What a surprise."

We veered onto a paved walkway leading into the grounds and took an immediate left on the main, winding perimeter road. It led us upward among grassy, densely filled paddocks of graves dating from the nineteenth century to the present day. West Laurel Hill was established in 1869 and originally designed as a rural cemetery in the spirit of Green-Wood and Mount Auburn. We came there to see its newest portion, a three-acre sliver of green space called Nature's Sanctuary. The site is the result of a decade-long land reclamation effort that began in 2008 and transformed it into the most earth-friendly burial spot in America.

Nature's Sanctuary eliminates nearly all the expensive, eco-hostile burial must-haves placed upon people by the Death Industrial Complex. It forgoes caskets, vaults, embalmment, and gravestones. Its permanent residents are placed into their eternal homes with the sole purpose of their physical essences vanishing into the soil. It stands at the forefront of a larger American artisanal death movement that brings the end of life back to the home and out of hospitals, and interments back to nature.

What's striking about Nature's Sanctuary is how familiar it seems—how this new, modern version of burials takes us full circle to America's earliest colonial days.

A BODY BURIED in America today doesn't actually become food for worms or push up daisies. Typical graves are like mini Superfund sites. America deposits about 4.3 million gallons of toxic embalming fluids— including 800,000 gallons of formaldehyde—into the ground yearly, according to the Green Burial Council. We also inter 20 million board feet of wood, 1.6 million tons of concrete, and 81,000 tons of metal. In addition, human remains contain mercury from fillings, metals from pacemakers and other devices, and potent pharmaceuticals like chemotherapy drugs, which leach into the soil. Then there are the chemical fertilizers, herbicides, and pesticides cemeteries use to keep the grass above the graves looking pristine, which requires regular mowing from exhaust-belching, fossil-fuel-guzzling machines.

However, death doesn't need to turn resting places into mini Chernobyl blooms, as a growing number of burial grounds have begun offering varying degrees of sustainable options. The pioneer of modern, all-natural cemeteries in the United States is Ramsey Creek Preserve, which opened in 1998 in the hills of northwestern South Carolina, near the Chattahoochee-Oconee National Forest. A local couple established Ramsey Creek on a thirty-three-acre piece of overgrown farmland, and its spread has more than doubled in size since.

All graves are hand dug at Ramsey Creek, which is no easy process, as I know from my own limited grave-digging experience. Bodies are placed in a simple shroud or biodegradable casket with no vault for interment. Markers are made of natural stone—if any are placed at a grave site at all. The property protects and encourages the growth of native plants and wildflowers. Only 10 percent of Ramsey Creek can be used for graves or cemetery infrastructure, for sustainability reasons—to leave the rest wild and undisturbed by human hands. In 2006 the cemetery entered into an agreement with a nonprofit land trust to ensure that its expanses will never be developed, regardless of what happens to the operation's management or finances. As a result of these efforts, Ramsey Creek Preserve is not so much a cemetery that doubles as a wild area, but a wild area where people happen to be buried.

Although Ramsey Creek has served as an environmental model for other so-called green cemeteries, its overall financial model isn't so sustainable. It limits burial space to only twenty-one graves per acre, compared to roughly 1,000 in a traditional cemetery—which may work, revenue-wise, on inexpensive land, but would be destined for failure in a pricey real estate market. Besides, an argument could be made that it's more effective from a land-use perspective to cram bodies close together than so far apart. Just like someone converting a diesel car to run on recycled french fry grease, Ramsey Creek is *a* solution to one of our environmental challenges, not *the* solution.

The cemetery's founders tried a more suburban approach by teaming with Hollywood Forever's owner, Tyler Cassity, in 2004. They bought Fernwood Cemetery, a spacious burial ground established in the 1890s in Marin County, California, thirty minutes from the Chapel of the Chimes in Oakland, and created an all-natural burial space on the undeveloped half of its thirty-two acres. Nowhere was more fertile for a natural burial ground than Marin County. Located on the opposite end of the Golden Gate Bridge from San Francisco, it's known as an earth-loving haven for Tesla-driving, graduate-degree-holding tofu eaters.

More than 80 percent of its land area is protected—encompassing national treasures like Point Reyes National Seashore, Muir Woods National Monument redwood forest, and Mount Tamalpais State Park, where mountain biking was invented. Nearly three-quarters of its population of 250,000 lives within a half mile of a park. Marin boasts the highest median family income of any county in California, and its life expectancy of eighty-five years is eight years above the national average.

Cassity used his prodigious marketing talents to garner the same kind of breathless national reporting and publicity for Fernwood that he did initially for Hollywood Forever. But in 2005, the Ramsey Creek owners split from the venture, reportedly because they disagreed with his profit-minded focus, and he took over the entire operation. I made a quick visit there, once, climbing up its steep, narrow main road. I passed the traditional granite graves of the old cemetery, ascended into the new, natural burial area, and stopped at the highest point where the road ended abruptly at a spot called Founders' Forest. Fieldstones that served as grave markers, engraved with names and dates, filled the adjacent slope, canopied by massive old-growth oak trees. A couple of the plots seemed fresh, with the brown, stony soil bare of the brown grass clumps that splotched the terrain, while most showed no trace of a shovel's work.

Like at Ramsey Creek, the resting places there are dug by hand, the bodies placed in them are not embalmed and are encased either in a simple shroud or a biodegradable casket. The graves overlooked an elementary school in the valley below, where I could see kids on the playground and hear their shouts and yells.

Fernwood Cemetery's back-to-earth burial options are a natural extension of the artisanal death movement taking root in Marin County and Sonoma next door. The area has become an epicenter of old-school, custom end-of-life options that circumvent the Death Industrial Complex. There, you can find death midwives, those in the profession of facilitating a person's final passage at home, and coordinators for home funerals who guide families through do-it-yourself cleaning and preparation of the body and memorial services. And there's a local artists' collective specializing in handmade urns and memorial art.

When Fernwood's sustainable spaces first opened in 2004, fewer than two hundred modern natural burials had been performed across the country. The next year, the Green Burial Council, a national non-profit dedicated to promoting and setting environmental standards for eco-friendly burial grounds, was founded. Soon, other sustainable cemeteries opened, and some older, traditional ones—like Mount Auburn, and Congressional Cemetery in Washington, D.C.—established natural-only sections on their grounds. By the end of 2021, there were thirty-one all-natural cemeteries operating in America, and forty-two traditional cemeteries offering green options, with the largest concentrations in the Northeast and on the West Coast.

WEST LAUREL HILL'S Nature's Sanctuary was created on a one-acre nook on the cemetery's northern edge that previously served as a dumping ground. The reclamation effort involved clearing debris, eradicating non-native plants, and adding a layer of fertile topsoil. Its footpaths were surfaced using crushed concrete, and crews installed three honeybee apiaries to pollenate the wildflowers. Its expanse has grown to three acres with enough planned space to fit 1,000 burials.

The hand-dug graves are unmarked, and the site's lone memorial marker is a long granite wall that spans the eastern edge along the main road, with the names of the deceased carved onto the top. Goats live on the property to graze away the encroachment of invasive fauna (sadly, Ann Marie and I didn't see them), and the vegetation on-site is planned to evolve from the current state of meadow flowers and grasses to saplings and eventually to forest.

It took us about five minutes jogging from West Laurel Hill's pedestrian entrance by the bike path to reach Nature's Sanctuary. Several hard-pedaling cyclists, also using the cemetery as a workout space, huffed by. We could hear the soft whoosh of traffic from the nearby interstate highway and smell decaying berries from a ginkgo tree down the hill.

Nature's Sanctuary looked simply like a collection of overgrown wildflower gardens, browned by the late-fall frost and connected by stone-bordered footpaths. One small section lay bare of plants, covered instead by a thick layer of leaf mulch. About one hundred burials had taken place there by the time of our visit, not that one could guess by looking.

In 2018, Nature's Sanctuary became the first and only cemetery space to earn SITES Gold certification, a top honor for sustainable landscapes based on an exhaustive set of earth-friendly standards established by the American Society of Landscape Architects. Despite these modern certifications of sustainability, what's striking about Nature's Sanctuary and the modern natural burial grounds like it is how far they take us back to the past. They're similar in intent to conservation areas such as Sleepy Hollow Cemetery in Concord, Massachusetts, established in the early 1800s with the help of Thoreau and Emerson. They're aimed at protecting land and wildlife from human encroachment, filled with bodies—free of embalming chemicals or vaults or metal caskets—that fully return to the natural realm in perfect transcendental harmony. The gravestones at Fernwood in California are even similar to Emerson's, etched into stone.

In design, modern natural cemeteries hearken back even further into the country's history, to early Jamestown and Plymouth, where the settlers buried the dead in simple shrouds in unmarked spots that the land eventually reclaimed, the exact locations forgotten. Nature's Sanctuary matter-of-factly returns us to the soil without perpetuating the myth that we're somehow lords over nature. Bodies there actually do become food for worms, their impressions on the earth quickly enveloped by soil, dust to dust.

Ann Marie and I walked its paths just long enough for the sweat to start to cool on our backs. I turned to her. "So. What do you think?"

I was breaking our unwritten rule of not discussing our own mortality—and burial options—during a cemetery visit. But in this place, I couldn't resist. She's environmentally conscious enough to make someone from Greenpeace or PETA seem like a shrinking violet. I wanted to know what she thought.

She deflected. "It's definitely interesting. What do *you* think?"

I deflected back. "Over my dead body."

The deep bass of a bell chimed, its *bong-bong-bong* loud enough to break our conversation. The sound must have come from the cemetery's nearby Gothic bell tower, built in 1887, which rings at the top of the hour and during funerals. It seemed like an omen. We walked back onto the main avenue and resumed our jog. I didn't feel ready at that moment to verbalize my own thoughts on weighty cemetery subjects, even as they filled my mind.

I recognize that our burial methods today are unsustainable, and there's no such thing as a truly eternal resting place. All cemeteries fill to capacity someday, and the resources and willpower to keep them going vanish as the generations pass and the names within them are forgotten.* Wait enough time, and one person's burial ground inevitably becomes another's archaeological dig.

It's a positive development that Nature's Sanctuary has come into existence and cremations are outnumbering traditional interments. The monopolistic Death Industrial Complex is too predatory and powerful. The way we preserve ourselves—embalmed and entombed like Egyptian mummies—is too environmentally harmful. And Digital Immortality now allows the body of our lives' experiences to endure in a much more lasting way than a hole in the ground can.

Still, reflexively, the new natural cemeteries violate my ingrained ideal of American individualism, how in death everyone gets a trophy— a little plot of earth to call their own and a gravestone announcing, *I was here.* My own life's actions have been driven, consciously or not, by some vain attempt at leaving a mark, through my role as a parent passing lessons and bad dad jokes on to my kids, as a teacher for much the same reason, as a military officer serving my country and participating in history, and as a writer hoping my words endure.†

On a larger level, think of what a cultural tragedy the demise of modern cemeteries would be. These places flowing with the human spirit, which spread across our landscape in far greater numbers than

---

* Not that this excuses the deliberate destruction or erasure of culturally important cemeteries.
† Except for an online how-to article on manscaping I once wrote. I truly hope those words don't endure.

The author stops during a run to snap a selfie inside the 3.5-acre Nature's Sanctuary, considered America's greenest natural burial site.

all of the Starbucks and McDonald's combined. These unfiltered lenses of truth through which we can view America—from the burial ground at Jamestown, to the enslaved people's graveyard at Monticello, to Boot Hill, Hollywood Forever, and all points in between. I'm riveted by the way each cemetery serves as the protagonist of its own larger-than-life American story. Every time one vanishes, a piece of our country's soul dies. We must celebrate them while we can and pay heed to what they're whispering to us.

But this wasn't the stuff of light conversation during a morning run. At that moment I was simply content to be a passing visitor in a cemetery as my wife and I returned to the bike path, beneath the sun peeking between the clouds in Philadelphia.

EPILOGUE

ON THE MORNING I reported to the navy unit that would dispatch me overseas to Afghanistan, a personnel officer handed me a form to complete. It asked a series of questions spelling out my final wishes in the event of my untimely death. The unit was well-versed in performing memorial services and burials for its members, and this paperwork made the process run more smoothly. It also eased the planning burden on the deceased person's family while steering the send-off to be more of a celebration of life—down to the song to be played in the person's honor after the eulogies.

My song choice came instantly: "Forever Young" by Bob Dylan. The fast version, not the slow one, and definitely not the crappy Rod Stewart song by the same name. When I reached the section on the form covering the final disposition of my body, I paused. Ann Marie and I had never discussed the topic fully. Burial or cremation? I reflexively circled cremation. As for where my ashes should be spread, I scribbled, "Near the top of Old Rag Mountain. In Shenandoah National Park in Virginia. With only my wife and kids present."

The odds of my returning from overseas in a flag-draped coffin were slim, I assumed. My job as a public affairs officer didn't involve blowing stuff up or pointing guns at people. I could pen a killer speech or tweet, but that was about it. I'm a writer, not a fighter. So I wasn't overly concerned with how I filled out the blanks, and my mind wasn't necessarily set on cremation over burial.

I soon embarked on my deployment, and quickly learned there's no such thing as being a part of the war machine while somehow separating yourself from war. Months later I returned home expecting the world to be exactly as I left it. But it wasn't. Nor was I.

I wasn't haunted by recurring flashback images of deaths. That would come later. Instead, I repeatedly awoke panic-stricken over my own mortality and the eyeblink of time we all spend on Earth—whether we're killed in action or live a full, long life. The night became my enemy. I spent a considerable amount of my wide-awake time under the covers dwelling on what should be done with my body. Would it truly be cremation? The thought of my physical self—which I've worked so hard to keep in shape, healthy, and alive—being turned to dust in minutes within a 2,000-degree blaze seemed so, I don't know, final.

How about a traditional cemetery? I like hanging out in them, clearly, but did I want to enter into a permanent relationship with one? There's the cemetery at the United States Naval Academy that I used to run past nearly every day during the four years I taught there. And the hilly, rural-style one in Asheville, North Carolina—a town I love. And Shawsheen, in my old hometown.

No, I didn't want to go the traditional burial route, as much as I understand how and why other people do. Embalming didn't appeal to me because I don't want someone injecting chemicals into my veins, nor did the expense of being dropped into a casket and hermetically sealed in an underground vault. As for natural burial, I like that it's the most earth-friendly alternative, and the most divorced from the clutches of the Death Industrial Complex. It's tempting, but ultimately, no. I didn't want to occupy space after I passed.

So cremation it was, then. As for a resting place, a columbarium turned me off for the same environmental, space-saving reasons traditional burial did. Cemeteries, mausoleums, tombs, and columbaria are amazing cultural artifacts. They're even worthy of books being written about them. They're just not quite the final home for me, despite my natural American desire to get a trophy for dying.

I contemplated Old Rag Mountain, my reflexive choice on the form. When Ann Marie and I started dating, we both moved to the D.C. area after graduation for work. Our first overnight hiking adventure—which she planned—took us into Shenandoah National Park to the top of Old Rag, a couple of hours from the city. Its bare, rocky, 3,400-foot-high peak offers views in every direction of the Blue Ridge Mountains, soft-ened by 470 million years of wind, snow, and rain. In the fall, as the leaves turn orange and red, the scenery looks as if it's aflame. When we were in our mid-twenties, we quit our jobs and spent four months backpacking 1,400 miles on the Appalachian Trail, which she planned, from Georgia to Connecticut. My favorite stretch was the 120 miles through Shenandoah National Park.

Old Rag makes me think of Ann Marie. It evokes happiness. I announced to her one evening, in the middle of dinner, that if the situ-ation arises, I wanted my ashes spread near the top of Old Rag Mountain with just her and the kids present. No need for ceremony.

She nodded and said nothing. It was decided.

Of course, there's no guarantee my final wishes will come to frui-tion. I could fall off a boat and get eaten by a whale, never to be seen again. Ann Marie could decide it's easier to dump my ashes into the Delaware River, or store them on a bookshelf in the living room next to the urn of our old hound dog. She could, on a whim—and I don't put it past her—donate my body to science or have it composted. Or some unfortunate series of events could arise, causing my remains to be sent to a potter's field like the one at Hart Island in New York City. After I breathe my last breath, will I really know or care what happens to my body?

Besides, the traditions surrounding the ultimate disposition of our bodies—how and where we place them—aren't etched in stone. They're dictated by ever-changing cultural, political, and spiritual trends. The burial practices of the 1620s, versus the 1820s, versus today (including cremations) all look immensely different.

If there's one lesson I've learned, starting with that summer job digging graves at Shawsheen Cemetery through my many tombstone travels, and finally in writing these pages, it's this: What's most sacred in this world isn't what happens to our bodies after death, but how and for whom we live our lives.

St. Louis Cemetery No. 1, known as the City of the Dead, in New Orleans.

APPENDIX

Three More Heart-Stopping Historic Cemeteries

—

St. Louis Cemetery No. 1
New Orleans, Louisiana
Established: 1789

BLOW OFF THE beignets and the bands blaring on Bourbon Street. Any trip to New Orleans should begin at the Southern Gothic resting place St. Louis Cemetery No. 1. Nicknamed the "city of the dead," its serpentine avenues are crowded by breathtakingly weathered above-ground tombs and mausoleums of varying size and levels of disrepair (and despair).

St. Louis No. 1 was the first major North American cemetery to be built untethered from a churchyard. Occupying about a city block, it was established on an unwanted piece of swampland fringing what, at that time, was the edge of town, when Louisiana was still a Spanish colony. Local leaders wanted to keep the new burial ground away from populated areas, out of fear that crowded graveyards would spread disease through the region's tropical air and water. The first interments were underground, but the high water table quickly rejected the idea and the coffins along with it.

Cincinnati's pastoral Spring Grove Cemetery, where the "lawn plan"
cemetery design was created.

Spring Grove Cemetery
Cincinnati, Ohio
Established: 1845

NEARLY EVERY MODERN American cemetery owes its look and layout to the grassy, tree-garnished expanses of 733-acre Spring Grove in Cincinnati. Its open "lawn plan" design—the masterwork of landscape architect Adolph Strauch—revolutionized the facade of the country's burial grounds. Spring Grove was originally intended to mimic the woodsy, eclectic rural designs of Mount Auburn in Massachusetts and Green-Wood in New York, featuring a mix of plots, plantings, mausoleums, and monuments. But when Strauch arrived as superintendent in 1855 he immediately began to economize the look, cost of upkeep, and price for burial in a new way.

He ripped down the ornate fences, hedges, and plantings that divided family plots. He removed overly ostentatious memorials, set size standards for gravestones, and lined the plots in symmetrical order. He carpeted the grounds with swathes of turf, shaded by a vast array of decorative trees and sprinkled with placid ponds. The parklike setting was more inviting to the public and enabled easier upkeep thanks to the newly invented power lawnmower. Strauch's Spring Grove instantly became a popular picnic destination and international tourist sensation—more than a decade before New York City's completion of Central Park, in 1876, which sparked the country's urban park movement.

The Carrie Eliza Getty Tomb, one of Chicago's most treasured architectural marvels, at Graceland Cemetery on the city's North Side.

Graceland Cemetery
Chicago, Illinois
Established: 1860

AT LEAFY GRACELAND Cemetery on the Chicago's North Side, the history of modern American architecture comes alive like absolutely nowhere else. Portions of its rural-style grounds were designed by William Le Baron Jenney, known for designing and building the world's first steel-framed skyscraper. And during the late nineteenth and early twentieth centuries, Graceland's 119 shady acres served as a creative testing ground and public competition arena between some of the country's most influential architects—all vying to outdo each other through the tombs, monuments, and mausoleums they were commissioned to create for the city's elite families.

Graceland's most breathtaking marvel is the arched Carrie Eliza Getty Tomb, built in 1890. The flat-topped cube-shaped limestone structure was designed by Louis Sullivan, called the "prophet of modern American architecture." He pioneered a new poetry of form in urban buildings that broke free from the historic Gothic, Renaissance, and Classical styles, and is still emulated today.

ACKNOWLEDGMENTS

PROFOUND THANKS ARE due to many people for their contributions to this book's completion. First, thank you, Ann Marie, Greer, and Kai for your patience during the entire research and writing process. (Although I'd like to add a small "you're welcome" for all of the side excursions to graveyards that have no doubt made your lives richer and more interesting.) Thanks next to superagent Lindsay Edgecombe for her patience, input, and unwavering support, and Daniel Greenberg for leading her the book's way.

I'm grateful to all the people who didn't run away screaming when I told them I was writing a book about graveyards and asked for their help. Naida García-Crespo constantly encouraged (and forced) me to work on the original proposal, unafraid to tell me in painfully clear terms what needed to be fixed until it reached a semi-presentable final product. Mike Parker, a walking encyclopedia of graveyard knowledge, was equally as supportive and helpful. Amy Kover Lox, my first editor—at the Kenyon College newspaper when we were undergrads—volunteered to reprise her role a couple of decades (or more) later as an early reader, for which I am eternally grateful. John Gans was the project's biggest cheerleader throughout the long process.

John Beckman and Jarrod Suess tolerated my randomly texting them draft sentences without responding with too much snark. Michelle Allen-Emerson, Charles Nolan, and Mark McWilliams always kindly pretended to care when I'd corner them to deliver, unsolicited, some long-winded graveyard story in the English Department's halls at the United States Naval Academy. Jason Shaffer and Phil Garrow often bore the brunt of my writing frustrations by receiving direct messages from me ranting about some ridiculous, completely unrelated tangent. Mary Senoyuit and Nicole Uchida were early readers whose time and insights I greatly appreciated (although Nicole had to be fired because she was too consistently positive in her feedback). I stopped asking Margaret Sullivan to read passages because her commentary was so incisive that I felt dumb. The hack consulting firm of Burke, Bogardus, Parsons, and Scroppo receive my eternal gratitude and loyalty. Members of the Circle of Trust (Burger, Farrant, Kibby, McVeigh) don't warrant a mention here, but they get one anyway.

Jeanine and John Persano and Lisa and Andrew Cope kindly provided much-needed logistical support during the research process.

Thanks finally to Zack Knoll, whose keen editorial talents made the book immeasurably better, and Jamison Stoltz for giving *Over My Dead Body* a wonderful home at Abrams Press.

BIBLIOGRAPHY

ADDITIONAL READING/INVALUABLE RESOURCES

Mitford, Jessica. *The American Way of Death Revisited.* New York: Vintage Books, 2000.

Sloane, David Charles. *The Last Great Necessity: Cemeteries in American History (Creating the North American Landscape).* Baltimore: Johns Hopkins University Press, 1995.

CHAPTER 1

"Ancient Human Remains Come from Montana Ancestor of Most Native Americans." Montana Public Radio, 2 Feb. 2014, mtpr.org/montana-news/2014-02-12/ancient -human-remains-come-from-montana-ancestor-of-most-native-americans.

Attreed, Lorraine C. "Preparation for Death in Sixteenth Century Northern England." *The Sixteenth Century Journal* 13, no. 3 (1982): 37–66. doi.org/10.2307/2539604.

Balter, Michael. "Native Americans Descend from Ancient Montana Boy." *Science*, 12 Feb. 2014, science.org/content/article/native-americans-descend-ancient -montana-boy.

Brown, David. "Burial Ground Yields New Clues About Jamestown Life." *Washington Post*, 6 Apr. 2001, washingtonpost.com/archive/politics/2001/04/06/burial-ground -yields-new-clues-about-jamestown-life/de321eef-2a6f-4d6d-be60-04b87c182dc2.

Colonial Ghosts. "The Graves of the Powhatan." 30 Aug. 2017, colonialghosts.com /the-graves-of-the-powhatan.

Curry, Andrew. "Ancient Egyptian 'Funeral Home' Was One-Stop Shop for the Afterlife." *National Geographic*, 3 May 2021, nationalgeographic.com/history/article/ancient -egyptian-funeral-home-one-stop-shop-afterlife.

Dunning, Hayley. "A History of Burial in London." Natural History Museum, accessed 18 Jan. 2022, nhm.ac.uk/discover/a-history-of-burial-in-london.html.

French, Brett. "Child's Remains, Artifacts from Oldest-Known Burial Site in North America Are from Same Era, Study Shows." *Billings Gazette*, 19 June 2018, billingsgazette.com /news/state-and-regional/montana/childs-remains-artifacts-from-oldest-known -burial-site-in-north-america-are-from-same-era/article_bodddf0e-40da-56d2-8d49 -0006888e0298.html.

Historic Jamestowne. "Captain's Burial." Accessed 18 Jan. 2022, historicjamestowne .org/archaeology/map-of-discoveries/captains-burial.

Moskowitz, Clara. "The Secret Tomb of China's 1st Emperor: Will We Ever See Inside?" LiveScience, 17 Aug. 2012, livescience.com/22454-ancient-chinese-tomb-terracotta-warriors.html.

Muir, Hazel. "Pyramid Precision." *New Scientist*, 15 Nov. 2000, newscientist.com/article/dn174-pyramid-precision.

Nadel, Dani, Avinoam Danin, Robert C. Power, Arlene M. Rosen, Fanny Bocquentin, Alexander Tsatskin, Danny Rosenberg, Reuven Yeshurun, Lior Weissbrod, Noemi R. Rebollo, Omry Barzilai, and Elisabetta Boaretto. "Earliest Floral Grave Lining from 13,700–11,700-y-old Natufian Burials at Raqefet Cave, Mt. Carmel, Israel." *Proceedings of the National Academy of Sciences* 110, no. 29 (2013): 11774–78.

National Museum of Natural History. "A Highly Unusual Case." Accessed 18 Jan. 2022, naturalhistory.si.edu/education/teaching-resources/written-bone/forensic-case-files/highly-unusual-case.

O'Brien, Jane. "'Proof' Jamestown Settlers Turned to Cannibalism." BBC News, 1 May 2013, bbc.com/news/world-us-canada-22362831.

Rasmussen, Morten, Sarah L. Anzick, and Eske Willerslev. "The Genome of a Late Pleistocene Human from a Clovis Burial Site in Western Montana." *Nature* 506, no. 7487 (2014): 225–29, doi.org/10.1038/nature13025.

Rolfe, John. "'Twenty and Odd Negroes'; an Excerpt from a Letter from John Rolfe to Sir Edwin Sandys (1619/1620) – Encyclopedia Virginia." *Encyclopedia Virginia*, encyclopediavirginia.org/entries/twenty-and-odd-negroes-an-excerpt-from-a-letter-from-john-rolfe-to-sir-edwin-sandys-1619-1620. Accessed 19 Feb. 2022.

Stromberg, Joseph. "Starving Settlers in Jamestown Colony Resorted to Cannibalism." *Smithsonian Magazine*, 30 Apr. 2013, smithsonianmag.com/history/starving-settlers-in-jamestown-colony-resorted-to-cannibalism-46000815.

Wilford, John Noble. "With Escorts to the Afterlife, Pharaohs Proved Their Power." *New York Times*, 16 Mar. 2004, nytimes.com/2004/03/16/science/with-escorts-to-the-afterlife-pharaohs-proved-their-power.html.

CHAPTER 2

Bennett, M. K. "The Food Economy of the New England Indians, 1605–75." *Journal of Political Economy* 63, no. 5 (1955): 369–97, doi.org/10.1086/257706.

Bongiovanni, Domenica. "What Happened to the Thousands of Artifacts, Human Bones the FBI Found on Indiana Farm." *Indianapolis Star*, last modified 28 Feb. 2019, indystar.com/story/entertainment/arts/2019/02/27/what-happened-don-miller-artifacts-fbi-found-indiana-farm/2990542002.

Boston Research Center. "Native American Executions on Boston Common." Accessed 18 Jan. 2022, bostonresearchcenter.org/projects_files/eob/single-entry-executions.html.

Breed, Allen. "Some See Irony in Virus' Impact on Mayflower Commemoration." *Washington Post*, 22 Sept. 2020, www.washingtonpost.com/health/some-see-irony-in-covids-impact-on-mayflower-commemoration/2020/09/22/0c365f88-fc92-11ea-b0e4-350e4e60cc91_story.html.

Delabarre, Edmund B., and Harris H. Wilder. "Indian Corn-Hills in Massachusetts." *American Anthropologist* 22, no. 3 (July–September 1920): 203–25, doi.org/10.1525 /aa.1920.22.3.02a00010.

Devereaux, Ryan. "The Border Patrol Invited the Press to Watch It Blow Up a National Monument." *Intercept*, 27 Feb. 2020, theintercept.com/2020/02/27/border-wall -construction-organ-pipe-explosion.

Dickinson, Elizabeth Evitts. "The Endless Robbing of Native American Graves." *Washington Post*, 8 July 2021, washingtonpost.com/magazine/2021/07/08/will-mass -robbery-native-american-graves-ever-end.

Goodwin, John. *The Pilgrim Republic: An Historical Review of the Colony of New Plymouth; With Sketches of the Rise of Other New England Settlements, the History of Congregationalism, and the Creeds of the Period.* London: Forgotten Books, 2018.

Harrigan, Stephen. "First Encounter." HistoryNet, accessed 21 Feb. 2022, historynet .com/first-encounter.htm.

History.com Editors. "King Philip's War Ends." History.com, last modified 20 Sept. 2021, history.com/this-day-in-history/king-philips-war-ends.

Lang, John S. "Guess Who's Not Coming to Thanksgiving Dinner." *Washington Post*, 21 Nov. 1989, washingtonpost.com/archive/lifestyle/wellness/1989/11/21/guess -whos-not-coming-to-thanksgiving-dinner/e951a901-2cd7-41a0-afa7-15f044e11bae.

Little, Becky. "A Few Things You (probably) Don't Know about Thanksgiving." *National Geographic*, 20 Nov. 2018, nationalgeographic.com/history/article/151121-first -thanksgiving-pilgrims-native-americans-wampanoag-saints-and-strangers.

Maffly, Brian, Matt Canham, and Zak Podmore. "Biden Is Poised to Expand Bears Ears and Grand Staircase Monuments. The Real Question Is by How Much?" *Salt Lake Tribune*, 11 Apr. 2021, sltrib.com/news/environment/2021/04/11/biden-is-poised -expand.

Mann, Charles C. "Native Intelligence." *Smithsonian Magazine*, Dec. 2005, smithsonian mag.com/history/native-intelligence-109314481.

Marr, John S., and John T. Cathey. "New Hypothesis for Cause of Epidemic among Native Americans, New England, 1616–1619." *Emerging Infectious Diseases* 16, no. 2 (2010): 281–86.

Medrano, Lourdes. "The Border Wall Has Been 'Absolutely Devastating' for People and Wildlife." *Audubon Magazine*, Winter 2020, audubon.org/magazine/winter-2020 /the-border-wall-has-been-absolutely-devastating.

Midtrød, Tom Arne. "'Calling for More Than Human Vengeance': Desecrating Native Graves in Early America." *Early American Studies: An Interdisciplinary Journal* 17, no. 3 (Summer 2019): 281–314.

Mourt's Relation: A Journal of the Pilgrims at Plymouth. United States, 1849.

National Park Service. "Native American Graves Protection and Repatriation Act." Accessed 18 Jan. 2022, nps.gov/subjects/nagpra/index.htm.

New England Historical Society. "Exactly How New England's Indian Population Was Decimated." Accessed 18 Jan. 2022, newenglandhistoricalsociety.com/exactly-new -englands-indian-population-decimated.

Ostler, Jeffrey. "Disease Has Never Been Just Disease for Native Americans." *The Atlantic*, 29 Apr. 2020, theatlantic.com/ideas/archive/2020/04/disease-has-never-been-just-disease-native-americans/610852.

Philbrick, Nathaniel. *Mayflower: A Story of Courage, Community, and War.* New York: Viking, 2006.

CHAPTER 3

Abrahams, Edmund. "Some Notes on the Early History of the Sheftalls of Georgia." *Publications of the American Jewish Historical Society* 17 (1909): 167–86, www.jstor.org/stable/43057798.

Amanik, Allan. *Dust to Dust: A History of Jewish Death and Burial in New York.* New York: NYU Press, 2019.

Berkovitz, Jay R. "The French Revolution and the Jews: Assessing the Cultural Impact." *AJS Review* 20, no. 1 (1995): 25–86. Crossref, https://doi.org/10.1017/s0364009400006309.

Barazesh, Solmaz. "Probing Question: Was Christopher Columbus Jewish?" Pennsylvania State University, last modified 11 Nov. 2013, psu.edu/news/research/story/probing-question-was-christopher-columbus-jewish.

Borschel-Dan, Amanda. "Christopher Columbus—the Hidden Jew?" *Times of Israel*, 9 Oct. 2018, timesofisrael.com/christopher-columbus-the-hidden-jew.

Chabad.org. "Proverbs, Chapter 22." Accessed 19 Feb. 2022, chabad.org/library/bible_cdo/aid/16393.

Congregation Shearith Israel. "Chatham Square Cemetery." Accessed 18 Jan. 2022, shearithisrael.org/content/chatham-square-cemetery.

———. "Congregational History." Accessed 18 Jan. 2022, shearithisrael.org/content/congregational-history.

Davis, Kenneth C. "America's True History of Religious Tolerance." *Smithsonian Magazine*, Oct. 2010, smithsonianmag.com/history/americas-true-history-of-religious-tolerance-61312684.

Epstein, Kayla. "The Disturbing History of Vandalizing Jewish Cemeteries." *Washington Post*, 21 Feb. 2017, washingtonpost.com/news/acts-of-faith/wp/2017/02/21/the-disturbing-history-of-vandalizing-jewish-cemeteries.

Feldberg, Michael, PhD. "New Amsterdam's Jewish Crusader." Jewish Virtual Library, accessed 18 Jan. 2022, jewishvirtuallibrary.org/new-amsterdam-s-jewish-crusader.

Harris, Kathryn. "Moses Seixas." George Washington's Mount Vernon, accessed 18 Jan. 2022, mountvernon.org/library/digitalhistory/digital-encyclopedia/article/moses-seixas.

Israel, Jonathan. "Religious Toleration in Dutch Brazil (1624–1654)." In *The Expansion of Tolerance: Religion in Dutch Brazil (1624–1654)*, edited by Jonathan Israel and Stuart Schwartz. Amsterdam: Amsterdam University Press, 2007.

Karp, Abraham J. *Jewish Continuity in America: Creative Survival in a Free Society.* Tuscaloosa, AL: University of Alabama Press, 2015.

Langham, Barker. "Jewish Burial Grounds: Understanding Values." Historic England, 18 Oct. 2017, historicengland.org.uk/research/results/reports/74-2016.

Lazarus, Emma. "The New Colossus." Poetry Foundation, 1883, www.poetryfoundation
.org/poems/46550/the-new-colossus.

———. "In the Jewish Synagogue at Newport." Religion in America, 1883, religionin
america.org/rahp_objects/in-the-jewish-synagogue-at-newport.

National Park Service. "Royal Charter (1644–1663)." Accessed 18 Jan. 2022, nps.gov
/rowi/learn/historyculture/charter.htm.

O'Callaghan, Edmund Bailey, and Berthold Fernow. *The Records of New Amsterdam from
1653 to 1674 Anno Domini.* Nabu Press, 2010.

Oppenheim, Samuel. *The Early History of the Jews in New York, 1654–1664.* New York,
1909.

Roberts, Sam. "Podcast: Our Dutch Heritage" [New York, NY]. *New York Times,* 7 July
2017, cityroom.blogs.nytimes.com/2008/09/25/podcast-our-dutch-heritage.

Temkin, Sefton D. "Cemetery." Jewish Virtual Library, accessed 18 Jan. 2022, jewish
virtuallibrary.org/cemetery.

Washington, George. George Washington to the Hebrew Congregation in Newport, Rhode
Island, 18 Aug. 1790. In *July–November 1790,* ed. Dorothy Twohig. Volume 6 of *The
Papers of George Washington.* Charlottesville, VA: University of Virginia Press, 1996.

Wertheimer, Jack. *The American Synagogue: A Sanctuary Transformed.* New York: Cambridge University Press, 2003.

Wiznitzer, Arnold. "The Exodus from Brazil and Arrival in New Amsterdam of the Jewish Pilgrim Fathers, 1654." *Publications of the American Jewish Historical Society* 44,
no. 2 (December 1954): 80–97, jstor.org/stable/43058879.

CHAPTER 4

Associated Press. "Slave Cemetery Poses Questions for Country Club in Florida's capital
City." NBC News, 26 Dec. 2019, nbcnews.com/news/us-news/slave-cemetery-poses
-questions-country-club-florida-s-capital-city-n1107236.

Gamerman, Ellen. "Slaves' Remains Reveal Stories of Their Ordeal: Howard Collection
Oldest in N. America." *Baltimore Sun,* 10 Feb. 1997, baltimoresun.com/news/bs
-xpm-1997-02-10-1997041013-story.html.

Hacker, J. David. "From '20. and Odd' to 10 Million: The Growth of the Slave Population
in the United States." *Slavery & Abolition* 41, no. 4 (2020): 840–55, doi.org/10.1080
/0144039X.2020.1755502.

Jefferson, Thomas. Thomas Jefferson to Thomas Mann Randolph, 23 Jan. 1801. Founders Online, accessed 18 Jan. 2022, founders.archives.gov/documents/Jefferson/01
-32-02-0354.

———. Thomas Jefferson to James Lyle, 10 July 1795. Accessed 19 Feb. 2022, tjrs
.monticello.org/letter/156.

Kazek, Kelly. "When You Visit These 4 Public Places in Alabama, You're Probably
Walking across Graves." AL.com, last modified 13 Jan. 2019, al.com/living/2015/02
/when_you_visit_these_4_public.html.

McGill, Kevin. "As Shell Preserves Louisiana Slave Burial Ground, Question Persists:
Where Are the Rest?" *The Advocate,* 14 June 2018, theadvocate.com/baton_rouge
/news/article_5a1abofa-6fdb-11e8-b6d6-932aad7138e2.html.

Monticello. "Enslaved Families of Monticello." Accessed 18 Jan. 2022, monticello.org
    /slavery/paradox-of-liberty/enslaved-families-of-monticello.
———. "James Hubbard." Accessed 18 Jan. 2022, monticello.org/site/research-and
    -collections/james-hubbard.
———. "Jefferson's Attitudes Toward Slavery." Accessed 19 Feb. 2022, www.monticello
    .org/thomas-jefferson/jefferson-slavery.
———. "The Life of Sally Hemings." Accessed 18 Jan. 2022, monticello.org
    /sallyhemings.
———. "Monticello Affirms Thomas Jefferson Fathered Children with Sally Hemings."
    Accessed 18 Jan. 2022, monticello.org/thomas-jefferson/jefferson-slavery/thomas
    -jefferson-and-sally-hemings-a-brief-account/monticello-affirms-thomas-jefferson
    -fathered-children-with-sally-hemings.
———. "Nailery." Accessed 18 Jan. 2022, monticello.org/site/research-and-collections
    /nailery.
National Archives. "Executive Order 10631—Code of Conduct for Members of the
    Armed Forces of the United States." 15 Aug. 2016, www.archives.gov/federal
    -register/codification/executive-order/1063.
Oldham, James. James Oldham to Thomas Jefferson, 26 Nov. 1804. Founders Online,
    accessed 18 Jan. 2022, founders.archives.gov/documents/Jefferson/99-01-02-0722.
Perry, Douglas. "Do You Know Where the Bodies Are Buried? The Common Phrase's
    Dark Hollywood Origins." *Oregonian*, 2 June 2015, www.oregonlive.com/movies
    /2015/06/do_you_know_where_the_bodies_a.html.
Truscott, Lucian K. "Children of Monticello." *American Heritage* 52, no. 1 (Feb./Mar.
    2001), americanheritage.com/children-monticello.
Wiencek, Henry. "The Dark Side of Thomas Jefferson." *Smithsonian Magazine*, Oct.
    2012, smithsonianmag.com/history/the-dark-side-of-thomas-jefferson-35976004.
Williams, Yohuru. "Why Thomas Jefferson's Anti-Slavery Passage Was Removed from
    the Declaration of Independence." History.com, 29 June 2020, history.com/news
    /declaration-of-independence-deleted-anti-slavery-clause-jefferson.

CHAPTER 5

Bigelow, Jacob. *A History of the Cemetery of Mount Auburn, Scholar's Choice Edition.*
    Wolcott, NY: Scholar's Choice, 2015.
Doyle, Arthur Conan. *Our American Adventure (Cambridge Scholars Publishing Classics
    Texts)*. New edition, CSP Classic Texts, 2009.
Emerson, Ralph Waldo. *Emerson in His Journals.* Edited by Joel Porte. Cambridge, MA:
    Harvard University Press, 1982.
Fondation Napoleon. "Père Lachaise Cemetery." Accessed 18 Jan. 2022, napoleon.org
    /en/magazine/places/pere-lachaise-cemetery.
Giguere, Joy M. "Localism and Nationalism in the City of the Dead: The Rural Cemetery
    Movement in the Antebellum South." *Journal of Southern History* 84, no. 4 (Nov.
    2018): 845–82, doi.org/10.1353/soh.2018.0244.
Goldsmith, Oliver. "The Deserted Village." Poetry Foundation, 1950, www.poetry
    foundation.org/poems/44292/the-deserted-village.

Kendrick, Stephen. *The Lively Place: Mount Auburn, America's First Garden Cemetery, and Its Revolutionary and Literary Residents*. Boston: Beacon Press, 2016.

Lee, Pamela M. "On the Holes of History: Gordon Matta-Clark's Work in Paris." *October* 85 (Summer 1998): 65–89, doi.org/10.2307/779183.

Linden-Ward, Blanche. *Silent City on a Hill: Landscapes of Memory and Boston's Mount Auburn Cemetery*. Columbus, OH: Ohio State University Press, 1989.

Manning, Robert. *History of the Massachusetts Horticultural Society. 1829–1878*. Boston: Printed for the Society, 1880, doi.org/10.5962/bhl.title.139737.

Meier, Allison C. "How the Paris Catacombs Solved a Cemetery Crisis." *JSTOR Daily*, 23 July 2019, daily.jstor.org/how-the-paris-catacombs-solved-a-cemetery-crisis.

Mount Auburn Cemetery. "Boston Courier's Account of the Consecration." Accessed 19 Feb. 2022, mountauburn.org/boston-courier-account-of-the-consecration.

———. "Joseph Story's Consecration Address." Accessed 19 Feb. 2022, mountauburn .org/joseph-storys-consecration-address.

The Picturesque Pocket Companion, and Visitor's Guide, Through Mount Auburn: Illustrated with Upwards of Sixty Engravings on Wood. Boston, 1839.

Saifulina, Nuriya. "Harvard's Habeas Corpus: Grave Robbing at Harvard Medical School." *Harvard Crimson*, 28 Sept. 2017, thecrimson.com/article/2017/9/28/grave -robbers.

Wakeman, Rosemary. "Fascinating Les Halles." *French Politics, Culture & Society* 25, no. 2 (1 June 2007), doi.org/10.3167/fpcs.2007.250205.

CHAPTER 6

Academy of American Poets. "A Guide to Walt Whitman's Leaves of Grass." Accessed 19 Feb. 2022, poets.org/text/guide-walt-whitmans-leaves-grass.

Cleaveland, Nehemiah. *Green-Wood, a Directory for Visitors*. New York, 1850.

Della Zazzera, Elizabeth. "Walt Whitman's Brooklyn." *Lapham's Quarterly*, 26 June 2019, laphamsquarterly.org/whitman-brooklyn/index.html.

Dunlap, David W. "For Historic Cemeteries, New Chapters." *New York Times*, 2 June 2002, nytimes.com/2002/06/02/realestate/for-historic-cemeteries-new-chapters .html.

Eaton, Leslie. "Hoping to Lure a Livelier Crowd; Historic Graveyard in Brooklyn Wants Tourists to Stroll Its Lawns." *New York Times*, 29 Aug. 1999, nytimes.com /1999/08/29/nyregion/hoping-lure-livelier-crowd-historic-graveyard-brooklyn -wants-tourists-stroll-its.html.

Giguere, Joy M. "'Too Mean to Live, and Certainly in No Fit Condition to Die': Vandalism, Public Misbehavior, and the Rural Cemetery Movement." *Journal of the Early Republic* 38, no. 2 (Summer 2018): 293–324, doi.org/10.1353/jer.2018.0028.

Green-Wood Cemetery (website). Accessed 19 Jan. 2022, green-wood.com.

Hellman, Peter. "Where History Is at Rest." *New York Times*, 6 Sept. 1996, nytimes .com/1996/09/06/arts/where-history-is-at-rest.html.

Henderson, Desirée. "'What Is the Grass?': The Roots of Walt Whitman's Cemetery Meditation." *Walt Whitman Quarterly Review* 25, no. 3 (2008): 89–107, doi .org/10.13008/2153-3695.1841.

Margolies, Jane. "Real Estate for the Afterlife." *New York Times*, 15 Mar. 2019, nytimes
.com/2019/03/15/realestate/real-estate-for-the-afterlife.html.

Meade, Natalie. "Unearthing Black History at Green-Wood Cemetery." *New Yorker*,
6 Mar. 2019, newyorker.com/culture/culture-desk/unearthing-black-history-at
-green-wood-cemetery.

Mondello, Bob. "A History of Museums, 'The Memory of Mankind.'" NPR, 24 Nov.
2008, npr.org/templates/story/story.php?storyId=97377145.

Pitman, Bonnie. "Muses, Museums, and Memories." *Daedalus* 128, no. 3 (Summer
1999): 1–31, jstor.org/stable/20027565.

Strong, George Templeton. *The Diary of George Templeton Strong*. University of Washington Press, 1988.

Voorsanger, Catherine Hoover, and John K. Howat, eds. *Art and the Empire City:
New York, 1825–1861*. New York: Metropolitan Museum of Art, 2000. Exhibition
catalog.

Wadler, Joyce. "PUBLIC LIVES; The Cemetery as Destination, and Not the Final One."
New York Times, 25 June 2002, nytimes.com/2002/06/25/nyregion/public-lives-the
-cemetery-as-destination-and-not-the-final-one.html.

Whitman, Walt. "Song of Myself (1892 Version)." Poetry Foundation, www.poetry
foundation.org/poems/45477/song-of-myself-1892-version.

———. *Walt Whitman's Selected Journalism*. Edited by Douglas A. Noverr and Jason
Stacy. Iowa City, IA: University of Iowa Press, 2014.

Williams, Tate. "In the Garden Cemetery: The Revival of America's First Urban Parks."
American Forests Magazine, Spring/Summer 2014, americanforests.org/magazine
/article/in-the-garden-cemetery-the-revival-of-americas-first-urban-parks.

CHAPTER 7

Catron, Susan, ed. *Stories from Our Souls: The Living Narratives of Savannah's Burial
Grounds*. Savannah, GA: Savannah Morning News, 2016, issuu.com/christopher
sweat/docs/storiesfromoursouls.

Dart, Tom. "'Racism from Cradle to Grave': Texas Cemetery Sued for 'Whites Only' Policy." *Guardian*, 6 May 2016, theguardian.com/us-news/2016/may/06/san-domingo
-cemetery-texas-hispanic-lawsuit.

Fandos, Nicholas. "At 2 Georgetown Cemeteries, History in Black and White." *New York
Times*, 20 Oct. 2016, nytimes.com/2016/10/21/us/georgetown-washington-mount
-zion-oak-hill-cemetery.html.

Gamerman, Ellen. "Black Cemetery Now a Place of Remembrance." *Baltimore Sun*,
28 Nov. 1994, baltimoresun.com/news/bs-xpm-1994-11-28-1994332060-story.html.

Hayes-Williams, Janice. "Our Legacy: Brewer Hill Cemetery in Annapolis Needs Our
Help." *Capital Gazette*, 12 Aug. 2016, capitalgazette.com/opinion/columns/ph-ac
-ce-column-williams-0812-20160810-story.html.

Hern, Nelson. "When the Area's White Lynch Mob Acted." *Washington Post*, 20 Dec.
2001, washingtonpost.com/archive/local/2001/12/20/when-the-areas-white-lynch
-mob-acted/a3270dd2-7102-46b3-b339-8b965f6e365f.

Holley, Peter. "A Segregated Cemetery Divides a Texas Town: 'That Should Have Been Taken Out 75 Years Ago.'" *Washington Post*, 7 June 2016, washingtonpost.com/news /post-nation/wp/2016/06/07/a-segregated-cemetery-divides-a-texas-town-that -should-have-been-taken-out-75-years-ago.

James, Jacqueline B. "A Plot of History Crumbling." *Washington Post*, 16 Nov. 1989, washingtonpost.com/archive/local/1989/11/16/a-plot-of-history-crumbling /419d3a69-e704-4664-a120-e39dc7b2bd7b.

McConnaughey, Janet. "Cemetery Changes Contract after Black Deputy Denied Burial." AP News, 29 Jan. 2021, apnews.com/article/race-and-ethnicity-louisiana-1bc5dd398 b17fc70d69062a3b05bd508.

McGreevy, Nora. "New Legislation Seeks to Protect the U.S' Historic Black Cemeteries." *Smithsonian Magazine*, 29 Dec. 2020, www.smithsonianmag.com/smart-news /legislation-protect-african-american-burial-grounds-passes-senate-180976642.

Mount Zion/Female Union Band Society Cemetery (website). Accessed 19 Jan. 2022, mtzion-fubs.org.

Oak Hill Cemetery (website). Accessed 20 Feb. 2022, oakhillcemeterydc.org.

Stodghill, Ron. "Savannah, Both Sides." *New York Times*, 3 Oct. 2014, nytimes .com/2014/10/05/travel/savannah-both-sides.html.

Thanh Dang, Dan. "Historic Annapolis Cemetery Gets Face Lift: Community Celebrates Brewer Hill Restoration." *Baltimore Sun*, 25 Oct. 1998, baltimoresun.com/news /bs-xpm-1998-10-25-1998298053-story.html.

Vargas, Theresa. "While Working to Restore Two Historic Black Cemeteries, She Discovered a Construction Crew Digging on Burial Grounds." *Washington Post*, 9 Oct. 2021, washingtonpost.com/local/black-cemetery-georgetown-construction-crew /2021/10/08/2afc5834-2890-11ec-8831-a31e7b3de188_story.html.

Villemaire, Lois. "Historic Brewer Hill Cemetery." Visit Annapolis, 10 Feb. 2021, visit annapolis.org/blog/stories/post/historic-brewer-hill-cemetery.

CHAPTER 8

Emerson, Ralph Waldo. *The Complete Works of Ralph Waldo Emerson*. Boston: Houghton Mifflin Company, 1875.

———. "The Problem." Academy of American Poets. Accessed 20 Feb. 2022, poets .org/poem/problem.

Garrelick, Renee. "Walking Tour of Sleepy Hollow Cemetery: Marian Wheeler." Concord Free Public Library, 11 July 2005, concordlibrary.org/uploads/scollect/OH _Texts/wheeler_2005.html.

Hawthorne, Nathaniel. "Passages from Hawthorne's Note-Books (Part XI)." *The Atlantic*, Nov. 1866.

The Home of Ralph Waldo Emerson. "Emerson's Walks in Concord." Accessed 19 Jan. 2022, ralphwaldoemersonhouse.org/emersons-walks-2.

Jones, Buford. "'The Hall of Fantasy' and the Early Hawthorne-Thoreau Relationship." *Publications of the Modern Language Association of America* 83, no. 5 (Oct. 1968): 1429–38, doi.org/10.2307/1261316.

Keyes, John S. Autobiography of Hon. John S. Keyes. Transcribed from ms. in John Shepard Keyes Papers, William Munroe Special Collections, Concord Free Public Library, Concord, MA, concordlibrary.org/uploads/scollect/doc/Autobiography _final.pdf.

National Park Service. "The Old Manse." Accessed 19 Jan. 2022, nps.gov/places/the -old-manse.htm.

Person, Leland S. The Cambridge Introduction to Nathaniel Hawthorne. New York: Cambridge University Press, 2007.

Thoreau, Henry David. Walden and Civil Disobedience. New York: Signet, 2012.

Walden Woods Project. "Thoreau and the Environment." Accessed 20 Feb. 2022, www .walden.org/what-we-do/library/thoreau/thoreau-and-the-environment.

Whitney, Gordon G., and William C. Davis. "From Primitive Woods to Cultivated Woodlots: Thoreau and the Forest History of Concord, Massachusetts." Journal of Forest History 30, no. 2 (Apr. 1986): 70–81, doi.org/10.2307/4004930.

Whitney, Terri. "Introduction to Henry David Thoreau and Nathaniel Hawthorne." Hawthorne in Salem, accessed 19 Jan. 2022, hawthorneinsalem.org/Hawthornes Circle/Thoreau/Introduction.html.

Wilson, Leslie Perrin. "New England Transcendentalism." Concord Free Public Library, accessed 19 Jan. 2022, concordlibrary.org/special-collections/essays-on-concord -history/new-england-transcendentalism.

CHAPTER 9

Central Park Conservancy. "Before Central Park: The Story of Seneca Village." 18 Jan. 2018, centralparknyc.org/articles/seneca-village.

Cummins, Eleanor. "Your Favorite Park Is Probably Built on Dead Bodies." Vice, 6 Apr. 2020, vice.com/en/article/akwp8e/your-favorite-park-is-probably-built-on-dead -bodies.

Downing, Andrew Jackson. Rural Essays. By A. J. Downing. Ed., With a Memoir of the Author, by George William Curtis, and a Letter to His Friends, by Frederika Bremer. New York: Leavitt & Allen, 1858.

———. A Treatise on the Theory and Practice of Landscape Gardening: Adapted to North America. New York: Wiley and Putnam, 1844.

Drusus, Livius. "Seneca Village: When New York City Destroyed a Thriving Black Community to Make Way for Central Park." Mental Floss, 15 Apr. 2015, mentalfloss.com /article/63039/seneca-village-community-died-so-central-park-could-live.

Fisher, Colin. "Nature in the City: Urban Environmental History and Central Park." OAH Magazine of History 25, no. 4 (Oct. 2011): 27–31, doi.org/10.1093/oahmag /oar038.

Hendrix, Steve. "A Public Park for Ashes? As Cremations Soar, Demand for Scatter Gardens Grows." Washington Post, 27 Nov. 2016, washingtonpost.com/local/a-public-park-for -ashes-as-cremations-soar-demand-for-scatter-gardens-grows/2016/11/27/319e9448 -ad18-11e6-8b45-f8e493f06fcd_story.html.

Jones, Karen R. "'The Lungs of the City': Green Space, Public Health and Bodily

Metaphor in the Landscape of Urban Park History." *Environment and History* 24, no. 1 (Feb. 2018): 39–58, doi.org/10.3197/096734018x15137949591837.

The Living Urn. "New York City Memorials & Ash Scatterings." 6 Jan. 2021, theliving urn.com/blogs/news/new-york-city-memorials-ash-scatterings.

"Local Intelligence: Central Park. What's to Be Seen There and How to See It—What It Has Cost and How the Money Goes." *New York Times*, 19 Aug. 1866.

Lubove, Roy. "Review of *Social History and the History of Landscape Architecture*, by Elizabeth Barlow, William Alex, Jens Jensen, Leonard K. Eaton, Gordon T. Milde, V. Michael Weinmayr, Julius Gy. Fabos, et al." *Journal of Social History* 9, no. 2 (1975): 268–75, jstor.org/stable/3786255.

Martin, Douglas. "Before Park, Black Village; Students Look into a Community's History." *New York Times*, 7 Apr. 1995, nytimes.com/1995/04/07/nyregion/before-park -black-village-students-look-into-a-community-s-history.html.

Menard, Andrew. "The Enlarged Freedom of Frederick Law Olmsted." *New England Quarterly* 83, no. 3 (Sept. 2010): 508–38, doi.org/10.1162/tneq_a_00039.

NYC Parks. "Scattering Ashes and Cremated Remains in NYC Parks." Accessed 19 Jan. 2022, nycgovparks.org/facility/rules/cremation.

Pattee, Sarah Lewis. "Andrew Jackson Downing and His Influence on Landscape Architecture in America." *Landscape Architecture Magazine* 19, no. 2 (Jan. 1929): 79–83, jstor.org/stable/44660685.

Schuyler, David. "Parks in Urban America." *Oxford Research Encyclopedia of American History*, 3 Nov. 2015, doi.org/10.1093/acrefore/9780199329175.013.58.

Staples, Brent. "Opinion: The Death of the Black Utopia." *New York Times*, 28 Nov. 2019, nytimes.com/2019/11/28/opinion/seneca-central-park-nyc.html.

Taylor, Dorceta E. "Central Park as a Model for Social Control: Urban Parks, Social Class and Leisure Behavior in Nineteenth-Century America." *Journal of Leisure Research* 31, no. 4 (1999): 420–77, doi.org/10.1080/00222216.1999.11949875.

Tucker, Reed. "The Hidden Cemeteries of NYC." *New York Post*, 25 Oct. 2014, nypost .com/2014/10/25/the-hidden-cemeteries-of-nyc.

WNET Group. "A Walk Through Central Park." Accessed 19 Jan. 2022, thirteen.org /centralpark/centralpark.html.

CHAPTER 10

American Battlefield Trust. "Civil War Casualties." Accessed 24 Aug. 2021, battlefields .org/learn/articles/civil-war-casualties.

Carson, Herbert L. "Nor Long Remember: Lincoln at Gettysburg." *Pennsylvania History: A Journal of Mid-Atlantic Studies* 28, no. 4 (Oct. 1961): 365–71, jstor.org/stable /27770061.

Chiappelli, Jeremiah, and Ted Chiappelli. "Drinking Grandma: The Problem of Embalming." *Journal of Environmental Health* 71, no. 5 (Dec. 2008): 24–29, jstor .org/stable/26327817.

"The Complete Embalmer." *Southern Calls*, 26 June 2020, southerncalls.com/article /the-complete-embalmer.

Edwards, Owen. "The Death of Colonel Ellsworth." *Smithsonian Magazine*, Apr. 2011, smithsonianmag.com/history/the-death-of-colonel-ellsworth-878695.

Faust, Drew Gilpin. "Death and Dying." National Park Service, accessed 20 Jan. 2022, nps.gov/nr/travel/national_cemeteries/death.html.

———. *This Republic of Suffering: Death and the American Civil War*. New York: Vintage Books, 2009.

Fitzharris, Dr. Lindsey. "Embalming and the Civil War." National Museum of Civil War Medicine, 20 Feb. 2016, civilwarmed.org/embalming1.

Georg, Kathleen R. "'This Grand National Enterprise': The Origins of Gettysburg's Soldiers' National Cemetery." Gettysburg Discussion Group, May 1982, gdg.org/research/BattlefieldHistories/kghgrand.html.

Gilliland, Donald. "Living on the Wrong Side of History? The Harrisburg Patriot & Union's Notorious 'Review' the Gettysburg Address." *Patriot-News*, last modified 5 Jan. 2019, pennlive.com/gettysburg-150/2013/11/lincoln_gettysburg_address_har.html.

———. "Seven Things You May Not Have Known about Lincoln's Gettysburg Address." *Patriot-News*, last modified 5 Jan. 2019, pennlive.com/gettysburg-150/2013/11/seven_things_you_may_not_have.html.

History.com Editors. "The Gettysburg Address." History.com, last modified 18 Nov. 2019, history.com/topics/american-civil-war/gettysburg-address.

Merrifield, Kelly. "From Necessity to Honor: The Evolution of National Cemeteries in the United States." National Park Service, accessed 20 Jan. 2022, nps.gov/nr/travel/national_cemeteries/development.html.

Moynihan, Colin. "A Quest to Recognize Forgotten Achievements Still Relevant in Everyday Life." *New York Times*, 26 May 2014, nytimes.com/2014/05/27/nyregion/recognizing-bits-of-our-forgotten-history.html.

National Cemetery Administration. "Dates of Establishment: National Cemeteries & NCA Burial Sites." Accessed 20 Jan. 2022, cem.va.gov/facts/Dates_of_Establishment_1.asp.

———. "Facts: NCA History and Development." Accessed 20 Jan. 2022, cem.va.gov/facts/NCA_History_and_Development_1.asp.

———. "Timeline." Accessed 20 Feb. 2022, www.cem.va.gov/cem/history/timeline/timeline-1870.asp.

National Park Service. "Andrew Curtin." Accessed 20 Jan. 2022, nps.gov/people/andrew-curtin.htm.

"News and Miscellany." *Medical Herald* 14 (1895): 375.

"Obsequies of Col. Ellsworth." *New York Times*, 27 May 1861.

Okrent, Arika. "How Morticians Reinvented Their Job Title." Mental Floss, 5 Jan. 2016, mentalfloss.com/article/68177/how-morticians-reinvented-their-job-title#:%7E:text=So%20Embalmers'%20Monthly%20put%20out,connection%20with%20the%20medical%20profession.

Scandura, Jani. "Deadly Professions: *Dracula*, Undertakers, and the Embalmed Corpse." *Victorian Studies* 40, no. 1 (Autumn 1996): 1–30, jstor.org/stable/3828796.

Taylor, Michael L. "The Civil War Experiences of a New Orleans Undertaker." *Louisiana History: The Journal of the Louisiana Historical Association* 55, no. 3 (Summer 2014): 261–81, jstor.org/stable/24396704.

United States War Department. *General Orders Affecting the Volunteer Force: Adjutant General's Office, 1862.* hansebooks, 2019.

Welch, Daniel. "'Acting as an Agent for Governor Curtin': David Wills and His Mark on Gettysburg." In *The Unfinished Work: Abraham Lincoln, David Wills, and the Soldiers' National Cemetery. Papers of the Fifteenth Semi-Annual Gettysburg National Military Park Seminar,* 15–33. National Park Service, 2015, npshistory.com/series/symposia /gettysburg_seminars/15/essay2.pdf.

Wisconsin Historical Society. "A Captain Describes the New Process of Embalming." Accessed 20 Feb. 2022, wisconsinhistory.org/Records/Article/CS3376.

Zeller, Bob. "How Many Died in the American Civil War?" History.com, 6 Jan. 2022, history.com/news/american-civil-war-deaths.

CHAPTER 11

Adkins, Trace. "Trace Adkins—Arlington (Official Music Video)." YouTube, 26 Feb. 2009, youtube.com/watch?v=rJO7lJIxG10.

American Battle Monuments Commission. "Normandy American Cemetery." Accessed 20 Jan. 2022, abmc.gov/multimedia/videos/normandy-american-cemetery.

Annette. "The African-American Experience in Arlington (Virtual Exhibit)." Arlington Historical Society, 30 Jan. 2021, arlingtonhistoricalsociety.org/2021/01/the-african -american-experience-in-arlington-virtual-exhibit.

Arlington National Cemetery. "Freedman's Village." Accessed 20 Jan. 2022, arlington-cemetery.mil/Explore/History-of-Arlington-National-Cemetery/Freedmans-Village.

———. "History of Arlington National Cemetery." Accessed 20 Jan. 2022, arlington cemetery.mil/Explore/History-of-Arlington-National-Cemetery.

———. "President John Fitzgerald Kennedy Gravesite." Accessed 20 Jan. 2022, arlingtoncemetery.mil/Explore/Monuments-and-Memorials /President-John-F-Kennedy-Gravesite.

Barre Granite Association. "Historical Timeline." Accessed 20 Jan. 2022, barregranite .org/historical-timeline.

Bergman, Teresa. "The Politics of Mourning: Death and Honor in Arlington National Cemetery." *Journal of American History* 104, no. 3 (Dec. 2017): 783–84, doi .org/10.1093/jahist/jax368.

Coates, Ta-Nehisi. "The Other Decoration Day Speech." *The Atlantic,* 19 Jan. 2011, theatlantic.com/national/archive/2011/01/the-other-decoration-day-speech/69782.

Douglass, Frederick. "Address at the Graves of the Unknown Dead at Arlington, Va." Library of Congress, 30 May 1871, loc.gov/item/mfd.22021.

Elliott, Bruce S. "Memorializing the Civil War Dead: Modernity and Corruption under the Grant Administration." In *Markers XXVII: Annual Journal of the Association for Gravestone Studies,* edited by June Hadden Hobbs, 15–55. Greenfield, MA: Association for Gravestone Studies, 2011.

"Gen. Lee's Lands Appropriately Confiscated." *Morning Chronicle*, 17 June 1864.

History.com Editors. "Arlington National Cemetery." History.com, last modified 20 Jan. 2021, history.com/topics/landmarks/arlington-national-cemetery.

———. "JFK Buried at Arlington National Cemetery." History.com, last modified 30 Nov. 2021, history.com/this-day-in-history/jfk-buried-at-arlington-national -cemetery.

John F. Kennedy Presidential Library and Museum. "President Kennedy's Grave in Arlington National Cemetery." Accessed 20 Jan. 2022, jfklibrary.org/learn/about -jfk/life-of-john-f-kennedy/fast-facts-john-f-kennedy/president-kennedys-grave-in -arlington-national-cemetery.

Lemay, Kate Clarke. "How the U.S. Designed Overseas Cemeteries to Win the Cold War." What It Means to Be American, 14 Feb. 2019, whatitmeanstobeamerican.org /places/how-the-u-s-designed-overseas-cemeteries-to-win-the-cold-war.

———. *Triumph of the Dead: American World War II Cemeteries, Monuments, and Diplomacy in France*. Tuscaloosa, AL: University Alabama Press, 2018.

McElya, Micki. *The Politics of Mourning: Death and Honor in Arlington National Cemetery*. Cambridge, MA: Harvard University Press, 2016.

Military Women's Memorial (website). Accessed 14 Jan. 2022, womensmemorial.org.

National Cemetery Administration. "History of Government Furnished Headstones and Markers." Accessed 20 Jan. 2022, cem.va.gov/history/hmhist.asp.

National Park Service. "Arlington House: The Robert E. Lee Memorial." Accessed 20 Jan. 2022, npshistory.com/publications/arho/index.htm#:%7E:text=Robert%20E.%20 Lee%2C%20who%20called,torn%20apart%20by%20civil%20war.

———. "Decoration Day Speech 1971 and Context." Accessed 20 Jan. 2022, nps.gov /frdo/learn/kidsyouth/upload/Decoration-Day-Speech-1871-and-context-1.docx.

———. "First Official National Decoration Day." Accessed 20 Jan. 2022, nps.gov /articles/first-official-national-decoration-day.htm.

———. "Freedman's Village." Accessed 20 Jan. 2022, nps.gov/arho/learn/history culture/emancipation.htm.

Normandy Tourism. "The Normandy American Cemetery." Last modified 14 Dec. 2020, en.normandie-tourisme.fr/the-normandy-american-cemetery.

Owen, Wilfred. "Dulce et Decorum Est." 1921. Poetry Foundation, www.poetryfoundation .org/poems/46560/dulce-et-decorum-est.

Poole, Robert M. "How Arlington National Cemetery Came to Be." *Smithsonian Magazine*, Nov. 2009, smithsonianmag.com/history/how-arlington-national-cemetery -came-to-be-145147007.

———. *On Hallowed Ground: The Story of Arlington National Cemetery*. New York: Bloomsbury, 2010.

Railton, Ben. "Considering History: The Lessons of Memorial Day's Decoration Day Origins." *Saturday Evening Post*, 20 May 2020.

"Sen. Kennedy Joins Brothers at Arlington." CBS News, 29 Aug. 2009, cbsnews.com /news/sen-kennedy-joins-brothers-at-arlington.

Shane, Leo, III. "As Space Dwindles, Final Rules on Burial Eligibility for Arlington Cemetery Expected This Fall." *Military Times*, 5 May 2021, militarytimes.com/news

/pentagon-congress/2021/05/05/as-space-dwindles-final-rules-on-burial-eligibility
-for-arlington-cemetery-expected-this-fall.

Chapter 12

Bady, David. "Woodlawn Cemetery." Lehman College Art Gallery: Bronx Architecture, accessed 20 Jan. 2022, lehman.edu/vpadvance/artgallery/arch/buildings /Woodlawn.html.

Barton, Mary Ann. "Undertakers of Last Resort: Indigent Burials on the Rise, Denting County Budgets." *County News*, 10 Dec. 2018, naco.org/articles/undertakers-last -resort-indigent-burials-rise-denting-county-budgets.

Burt, Geoffrey. "Adolph Strauch and Spring Grove Cemetery." National Park Service, accessed 20 Jan. 2022, nps.gov/articles/adolph-strauch-and-spring-grove-cemetery .htm.

"The Cemeteries of New-York.; Some Interesting Statistics How the Remains of Poor Persons Are Treated The Necessity for a Free Public Burial-Ground." *New York Times*, 7 July 1872, nytimes.com/1872/07/07/archives/the-cemeteries-of-newyork-some -interesting-statistics-how-the.html.

"Cemetery Upheld on Tax; Appeals Court Finds Kensico Is Not Run for Profit." *New York Times*, 3 May 1938, nytimes.com/1938/05/03/archives/cemetery-upheld-on-tax -appeals-court-finds-kensico-is-not-run-for.html.

CNS Editors. "One in 10 Local COVID Victims Destined for Hart Island, NYC's Potter's Field." Columbia News Service, 25 Mar. 2021, columbianewsservice .com/2021/03/25/one-in-10-local-covid-victims-destined-for-hart-island-nycs -potters-field.

The Cultural Landscape Foundation. "Adolph Strauch." Accessed 20 Jan. 2022, tclf.org /pioneer/adoph-strauch.

Dolan, Michael. "How Did the White Picket Fence Become a Symbol of the Suburbs?" *Smithsonian Magazine*, April 2019, smithsonianmag.com/history/history-white -picket-fence-180971635.

Dunlap, David W. "For Historic Cemeteries, New Chapters." *New York Times*, 2 June 2002, nytimes.com/2002/06/02/realestate/for-historic-cemeteries-new-chapters .html.

Elidrissi, Rajaa. "How This New York Island Became a Mass Grave." Vox, 7 Apr. 2021, vox .com/2021/4/7/22370410/new-york-city-hart-island-coronavirus-pandemic.

"Fortunes in a Cemetery; Profits and Demands of the Owners of Woodlawn." *New York Times*, 24 Apr. 1883, nytimes.com/1883/04/24/archives/fortunes-in-a-cemetery -profits-and-demands-of-the-owners-of.html.

Gleick, Peter H. "Ditch the Water-Wasting Lawns." *Mercury News*, 16 Apr. 2015, www .mercurynews.com/2015/04/16/peter-h-gleick-ditch-the-water-wasting-lawns.

Lange, Alexandra. "The Past and Future of Cemeteries." *The New Yorker*, 23 Oct. 2014, newyorker.com/culture/culture-desk/past-future-cemeteries.

Lasky, Julie. "Levittown, N.Y.: The Original Starter Community." *New York Times*, 19 Dec. 2018, nytimes.com/2018/12/19/realestate/levittown-ny-the-original-starter -community.html.

Linden-Ward, Blanche. "The Greening of Cincinnati: Adolph Strauch's Legacy in Park Design." *Queen City Heritage* 51 (Spring 1993): 20–39, library.cincymuseum.org /journals/files/qch/v51/n1/qch-v51-n1-gre-020.pdf.

Marshall, Colin. "Levittown, the Prototypical American Suburb—a History of Cities in 50 Buildings, Day 25." *Guardian*, 28 Apr. 2015, theguardian.com/cities/2015/apr/28 /levittown-america-prototypical-suburb-history-cities.

Mausoleums.com. "Mausoleum Art Exhibition Brings Back Figures of the Gilded Age." 15 Sept. 2014, mausoleums.com/mausoleum-art-exhibition-brings-back-figures -gilded-age.

McAree, J. V. "'Non-Profit' Cemeteries." *Globe and Mail*, 9 Sept. 1949.

Meier, Allison C. "Pandemic Victims Are Filling NYC's Hart Island. It Isn't the First Time." *National Geographic*, 13 Apr. 2020, nationalgeographic.com/history/article /unclaimed-coronavirus-victims-being-buried-on-hart-island-long-history-as-potters -field.

Repka-Franco, Virginia. "History of Levittown and the American Dream." Classic NewYorkHistory.com, 5 Mar. 2020, classicnewyorkhistory.com/history-of-levittown -and-the-american-dream.

Ruff, Joshua. "Levittown: The Archetype for Suburban Development." HistoryNet, accessed 20 Feb. 2022, historynet.com/levittown-the-archetype-for-suburban -development.htm.

Samuels, Elyse, and Adriana Usero. "'New York City's Family Tomb': The Sad History of Hart Island." *Washington Post*, 27 Apr. 2020, washingtonpost.com/history /2020/04/27/hart-island-mass-grave-coronavirus-burials.

Sondak, Robert. "Boston Funeral Home Provides Free Burials for the Homeless." *Spare Change News*, 5 July 2016, sparechangenews.net/2016/07/11790.

Streeter, Edward. *The Story of Woodlawn Cemetery*. New York: Woodlawn Cemetery, 1963.

Tobey, George B. "Adolph Strauch, Father of the Lawn Plan." *Landscape Planning* 2 (1975): 283–94, doi.org/10.1016/0304-3924(75)90032-5.

Troshynski, Serena. "Land of the Unknown: A History of Hart Island." New York Public Library, 6 Jan. 2021, nypl.org/blog/2021/01/07/land-unknown-history-hart-island.

Truelove, Meeghan. "This Cemetery Is a Design Lover's Dream." *Frederic Magazine*, 5 Oct. 2019, fredericmagazine.com/2019/10/woodlawn-cemetery-bronx-design -architecture.

Wick, Julia. "This Is How Los Angeles Buries Their Unclaimed Dead." LAist, 1 Dec. 2016, laist.com/news/unclaimed.

Woodlawn Cemetery (website). Accessed 20 Jan. 2022.

"Woodlawn, Historic Districts Council's Six to Celebrate—Part 2." Historic Districts Council, 3 Jan. 2017, 6tocelebrate.org/neighborhoods/woodlawn/page/2.

CHAPTER 13

Abraham, Terry, and Priscilla Wegars. "Urns, Bones and Burners: Overseas Chinese Cemeteries." *Australasian Historical Archaeology* 21 (2003): 58–69, jstor.org/stable /29544506.

Black, Rachael. "Chinese History in Arizona: Highlights from the Journal of

Arizona History." Arizona Historical Society, 28 May 2021, arizonahistoricalsociety
.org/2021/05/28/chinese-history-in-arizona-highlights-from-the-journal-of-arizona
-history.

Campney, Brent M. S. "'Standing in the Crater of a Volcano': Anti-Chinese Violence and
International Diplomacy in the American West." *California History* 98, no. 3 (Fall
2021): 2–27, doi.org/10.1525/ch.2021.98.3.2.

Chang, Gordon G. "Op-Ed: Remember the Chinese Immigrants Who Built America's First Transcontinental Railroad." *Los Angeles Times*, 10 May 2019, latimes.com
/opinion/op-ed/la-oe-chang-transcontinental-railroad-anniversary-chinese-workers
-20190510-story.html.

Chen, Yong. "Uncovering and Understanding the Experiences of Chinese Railroad
Workers in Broader Socioeconomic Contexts." Chinese Railroad Workers in North
America Project at Stanford University, 2020, web.stanford.edu/group/chinese
railroad/cgi-bin/website/wp-content/uploads/2020/04/Chen-Y-Uncovering-and
-Understanding.pdf.

Cheung, Floyd. "Performing Exclusion and Resistance: Anti-Chinese League and Chee
Kung Tong Parades in Territorial Arizona." *The Drama Review* 46, no. 1 (Spring
2002): 39–59, doi.org/10.1162/105420402753555840.

Fong, Lawrence Michael. "Sojourners and Settlers: The Chinese Experience in Arizona." *Journal of Arizona History* 21, no. 3 (Autumn 1980): 227–56, jstor.org/stable
/42678261.

Franz, Kathy. *Forget Me Not: A Boothill Remembrance*. Littleton, CO: LifeHouse Publishing, 2019.

Fuchs, Chris. "150 Years Ago, Chinese Railroad Workers Risked Their Lives in Pursuit of the American Dream." NBC News, 24 Apr. 2019, nbcnews.com/news/asian
-america/150-years-ago-chinese-railroad-workers-risked-their-lives-pursuit-n992751.

———. "The Chinese Railroad Workers Who Helped Connect the Country: Recovering an Erased History." NBC News, 22 Apr. 2019, nbcnews.com/news
/asian-america/recovering-erased-history-chinese-railroad-workers-who-helped
-connect-country-n991136.

Joyce, Matt. "Western Specters: Concordia Cemetery Holds the Legends of El Paso."
Texas Highways, 22 Aug. 2014, texashighways.com/culture/history/western
-specters-el-paso-concordia-cemetery.

Lednicer, Lisa. "Portland Filmmaker Traces Remains of Portland Railroad Workers Back
to China." *Oregonian*, last modified 10 Jan. 2019, oregonlive.com/portland/2009/09
/portland_filmmaker_traces_rema.html.

McGowan, Joe, Jr. "Wyoming's Memory Revived of Massacre of Chinese Mine Workers
a Century Ago." *Los Angeles Times*, 9 Feb. 1986, latimes.com/archives/la-xpm-1986
-02-09-mn-5997-story.html.

National Parks Conservation Association. "Golden Spike Redux." Accessed 21 Feb.
2022, www.npca.org/articles/2192-golden-spike-redux#.

NewsCenter1 Staff. "Looking Back on Deadwood's Chinese Immigrant Community."
KNBN NewsCenter1, 10 May 2018, newscenter1.tv/looking-back-on-deadwoods
-chinese-immigrant-community.

Ni, Ching-Ching. "The Site Where Chinese Laborers Were Interred, Their Graves Later Forgotten, Gets a Memorial." *Los Angeles Times*, 9 Mar. 2010, latimes.com/archives /la-xpm-2010-mar-09-la-me-chinese-burial9-2010mar09-story.html.

Obenzinger, Hilton. "Geography of Chinese Workers Building the Transcontinental Railroad." Stanford Chinese Railroad Workers in North America Project. Accessed 21 Feb. 2022, web.stanford.edu/group/chineserailroad/cgi-bin/website/virtual.

Pierson, David. "Reminders of Bigotry Unearthed." *Los Angeles Times*, 15 Mar. 2006, latimes.com/archives/la-xpm-2006-mar-15-me-chinagrave15-story.html.

Stanford, Leland. "Leland Stanford. Inaugural Address." The Governors Gallery. Accessed 21 Feb. 2022, governors.library.ca.gov/addresses/08-Stanford.html.

Qin, Yucheng. "A Century-Old 'Puzzle': The Six Companies' Role in Chinese Labor Importation in the Nineteenth Century." *Journal of American-East Asian Relations* 12, no. 3–4 (2003): 225–54, doi.org/10.1163/187656103793645289.

Rasmussen, Cecilia. "A Forgotten Hero from a Night of Disgrace." *Los Angeles Times*, 16 May 1999, latimes.com/archives/la-xpm-1999-may-16-me-37851-story.html.

Shao, Elena. "Remembering the Chinese Railroad Workers That Built Stanford's Fortune." *Stanford Daily*, 23 May 2019, stanforddaily.com/2019/05/23/chinese-railroad -workers.

Shueh, Sam, and Eric Chen. "Chinese Residents in Tombstone Arizona." *Tombstone Times*, Dec. 2006, tombstonetimes.com/chinese-in-tombstone-arizona.

Shyong, Frank. "The 1871 Los Angeles Chinese Massacre Still Resonates Today." *Los Angeles Times*, 24 Oct. 2021, latimes.com/california/story/2021-10-24/150th-anniversary -los-angeles-chinese-massacre.

Traywick, Ben T. "History: Quong Gee Kee: Tombstone's Last Celestial." *Tombstone News*, 25 June 2021.

Twain, Mark. *Roughing It*. New York: Signet, 2008.

Wishart, David J., ed. "Deadwood Chinatown." Encyclopedia of the Great Plains, accessed 20 Jan. 2022, plainshumanities.unl.edu/encyclopedia/doc/egp.asam.008.

Yen, Robert. "Chinese Immigrants Built a Lot More of America than the Transcontinental Railroad." *Arizona Republic*, 19 May 2019, azcentral.com/story/opinion /op-ed/2019/05/19/transcontinental-railroad-anniversary-should-honor-chinese -immigrants/3671499002.

CHAPTER 14

Bart, Peter. "Founder of Forest Lawn Is Entombed." *New York Times*, 27 Sept. 1966, timesmachine.nytimes.com/timesmachine/1966/09/27/82511541.html.

Consumer Federation of America. "Nation's Largest Funeral Home Company Charges High Prices and Refuses to Disclose These Prices on Their Websites." 6 Mar. 2017, consumerfed.org/press_release/nations-largest-funeral-home-company-charges -high-prices-refuses-disclose-prices-websites.

Cummins, Eleanor. "How 'Big Funeral' Made the Afterlife So Expensive." *Wired*, 1 Oct. 2021, wired.com/story/death-funeral-industry-lobbying-politics-health.

Donn, Jeff. "Insurance Firms Paying for Their Past Injustices." *Spokesman-Review*,

10 Oct. 2004, spokesman.com/stories/2004/oct/10/insurance-firms-paying-for
-their-past-injustices.

———. "Insurance Industry Facing Lawsuits, Restitution." NBC News, 11 Oct. 2004,
nbcnews.com/id/wbna6227370.

Eaton, Hubert. "The Builder's Creed." Accessed 21 Feb. 2022, www.huberteaton.com
/the-builders-creed.html.

Eckholm, Erik. "Burial Insurance, at $2 Per Week, Survives Skeptics." *New York Times*,
3 Dec. 2006, nytimes.com/2006/12/03/us/03bury.html.

Ehrenreich, Ben. "The End: What Really Happens After You Die?" *Los Angeles Magazine*,
30 Sept. 2016, lamag.com/longform/the-end.

Ferrell, Sarah. "If a Few of Forest Lawn's Million Visitors a Year Make Fun." *New York
Times*, 17 June 1979, nytimes.com/1979/06/17/archives/if-a-few-of-forest-lawns
-million-visitors-a-year-make-fun-of-it.html.

Forest Lawn Memorial-Parks (website). Accessed 18 Jan. 2022, forestlawn.com.

Heen, Mary L. "Ending Jim Crow Life Insurance Rates." *Northwestern Journal of Law
& Social Policy* 4, no. 2, (2009): 359–99, scholarlycommons.law.northwestern.edu
/njlsp/vol4/iss2/3.

"Hubert Eaton, Flamboyant Head of Forest Lawn, Is Dead at 85; Founder of Noted
Cemetery on Coast Revamped Many Funeral Practices." *New York Times*, 22 Sept.
1966, nytimes.com/1966/09/22/archives/hubert-eaton-flamboyant-head-of-forest
-lawn-is-dead-at-85-founder.html.

Kudler, Adrian Glick. "Los Angeles Is Killing Us." Curbed Los Angeles, 27 Oct. 2016,
la.curbed.com/2016/10/27/13396168/los-angeles-cemetery-hollywood-forever
-forest-lawn.

Lee, Wendy. "Forest Lawn Markets Funeral Services at Malls." KPCC, 3 Feb. 2014,
archive.kpcc.org/blogs/economy/2014/02/03/15753/forest-lawn-markets-funeral
-services-at-malls.

MarketResearch.com. "Death Care Services." Jan. 2021, marketresearch.com/Global
-Industry-Analysts-v1039/Death-Care-Services-14274177.

McNamara, Kevin. "Cultural Anti-Modernism and 'The Modern Memorial-Park':
Hubert Eaton and the Creation of Forest Lawn." *Canadian Review of American Studies* 32, no. 3 (Winter 2002): 301–20, doi.org/10.3138/cras-s032-03-04.

Oring, Elliott. "Icons of Immortality: Forest Lawn and the American Way of Death." In
Worldviews and the American West: The Life of the Place Itself, edited by Polly Stewart,
Steve Siporin, C. W. Sullivan, and Suzi Jones, 54–64. Louisville, CO: University
Press of Colorado, 2000, doi.org/10.2307/j.ctt46nx4g.9.

Picchi, Aimee. "A Buried Problem at Country's Top Funeral Home Chain?" CBS News,
6 Mar. 2017, cbsnews.com/news/a-buried-problem-at-the-countrys-top-funeral
-home-chain-service-corporation-international.

Pool, Bob. "Forest Lawn at 100: The Rest Is History." *Los Angeles Times*, 6 July 2006,
latimes.com/archives/la-xpm-2006-jul-16-me-forest16-story.html.

Ryon, Ruth. "Income Lags: Plot Sales No Gold Mine for Cemeteries." *Los Angeles Times*,
5 Apr. 1987, latimes.com/archives/la-xpm-1987-04-05-re-122-story.html.

Smith, Stacey Vanek. "The Price of Plots: A Look at the Cemetery Real Estate Business."
NPR, 27 Oct. 2017, npr.org/2017/10/27/560484054/the-price-of-plots-a-look-at
-the-cemetery-real-estate-business.

Tompor, Susan. "Graveyard Deals: Why Would You Buy a Cemetery Plot in Advance?"
Detroit Free Press, 24 Oct. 2018, freep.com/story/money/personal-finance/susan
-tompor/2018/10/24/buying-cemetery-plots/1698056002.

Trethewey, Natasha. "Collection Day." In *Domestic Work: Poems*, 54. Minneapolis, MN:
Graywolf Press, 2000.

Young, Robert O. "Hubert Eaton." *Los Angeles Times*, 20 Apr. 2000, latimes.com
/archives/la-xpm-2000-apr-20-me-21666-story.html.

CHAPTER 15

Boutelle, Sara Holmes. *Julia Morgan, Architect*. New York: Abbeville Press, 1995.

Connecting Directors. "Throwback Thursday Cremation Edition: Did You Know? Lawrence F. Moore." 2 Oct. 2014, connectingdirectors.com/44958-throwback-thursday
-cremation-edition-did-you-know-lawrence-f-moore.

Hawthorne, Christopher. "Gold Medal: Julia Morgan." *Architect*, 23 June 2014, archi-
tectmagazine.com/awards/aia-awards/gold-medal-julia-morgan_0.

Hearst Castle. "Julia Morgan." Accessed 20 Feb. 2022, hearstcastle.org/history-behind
-hearst-castle/historic-people/profiles/julia-morgan.

Kilgore, Clay. "Looking Back: LeMoyne Crematory." *Observer-Reporter*, last modified
16 June 2020, observer-reporter.com/news/looking_back/looking-back-lemoyne
-crematory/article_5d7dbd30-d185-11e8-8bbd-e7e798921a72.html.

Lange, Alexandra. "Overlooked No More: Julia Morgan, Pioneering Female Architect."
New York Times, 6 Mar. 2019, nytimes.com/2019/03/06/obituaries/julia-morgan
-overlooked.html.

Laskow, Sarah. "Here Lies E. Coli." Atlas Obscura, 22 Oct. 2018, atlasobscura.com
/articles/cemetery-soil-human-remains.

Leong, Eng-Choon, Hossam Abuel-Naga, Venkata Siva Naga Sai Goli, Bhagwanjee Jha,
Pankaj Pathak, and Devendra Narain Singh. "Design of Mass Burial Sites for Safe
and Dignified Disposal of Pandemic Fatalities." *Environmental Geotechnics* 8, no. 3
(May 2021): 208–16, doi.org/10.1680/jenge.20.00070.

McNeill, Karen. "Julia Morgan: Gender, Architecture, and Professional Style." *Pacific
Historical Review* 76, no. 2 (May 2007): 229–68, doi.org/10.1525/phr.2007.76.2.229.

———. "'WOMEN WHO BUILD': Julia Morgan and Women's Institutions." *California
History* 89, no. 3 (January 2012): 41–74, doi.org/10.2307/23215875.

Neptune Society. "Why Cremation Continues to Increase in Popularity." Accessed
20 Feb. 2022, neptunesociety.com/cremation-information-articles/why-cremation
-continues-to-increase-in-popularity.

Powell, Devin. "Dissolve the Dead? Controversy Swirls around Liquid Cremation."
Scientific American, 7 Sept. 2017, scientificamerican.com/article/dissolve-the-dead
-controversy-swirls-around-liquid-cremation.

Smith, Gregory. "U.S. Public Becoming Less Religious." Pew Research Center, 3 Nov.
2015, pewforum.org/2015/11/03/u-s-public-becoming-less-religious.

Solomon, Adina. "More States Legalize Dissolving Bodies in Water." *U.S. News*, 12 Mar. 2020.

UC Berkeley Environmental Design Archives. "Julia Morgan: Hidden Engineer." Accessed 21 Jan. 2022, exhibits.ced.berkeley.edu/exhibits/show/juliamorgan.

Washington County Historical Society. "The LeMoyne Crematory." Accessed 21 Jan. 2022, wchspa.org/creamatory.

Zavoral, Linda. "New York Times Writes Architect Julia Morgan's Obit—62 Years Later." *Mercury News*, last modified 8 Mar. 2019, mercurynews.com/2019/03/08/new-york-times-writes-architect-julia-morgans-obit-62-years-later.

Żychowski, Józef, and Tomasz Bryndal. "Impact of Cemeteries on Groundwater Contamination by Bacteria and Viruses—a Review." *Journal of Water & Health* 13, no. 2 (June 2015): 285–301, doi.org/10.2166/wh.2014.119.

CHAPTER 16

Ambrosino, Brandon. "Facebook Is a Growing and Unstoppable Digital Graveyard." *BBC*, 13 Mar. 2016, bbc.com/future/article/20160313-the-unstoppable-rise-of-the-facebook-dead.

Barekat, Houman. "Digital Immortality." *Los Angeles Review of Books*, 11 Jan. 2021, lareviewofbooks.org/article/digital-immortality.

Barol, Bill. "Death and the Salesman: Irreverence and death don't mix. Unless you're the Cassity brothers, who bring a show-biz sensibility to the staid funeral business." *Money*, 1 Mar. 2004, money.cnn.com/magazines/fsb/fsb_archive/2004/03/01/363872/index.htm.

Federal Bureau of Investigation. "National Prearranged Services, Inc. Controlling Officials Indicted." 22 Nov. 2010, archives.fbi.gov/archives/stlouis/press-releases/2010/sl112210.htm.

Holman, Gregory J. "J. Douglas Cassity, Businessman Ordered to Pay $435 Million in Funeral Scam, Dies in St. Louis." *Springfield News-Leader*, 2 June 2020, news-leader.com/story/news/local/missouri/2020/06/02/j-douglas-cassity-sentenced-prison-funeral-scam-dies-st-louis/3124092001.

———. "The Curious Case of Doug Cassity, 'Bernie Madoff of Missouri,' Is Back in the News." *Springfield News-Leader*, last modified 15 July 2019, news-leader.com/story/news/local/ozarks/2019/07/14/curious-case-doug-cassity-bernie-madoff-missouri-city-utilities-ponzi-funeral-preneed/1661826001.

Kneese, Tamara. "QR Codes for the Dead." *The Atlantic*, 21 May 2014, theatlantic.com/technology/archive/2014/05/qr-codes-for-the-dead/370901.

Kudler, Adrian Glick. "Los Angeles Is Killing Us." Curbed Los Angeles, 27 Oct. 2016, la.curbed.com/2016/10/27/13396168/los-angeles-cemetery-hollywood-forever-forest-lawn.

Leduff, Charlie. "Comeback for Resting Place of Movie Stars." *New York Times*, 1 Dec. 2002, nytimes.com/2002/12/01/us/comeback-for-resting-place-of-movie-stars.html.

Leibowitz, Ed. "The Hollywood Forever Way of Death." *The Atlantic*, Mar. 2001, theatlantic.com/magazine/archive/2001/03/the-hollywood-forever-way-of-death/302139.

Lever, Janet. "I Got My Dream Plot in Hollywood Forever Cemetery—Almost." *Los Angeles Magazine*, 2 Feb. 2018, lamag.com/culturefiles/got-dream-plot-hollywood -forever-cemetery-almost.

LiveScience. "'Mind Uploading' & Digital Immortality May Be Reality by 2045, Futurists Say." *HuffPost*, 18 June 2013, huffpost.com/entry/mind-uploading-2045 -futurists_n_3458961.

Mitchell, Kevin M. "The Future of Death." *St. Louis*, 6 Apr. 2007, stlmag.com/The -Future-of-Death.

Öhman, Carl J., and David Watson. "Are the Dead Taking Over Facebook? A Big Data Approach to the Future of Death Online." *Big Data & Society* 6, no. 1 (January–June 2019): 1–13, doi.org/10.1177/2053951719842540.

Patrick, Robert. "Funeral Scam Figures Get Prison Sentences in St. Louis Federal Court." *St. Louis Post Dispatch*, 14 Nov. 2013, stltoday.com/news/local/crime -and-courts/funeral-scam-figures-get-prison-sentences-in-st-louis-federal-court /article_68f2e563-bd91-55a4-a2e7-d202ac157df8.html.

Seibt, Sébastian. "The Digital Cemetery: When Facebook Controls Our History." France 24, last modified 29 Apr. 2019, france24.com/en/20190428-facebook-zuckerberg -dead-orwell-oxford-internet-institute.

Silverman, Jacob. "Burial Plots." *Tablet*, 22 Sept. 2011, tabletmag.com/sections/arts -letters/articles/burial-plots.

Tewksbury, Drew. "Cemetarian Tyler Cassity Finds Beauty in the Boneyard." KCET, 17 May 2012, kcet.org/shows/artbound/cemetarian-tyler-cassity-finds-beauty-in -the-boneyard.

Tucci, Linda. "Forever Enterprises Sold for $12 Million in Stock." *St. Louis Business Journal*, last modified 20 Feb. 2000, bizjournals.com/stlouis/stories/2000/02/21 /story8.html.

UC Riverside News. "Artificial Intelligence Is Bringing the Dead Back to 'Life'—but Should It?" 4 Aug. 2021, news.ucr.edu/articles/2021/08/04/artificial-intelligence -bringing-dead-back-life-should-it.

Vincent, Brandi. "Veterans Affairs Launches Digital National Cemetery." Nextgov, 26 Aug. 2019, nextgov.com/it-modernization/2019/08/veterans-affairs-launches -digital-national-cemetery/159450.

Chapter 17

Brown, Alex. "More People Want a Green Burial, but Cemetery Law Hasn't Caught Up." Stateline, 20 Nov. 2019, pewtrusts.org/en/research-and-analysis/blogs /stateline/2019/11/20/more-people-want-a-green-burial-but-cemetery-law-hasnt -caught-up.

Brown, Patricia Leigh. "Eco-Friendly Burial Sites Give a Chance to Be Green Forever." *New York Times*, 13 Aug. 2005, nytimes.com/2005/08/13/us/ecofriendly-burial-sites -give-a-chance-to-be-green-forever.html.

Conservation Burial Alliance. "The Ramsey Creek Preserve Story." Accessed 21 Jan. 2022, conservationburialalliance.org/ramsey_creek_preserve.html.

Davidson, Amy. "California Dying." *The New Yorker*, 21 Aug. 2005, newyorker.com /magazine/2005/08/29/california-dying.

Green Burial Council. "Disposition Statistics." Accessed 21 Jan. 2022, greenburialcouncil .org/media_packet.html.

Hoffner, Ann. "Ramsey Creek Preserve, America's First Modern Natural Burial Cemetery." Green Burial Naturally, 5 Feb. 2018, greenburialnaturally.org/blog/tag /Ramsey+Creek+Preserve.

Memorial Ecosystems. "Ramsey Creek Preserve History." Accessed 21 Jan. 2022, memorialecosystems.com/ramsey_creek_preserve_history.html.

Mulcahy, Alex. "Green Burials Are Good for the Environment. They Might Be Even Better for the Soul." *Grid Magazine*, 9 Apr. 2021, gridphilly.com/blog-home/2021/4/9 /green-burials-are-good-for-the-environment-they-might-be-even-better-for-the-soul.

Vatomsky, Sonya. "Thinking About Having a 'Green' Funeral? Here's What to Know." *New York Times*, 22 Mar. 2018, nytimes.com/2018/03/22/smarter-living/green -funeral-burial-environment.html.

PHOTOGRAPH CREDITS

ABOUT THE AUTHOR

Greg Melville is an adventure writer and former editor at *Men's Journal* and Hearst Magazines. His work has appeared in many national publications, including *Outside, National Geographic Traveler, Men's Health,* and the *Boston Globe Magazine,* and has been listed in *The Best American Sports Writing 2017.* He is a decorated navy veteran who served in Afghanistan and teaches writing and literature at the United States Naval Academy, where he was the recipient of the school's award for excellence in teaching in 2019. He lives with his wife and two kids in Delaware.